K. M. B … n

CW01662220

TH … EAGLE

A personal record of family life during the German Occupation of Guernsey, Channel Islands 1940 - 1945.

Line drawings by Diana de la Rue.

B PUBLICATIONS DIVISION

THE PREY OF AN EAGLE

ISBN 0 9509360 2 2

First published 1972
Reprinted 1980
This edition published by Burbridge Ltd 1985

Copyright © 1972 by K. M. Bachmann

Conditions of sale. This book is sold subject to the condition that it shall not, by way of trade or otherwise, be lent, re-sold, hired out, or otherwise circulated without the publishers prior consent in any form of binding or cover other than that in which it is published and without a similar condition including this condition being imposed on the subsequent purchaser.

ACKNOWLEDGEMENTS

To . . .

— L. A. Guillemette, Esq., O.B.E., for the Foreword.

— Pan Harmsworth for her interest and encouragement.

— My husband for details of his personal experiences and moral support.

— My daughter Diana de la Rue for the drawings and cover design.

— Mr. Carel Toms for the cover photograph.

— Miss Rita Spurdle for her encouragement.

Published by Burbridge Ltd,
Les Caches, St. Martin's, Guernsey, C.I.

Printed by The Guernsey Press Company Limited,
Guernsey, C.I.

CONTENTS

Cover photograph—Carel Toms Collection

" German troops in St. Peter Port "

To Mother

FOREWORD

by

Louis A. Guillemette, Esq., O.B.E.,
Guernsey States Supervisor,

Personal Secretary to the President of the States Controlling Committee throughout the German Occupation of Guernsey.

As one who helped in the administration in Guernsey during the German Occupation, I consider the author has presented a fair account of that period, and I can assure the reader that from the point of view of administration, it is an accurate record.

But it is more than that, of course. I would say that it is a valuable addition to the books already written about the Occupation because, unlike any other of them, it tells the story of a sensitive young woman who was subjected to all the trials which an Occupation can produce. First, parting with her child — and I know now as a parent and a grand-parent, the grief and anxiety which such a separation must have meant to her — then having to undergo a serious operation and, finally, giving birth to and bringing up a somewhat delicate child amid all the privations of an Occupation must all have taxed her to the utmost. Her story which reveals these and other tests of character and the way they were overcome with so much help from her husband and her many friends, compresses into one book experiences which might easily cover the occupation story of at least three somewhat hardpressed women.

I think though that for me — and I expect for any other reader who likes to know how people tick — the greatest charm of this diary is that, whether the author planned it or not, the Occupation was the catalyst which set her thinking and writing to her mother about her childhood as a member of a large and intelligent family in St. John's Parish in Guernsey. Seeing that I, too, was a member of a large family — living a hundred yards up the same road — and that we, too, filled a pew in St. John's Church, and remembering that we shared many friends in common, I feel qualified to assure anyone who happens to read this, that not only is this book a fine piece of writing, but that it records with sincerity the quality of our upbringing as members of large families in Guernsey in the first three decades of this century.

I really did enjoy this book and I am sure that it will give pleasure to many discerning readers.

PREAMBLE

I began these letters to my Mother, three weeks after the family had escaped to England in 1940.

Having suffered a virtual mass bereavement by their exodus, I felt a compulsive urge to keep in spiritual contact by the only means left to me. Time and inclination synchronized, and I was both able and very eager, in my emotional state, to unburden myself; and, at the same time, should we be absent on their return, to leave our scattered relatives some idea of the atmosphere of life in Guernsey under German Occupation.

Years after Liberation, friends began to ask if I ever managed to complete my record: as they were, and still are, eager to read it.

Inevitably, in letters to the absent members of one's family, there are many evocative comparisons between the peaceful years of one's youth, and the sudden changes that war brings. These I have been strongly urged to leave intact, as part of the fabric of life in Guernsey, past and present. In mitigation, I must therefore ask the reader to bear in mind that, at the time of writing, these letters were not intended for publication. And so the book remains unabridged, with glimpses of an untroubled Island, before Hitler "cried 'Havoc!!' and let slip the dogs of War."

K.M.B.

1940

To M.H. La Guelle. 13th July, 1940.

Three weeks ago you left us. To-day, sitting here on the lawn, beneath the old Mulberry tree, I look back on those three weeks that are more than three years to me.

This German Occupation is a heavy yoke for our British shoulders and we find it hard to accept. A lot of traditional grit, humour and dignity will be needed if we are to surmount it. I feel at times that this incredible situation cannot be. But there is no ignoring the metallic ring of jackboots in our little cobbled Town, Swastikas floating in the breeze over all the main buildings, the clipped, full-throated singing of their marching troops, the heel-clicking and arm-raising; and, above all, the shattering din of the German Band, a vigorous reminder of our change of fortune. If our little High Street were Whitehall, and Guernsey the Heart of the Empire, they could not look more triumphant.

Where, when and how will this strange, unwelcome and unhappy state of affairs come to an end? Oddly enough, it is no longer the War that weighs most heavily on me, but rather this enforced separation from you all. I dare not allow my thoughts on Diana full scope, or I would become too morbid to carry on. At first, life seemed unendurable. Your departure with Father and most of the family, was like a mass bereavement. I felt too weary to struggle against the current and vaguely wished that Peter would refrain from all attempts to bring me to the surface. I shall always be grateful to him for his patience and understanding, without which I would have groped and floundered indefinitely. It seems incredible that millions of other people of all classes, nationalities and creeds, have been subjected to this same ordeal—or indeed far worse—during the past year.

You will remember our parting with Diana on that black 20th of June, the day before you left Guernsey. Her going dealt us the worst blow of our lives. I thought my feelings would have been too numbed to register any further shocks for a long time. Your departure on the following day, however, shed brutal enlightenment on that point. You will also remember how we spent that fateful Thursday the 20th here with you, making and breaking plans for wholesale family evacuation. I can still picture Audrey and Pam, sitting in the stairs among bits of luggage, weighing the pros and cons. We were still vague and undecided when we left here in the afternoon. And so, Peter and I left our luggage in the hall intending to return the next morning for further discussion. You were in the garden when we left. Had I foreseen for one moment the events of the following day, I most certainly would have gone in search of you to say goodbye. Instead, I asked someone to say it for me. Perhaps the better way for both our sakes. Heaven knows I am not reproaching you for leaving the Island without us. No regular-boat service could be guaranteed. Berths had been offered you, to be claimed within an hour or the chance lost. We were at breakfast when you telephoned to say there was room for us on the boat, and begged us to join you. Audrey took the receiver, adding her entreaties to yours. I realise how you must have felt when, torn both ways, I gave you my answer. Peter could not bring himself to leave home and business at such short notice; neither would his old people entertain, for one moment, the idea of travelling.

He left me complete freedom of choice, with the promise never to reproach. I could go with you, or wait until we could decide the right course to take together. Well, I waited with him and have no regrets on that score. Of all the people left behind, the men who inveigled wives and children to go without them, and who are now isolated here by the influx of Germans, are truly the most pathetic.

Thus, Friday the 21st of June was another dark day; and the acute pain of Diana's going, only added to my desolation at your departure. I came up to "La Guelle" in a lorry that afternoon, sitting beside the man sent by George to fetch me. I roamed, bewildered and dazed, from room to room, as though sleep-walking. Signs of your rapid exodus were all about me. I stumbled against our trunk, and stopped to read the label which someone had glued there, with the address of your intended destination, little realising that it would never be used. On the table in the breakfast-room lay the mournful remnants of your hasty meal. At that moment I think I must have known that our long separation had begun, for my spirits sank once more to a new low-level, and I sank with them into the nearest chair: the whole room and its contents swimming before my eyes. The solid, immutable past vanished overnight, not to be restored for us, nor for countless millions, before the passing of many bleak dawns.

To M.H. La Guelle. 16th July, 1940.

As the days went by we pulled ourselves together for our mutual benefit. George, Felicia and her Mother (we call her Allie), decided to throw in their lot with us for moral support. Each of us soon realised, that to brood upon the past, to recoil from the future, and to refuse to come to terms with the present, would be to sabotage our return to sanity. So the five of us remain here at La Guelle for the time being. We shall return to Les Dunes if the Germans continue with their present attitude of seeming tolerance, leaving us more or less to our own devices.

I often wonder what you are thinking, and try to imagine your new way of life. How you must be wishing we had all left Guernsey, and visualising all manner of evils being forced upon us.

Oddly enough, life is almost normal on the surface; but within us lurks a feeling of nausea and a jumble of confused sensations.

I seldom give way to an acute attack of the blues nowadays. My last immersion was on hearing Saint Saëns' "Le Cygne" on the wireless a few days ago. I discovered then that my emotions are still too vulnerable for me to enjoy music in company; and, you will agree, "Le Cygne" is particularly moving. If I live to be very old, even the last of my generation, whenever I hear that plaintive air, I shall be in your dining room, standing at the window, looking across the fields, the trees, and the shipless sea beyond, observing none of them, yet, savouring to the full the torment and longing it stirred in me, so soon after you had all gone away to seek freedom and sanctuary elsewhere.

Herm and Jethou, from La Guelle.

What of our treatment by the Germans? They issued a Declaration on their arrival, announcing their intention to respect the people of Guernsey subject to certain conditions; the first being that we return that gesture. With typical British impartiality, and traditional sense of fair play, we are bound to say the conditions are reasonable enough. Curfew is 11 p.m. We are allowed to keep our wireless sets, and so forth. They point out that if we attempt resistance, our Town will be bombed.

They have appointed one of their officers—a Dr. Maas —as a liaison between themselves and us. He has fixed hours each day during which Islanders may call on him for advice, on any of the problems arising from the Occupation. Everyone appears to come away from his interview satisfied. Nevertheless, we have no illusions. This may be subtle propaganda, and we remain on our guard, at the same time rejoicing at the sedative effect of their present attitude.

Warily, we accept the Rule thrust upon us, and are gratified that we are not called upon to render homage "in good set terms". We are at least able to view the immediate future with fortitude, if not with enthusiasm.

To M.H. La Guelle. 18th July, 1940.

To-day I find myself once more at the small table in your bedroom window. The weather is brilliant, though gusty. The tree in the garden is rustling and swaying in melancholy fashion. The Church clock is striking four. Everything beautiful hurts for, to my mind, beauty has become a taunting irony, an ever retreating mirage. Felicia and I still sing at times, as in the first days: "O for the Wings of a Dove!" and now for some reason, continually hum the "Druids' Prayer". Perhaps this reflects a gradual change in the general pattern of our lives, from bitter frustration to grudging acceptance. I hope so, for here we are, and here we have to remain. There is nothing to be gained by wishing for a magic carpet, or the wings of a dove! Certainly in the years to come, when our hopes of peace are fulfilled, those simple old melodies will instantly recapture for us, the varied sensations and surging emotions of these early days of Occupation.

Although certain conditions of our lives differ widely, your reactions during these first weeks of uprooting, must surely be another version of our own; even to the point of sparing each other all we can of fruitless anxiety. Only when I sit here in spiritual contact with you all, do my secret ruminations emerge, shorn of all pretence and stay with me until I add them to these ramblings. Perhaps in years to come, when we find ourselves reverting to smug complacency, within the sheltered precincts of freedom, peace and comfort, they may serve to give our spirits a little judicious prodding.

I wonder how long it will be before you read this, and in what circumstances. If we could see through the haze into the future. Who knows? The intervening time might well be harder to bear. Never was the quotation made by the King in his broadcast of Christmas '39 more relevant: "We must go out into the darkness and put our hand into the Hand of God." A most comforting thought. Why ask to see the distant scene? If we are destined to bark our shins on a series of obstacles around innumerable corners, one step is surely enough.

Last night I dreamed about Diana. I met her frisking along the Esplanade with Kala bounding ahead. Armistice had been signed. Hugging her fiercely, I asked her if she had missed us; but she assured me that she had not had time. I certainly think she is too lively and interested in her new surroundings to pine for long. If only we could exchange letters, and if only the Germans had ignored our existence on the Map. This calls to mind one dramatic moment on the day before you left. We were all in the breakfast room discussing evacuation, when someone burst into the room shouting wildly: " Russia's in the War! On our side! " " It's all over Town! " I see you now sinking into your easy chair and saying: " That settles it. I'm staying here. The war will be over in six months." At that moment the pips sounded on the wireless for the one o'clock news. Instantly there was silence. Of course there was no mention of Russia at all; and once more, evacuation became the vital topic.

We sometimes imagine you visiting Diana wherever she may be, and making plans for her future. If only we had received even one letter from her, or from her new parents, before communications were cut. I often recall her final words as I tucked her into bed the night before she left: " I shall try to forget you and Daddy, then I shan't be too sad." She must have sensed that we would not be leaving Guernsey to join her in England. I often picture her as she lay the next morning, dishevelled after a restless night, sprawled across the bed, fast asleep, with flushed cheeks, her new identity disc on its silver chain slipped on to a bare shoulder, oblivious to the fact that I was standing there in mental agony, forcing myself to waken her and send her away, literally and irrevocably into the unknown.

To M.H. La Guelle. 20th July, 1940.

Twice since you left we have been to the cinema. A few Germans were dispersed among the audience. We could imagine their feelings. They also are separated from their families. Often they tell Peter in Town, that many of them have not seen their homes and relatives for years, and are hopelessly weary of war. Their appetite for glory—never as voracious as that of their Master—seems to have been satisfied long ago. A few of them already admit it: renouncing allegiance to Hitler's creeds and practices in no uncertain terms. They show photographs of their homes and families to anyone sufficiently interested to see them; admitting, in so many words, that all they want to do is to go home, and live in peace. They have had their fill of Hitler's Promised Land.

It was an unforeseen hazard that his armies would be dallying indefinitely in all the countries of Europe, waiting for the Invasion of Britain which, thanks to the R.A.F., has not come off. They have had ample time to compare their way of life with ours. They have seen true Democracy at work, and have discovered that it is not considered treason for us to air our views, however unpalatable to those in authority. They find us unburdened by secret police; neither have we to resort to subterfuge and deceit between friends and relatives. We do not live furtively, like rabbits afraid to leave their burrows. But how to stop this Frankenstein of their own creating? And to stem the flood which still sweeps them on? These are problems which only Time and the Allies can eventually solve.

Many houses, hotels and other buildings have now been commandeered by the Germans including the Victoria Hospital. Unice and I were with Matron Hall a few minutes after she had received her marching orders. She was quite overcome with sorrow and indignation. Only with the greatest effort was she able to pass any comment. Little did the general public suspect, when they contributed so generously to the recent appeal for funds, that their money would be spent on an up-to-date theatre and new beds for the Germans. Matron Hall is now in charge of the Câtel Hospital. It is the only civilian hospital in use in Guernsey for the Duration, and is now called "The Emergency Hospital."

Almost every day brings forth changes in the food situation. Bran will soon be mixed with flour to eke out our bread ration. Doubtful recipes appear daily in the Press for extracting salt from sea-water and for preserving vegetables. We are attempting to preserve tomatoes in sawdust and sand, and intend to pickle eggs and buy tomato purée. Cattle fodder is also alarmingly scarce. Lily, the cow, and her offspring appear to enjoy their new diet of tomatoes. As I write, a man is leading the cow to water, while her heifer is running wildly round and round her stake, blaring madly as though orphaned for ever.

This calls to mind that last afternoon spent in the field opposite the house where the men were hay-making. Audrey, with friends and their children at one end of the field; you, Diana and I at the other, segregated, because Diana was still in quarantine for chicken-pox. The sun beamed upon us as we ate our tea among the stooks and stubble in the hayfield. You will doubtless remember how Miss Ross came to tell us she had " just heard " that liners were coming to take us all to Canada! That was the first of a record crop of rumours, and also the first breath of the hurricane which was to sweep over us during the next few days. Little did we imagine that was to be our last cup of tea together, maybe for years, maybe for ever. What a dreadful thought! How worried we are about you all, and no doubt you are equally tormented when you try to imagine our plight.

I have just come in from the garden—your especial domain. I expected to see you at every corner, scissors in one hand, and freshly cut bouquet in the other, arranged as only you know how. I feel sure you left a wisp of your spirit out there, for it never fails to haunt me in many elusive ways; it lives in the song of a bird or in the wafted perfume of a rose.

Kala is pestering me to leave off writing, and to take him for a walk, so you are spared, for I was waxing lyrical, a rare disease in one of us.

On returning from the walk, I found a cup of tea awaiting me with Felicia and George. And now, I resume, since Peter is always later on Saturdays.

It seemed strange just now, walking at Beau Séjour; the whole place to myself at this time of year. So different from a few weeks ago, when school-tennis and other sports were in full swing. I expect the College Swimming Sports would have been held to-day. Diana would have been all agog over her races. Her new bathing suit is in the drawer beside me now. I also wonder what her part would have been in the School Concert, and whether she would have received a prize on Speech Day. But these are idle thoughts, for End-of-Term activities are elsewhere this year.

To M.H. La Guelle. 22nd July, 1940.

We are told that sixteen thousand people left Guernsey last month, and that approximately twenty three thousand remained. And yet, every time we go out and see the deserted streets, we feel it must surely be the other way about. There is an air of stillness which, at any other time would be so soothing but now seems to hold some hidden menace. One sees very few sunny faces in the streets and byways, as though all gaiety had dried up at its source; though we often find ourselves inordinately amused by endless inanities, seeking no doubt, to relieve our true feelings in a way which least betrays them. I fear we delude no one.

The food outlook we dare not contemplate. We use up perishables and rigidly conserve tinned stuff. We are not allowed to purchase beyond our immediate needs. No doubt we shall learn to overcome each obstacle as it presents itself.

With the lessening of our petrol supply, we see fewer and fewer cars. Horse-driven vehicles of all shapes and sizes are appearing like phantoms from the past, some of them are most amusing, almost derelict and seemingly resurrected from scrap-iron dumps. One van which passes this way is freshly painted, has a large hood like those on the old-time baker's cart, and is adorned with the wheels of a car complete with inflated rubber tyres; the whole contraption dwarfing the poor scrap of a pony between the shafts. Most of the cars contain Germans, chauffeured by our bus-drivers. Occasionally one sees the real owner of a car halt in his tracks and stand open-mouthed as his car races past him full of Germans. He resembles the rubber-necked man in the Shell advertisement: "That's mine . . . that was!"

Garage proprietors have been badly hit. Business for them is worse than stagnant. They are obliged to take brand new cars out of their showrooms for the Germans to use. Stan is reduced to selling vegetables and fruit in his showroom. We had to dodge the missiles when we smiled at his discomfiture.

There are men who, having developed unwieldy corporations through long years of car-riding and gastronomic indulgence, now have to balance themselves on bicycles; carrying the one and pushing the other up our many hills. Sometimes we have to practise self-control on meeting those devoid of humour, but there are many whose spirit is not so easily daunted. Among these stalwarts one sees many of the portly denizens of Men's Clubs.

To M.H. La Guelle. 24th July, 1940.

The myth of St. Swithin is daily being strengthened. Rain fell on the 15th and has continued to fall for part of every day since, sometimes persisting into late afternoon. Yesterday it cleared at 5.30 and I took Kala for his daily scamper on Beau Séjour. It was never so desolate. With the exception of a groundsman and a buffet attendant, I was the only person there. " I wandered lonely as a cloud "— the silence barely disturbed by the occasional drone of a distant plane, the rustling of leaves in the trees and the songs of birds. While Kala chased them whenever they settled on the ground, I sat in idle meditation. My spirits, like the trees, drooping and damp. The sky had turned a vivid blue and the air was pungent with the smell of steaming earth. A sudden chill breeze sighed in the trees, reflecting my mood. The branches above shuddered and, weeping, shed over me their surplus tears. The spell broken, with an answering sigh, I resumed my strolling, to Kala's delight.

Last evening we went to the Regal Cinema where we saw a German film based on the life of Tchaikovsky. This good production was marred for us by the preceding Propaganda Film. Morbid anti-British war scenes were depicted; including the sinking of a Battleship and Liner, the bombing of depôts and so on. It only tended to emphasise the futility of war. There we were, surrounded by an indifferent enemy, fortunately making no demonstration of approval or delight when their victims were displayed on the screen. Guernsey people would soon give up going to the cinema if they gloated.

This morning I went to College to collect Diana's books. A doleful job indeed, which in no way stimulated my 'joie de vivre'. The under-matron, the secretary and the caretaker were the only people there. I saw the children passing like phantoms before me, their laughter and shouting echoing everywhere. I heard once more their singing in Hall, the clanging luncheon bell, the banging of desks and doors, and the hundred and one familiar sounds associated with school life. I was completely absorbed into this atmosphere of the recent past; though it seemed years behind me instead of a few weeks. Like the little Match Girl in the fairy-tale, I ached for the vision to remain and materialize. Striking another match, I could see Diana singing her solo in her first school concert at the age of seven:

> " I had a little nut-tree."

I recalled my own final concert there seventeen years before. One song in particular echoing in my memory:

> " In the sunshine dance and sing and play
> " Let us all frolic while we may "

and ending

> " Each thing goes, be it foul or fair."

Well, all the fair things of life seem to have dissolved. Let us hope the foul ones will do likewise. And so I left the light and airy places, to dwell awhile in the sombre sphere of " Jerusalem," the last lines being all too painfully topical:

> " I will not cease from mental fight
> " Nor shall my sword sleep in my hand,
> " Till we have built Jerusalem
> " In England's green and pleasant land."

What words! How well I remember the lofty and dramatic resolve with which we used to adorn them, and send them echoing into the rafters. Yet, their full significance seemed to dawn on me yesterday for the first time. The most that we impotent creatures in Guernsey can do towards making them more than an empty boast, is to acquiesce—without alacrity certainly but, we hope, with dignity—to the dictates of those who are pledged to render Britain equally impotent.

Following the caretaker into Diana's Form Room, I collected her books on the very spot where she had left me quite happily on June 20th saying: " I must go now Mummy, for roll-call. Good-bye." For both our sakes I could not have wished our parting to have been different. I would not have changed her mood to mine for anything in the world. I walked back down the school drive, meeting—without daring to exchange glances—the stream of parents bringing their children like lambs to the slaughter, to be deposited and labelled for transport. Little did we know they would be at College all day and the boat delayed till nine o'clock in the evening. They had all been allowed home for lunch.

Diana had declined to return. Either the distance, or the fear that we might curb her adventurous spirit now that it had been aroused, induced her to remain with the main flock. One or two parents, we learned afterwards, whose children had returned home for lunch, had succumbed to the temptation not to take them back. I wonder how we would have reacted to the anguish of a second parting. The sheer physical and mental strain of her absence becomes ever more intense as the days pass, no matter how we strive to forget those last hours. I know that Peter feels it just as acutely as I do, though we never mention these things which lie so close to our hearts. It is unwise to subject one's emotions to too frequent exhumation. We have met numerous parents whose reactions are identical with ours. Guernsey is almost childless, as though a modern Pied Piper has enticed all the children away.

We heard a recorded talk on the wireless last night by Dorothy Thompson. What oratory! She almost out-Churchilled Churchill. When she had finished we all felt delivered of much that has been suffocating us for weeks. We also heard Lord Halifax talking on Sunday. He fearlessly brought Religion into his scheme of things. We here, can see so clearly what he meant when he said that the Rule of Force is contrary to God's Law. Freedom is everything. Freedom to do all the simple things which have given us joy in the past. Basking on the beach, tea in the hay, the sound of Diana's abandoned laughter as we raced with her through the gorse, Kala bouncing ahead. Our blackberrying expeditions and our return home over the Common with sticky fingers and numerous angry red scratches on arms and legs; to take it in turn with darning-needle and magnifying glass, digging out the tiny thorns from our purple-dyed fingers. But how worthwhile, when we ate our first slice of piquant jelly which we simply had to sample while it was still warm! All of which calls to mind a poem we were given to paraphrase at school:

> "If I have faltered more or less
> In my great task of happiness.
> If I have moved among my race,
> And shown no glorious morning face.

If beams from happy human eyes
Have moved me not, if morning skies
Books and my food and summer rain,
Knocked on my sullen heart in vain;
Lord Thy most pointed pleasure take
And stab my spirit broad awake.
Or Lord, if too obdurate I,
Take Thou before this spirit die
A piercing pain, a killing sin,
And to my dead heart run them in."

—*R.L.S.*

Our spirits have certainly suffered a bit of necessary stabbing. We lotus-eaters have been far too complacent over our freedom, and have taken it too much for granted; if indeed we have thought of it at all. Right now, we feel it to be the most precious thing in life. We covet it, dream of it, pray for it, and millions of people are being sacrificed to restore it to this demented world. We fervently pray that their sacrifice will not have been in vain.

To M.H. La Guelle. 26th July, 1940.

To-morrow will be Audrey's thirty-first birthday. I wonder what you will all be doing, and hope that the next celebration will be in Guernsey.

No doubt you were more than a little perturbed when you discovered that we had not sent on your luggage, as you had arranged with George. You will be readily appeased, I feel sure, when you learn that our first chance of doing so would have been on the evening of our memorable air-raid. We should have been among those present when the Harbour and Jetties were bombed. I was in the garden when it started. I ran for dear life, and leapt into an oatbin in the stable adjoining the garages. George decided to look for me, and seeing what a good refuge I had found, lifted the lid of another bin, and jumped in just as a salvo of bombs was released. The noise was deafening. Several times we heard the bump and rattle of objects running down the corrugated iron—a bomb obviously intended for the Fruit Export sheds over this hill, exploded on the beach across the road.

Occasionally we lifted the lids of our bins and stood up to stretch ourselves and breathe; promptly clamping them down again as the raiders returned, the bombers screaming and whining overhead.

How we have chortled since at our infantile capers, which rewarded us with stomach cramp for days. At the time, of course, we thought our hour had come. We had no idea of the enemy's objective. Judging by the din it might have been the destruction of the whole Island. We sat rigid, knees touching chins, waiting in tense silence, resigned to annihilation.

Suddenly the raid was over. Oddly enough, it seemed to have lasted only a few minutes: and we were amazed to find that we had spent almost an hour huddled in those containers. Peter arrived on the scene as we were clambering out. He had just left Town when the raid began, and hastened to join Elsie and his old people. Emil had hustled them all together under the stairs, before setting out on his Warden's duty. Having satisfied himself of their comparative safety, Peter came on here to find me. Little did I know that he was walking the streets while the raid was on. I pointed out to him—in case of future attentions by the Luftwaffe—that I was not alone, and was fully able to take advantage of any shelter available.

The Germans could have flattened Guernsey had they felt inclined for, of course, no resistance was offered. Nevertheless, nothing they may do or say hereafter, will justify their ruthless machine-gunning of defenceless civilians. The cargo and export sheds proved to have been their real objectives. Scarcely a whole window was left in the Royal Hotel, nor in many houses along the Esplanade. At the time of the raid, the jetties were crowded with growers' vans tomato-laden, and with people either going away or seeing relatives off. This accounted, to a large extent, for the distressing list of casualties. Unfortunately, some of the victims contributed to their own destruction, making targets of themselves, by leaving safe shelter in vain attempts to reach their cars; the idea being to drive away from the disaster with all possible speed. Others ventured into the thick of it from idle curiosity. Twenty-two people were killed on the spot, and thirty-five injured, some fatally.

The next day, Saturday June 29th, we set out with bolstered courage for the wedding of Felicia and George. The windows of Allie's house had been blown in by the raid; so she and Felicia decided to leave the Harbour vicinity at once to be here with us. Our future movements being unpredictable, Felicia and George thought it best to marry at once rather than wait for the original date fixed. Some of the Town Church windows had also been damaged, and we wondered if there would be a repetition during the wedding ceremony.

We left home in the late afternoon in glorious weather. George and I in the front seats of Father's car, representing our Family, while Felicia and Mrs. Allen sat behind. We covered the distance to the church with an eagle eye alert for bombers. Peter was George's Best man. We found him waiting at the North Door with Tom Benett, Mr. Béghin and Mr. Le Lièvre, who formed our only congregation. The details of that wedding will remain with us all, an indelible memory; so sadly different was it from the many colourful ceremonies we have witnessed there, including our own, in happier times. Across the aisle in the other front pew corresponding with mine, still numbed by the departure of their wives and children, sat the three grass-widowers; painfully conscious that these two persons, were about to enter into that blessed state which they had indefinitely relinquished a few hours before.

The Local Press would have said—and in this case rightly so—"The Bride looked charming, leaning on the arm of her Mother. She wore a Navy-blue edge-to-edge coat over a floral frock, and a Navy-blue toque with flowered crown." As they passed my pew I swallowed hard and felt infinitely sad. Felicia had been alone in their house the day before when it was damaged in the raid, and she was badly shaken. I felt that her one idea now, must be to get the wedding service over and done with. There was little delay. No waiting for dozens of guests to be ushered into the pews. There flashed through my mind, as I sat alone in my pew the words of Mr. Tabor twenty years before. You will remember how he dabbled in Palmistry, and that one night after supper as he read our hands (an odd adjunct for a Parson?), he told George that he would remain a bachelor until his late thirties, when he would be married under the most extraordinary conditions. Could he really have seen these things in his hand? Or was he endowed with some uncanny gift of prescience?

Half-way through the Service the Dean stopped abruptly to ask the Bridegroom for his Licence. George parried by saying that he thought it was his own personal property, and had left it at home. After a brief discussion—all very mysterious to the congregation—the Service proceeded. It was a deviation from strict ecclesiastical law admittedly; but why wrestle with trivialities, when bombs might drop at any moment, Kingdoms were falling like ninepins, and Empires being threatened?

As they turned from the Altar I rejoiced to see that Felicia and George had cast aside the cares of the past few days; and determined to hail this supreme moment as a blessed respite between sorrows newly endured, and the problems which assuredly lay ahead. Their consciousness of its very brevity caused them to seize such happiness as they could, with both hands, and make this their shining hour. Indeed this halcyon state prevailed overnight and into the dewy hours of the next morning; when Peter and I were brusquely awakened from a deep sleep by a sharp rapping on our bedroom door. Without more ado, the Bride stepped gaily into the room, clad in flowered négligée and feathered mules, carrying a tray with tea and biscuits, for all the world as though she had never heard of Hitler and his disciples.

We blinked at her as a pair of owls before a searchlight. But she laughed brightly and bade us sit up and partake. We were soon sharing her infectious laughter and enquiring if she was heralding a new era for brides. We were assured however, that she had been awake some time and unable to recapture sleep, had gone downstairs to make a pot of tea, giving George also an unexpected treat.

Remembering with sisterly relish, his aversion to early rising, I wondered, as I sipped my now very welcome tea, if George fully appreciated this almost nocturnal gusto on the part of his chosen; or was he vaguely apprehensive, lest this might prove to be one of many such Felician foibles.

With what glorious insanity we began that day. Convulsed with laughter over yesterday's incongruous revelry. Our little piece of Britain so soon to be swallowed up by an insatiable monster. Verily were we playing bowls with the Armada at our door.

But I digress. I must return you to the final stage of that incredible wedding.

The Service over, Dean Giffard escorted the happy pair from the Altar to the Vestry. He made a sign to me, and one towards the pew across the aisle. Mr. Le Lièvre raised what I interpreted to be an inviting eyebrow in my direction, to which, as I stepped out of my pew, I must have given suitable encouragement. For the next moment, we were walking up the aisle arm-in-arm at an alarming pace as though trying to overtake the chief participants.

The Dean came back to La Guelle for the licence, which George eventually found under a heap of garments and shoes on his bedroom floor. After drinking a toast to the Bride and Groom, His Reverence set off for the Deanery apparently satisfied that they were properly married.

What a pity you were not all there to share with us this memorable, though moving, event. Yet, I must own, we carried off the occasion "with one auspicious and one dropping eye", for Allie's sister had been killed in the raid the previous day, and her brother-in-law seriously injured. Unhappily, this created a classic example of "the funeral baked meats coldly furnishing forth the marriage tables." We are indeed becoming almost accustomed to truth being stranger than fiction.

We were an odd assortment of people at the " Reception " that evening; including a few of George's friends and ours, who, in all probability would never have met, but for the crazy trend of recent events. In defiance of all our combined disasters we numbered thirteen. The wedding feast embraced a menu of brawn, salad, raspberries and champagne, mostly collected by George and me in Town that morning between sirens, German planes zooming over us incessantly. At one time, at Mr. Luxon's kind invitation, we sat sheltering in some basement room of the Gas Company in Smith Street. There were several other people unknown to us. Among them, a woman with hair in curlers and head swathed in a towel, accompanied by her hairdresser. All driven underground by wailing sirens. I remember marvelling at the *sangfroid* which could conceivably allow anyone even to remember a hair appointment at such a time.

Unice and Winnie, Edna and her Mother, at my invitation, had spent a few days with us after you left. We all intended . . . travelling together should total evacuation be enforced. Unice and Winnie had returned to L'Ancresse a day or so before the raid, while Edna and her Mother had moved into Bill's house to await events and to make room for the newly-weds. They came to the reception, and with Emil and Elsie and several of George's friends whose wives and families had evacuated, we made a convivial gathering. Even I emerged from the depths causing polite ripples of laughter, by expressing my intention to follow Nelson's example and put my blind eye to the " doings ". We raised our glasses and sang, among other suitable ditties: " For to-night we'll merry merry be. To-morrow, we'll be sober! " We joked at the prospect of being left to revert into a nation of savages. Someone predicted: "We'll be wearing grass skirts and strings of beads when our folks return." For, by this time, we knew that we were indeed cut off from you all for the Duration; though, of course, we have no idea how long the period of incarceration will be.

Emil found himself sitting next to Mrs. Veal, of hitherto slight acquaintance. Like the rest of us, she had been very agitated by the upheaval of the past few days; and had also endured the most distressing nightmares during her brief snatches of sleep. With his inimitable brand of spontaneous wit, and by the surreptitious application of champagne, Emil set about raising her spirits to his own soaring heights. In fact they almost stole the show from the chief characters; much to the decorous Edna's consternation. She came round the next morning to redeem her Mother's good name; protesting that never before had she indulged in such licentious goings-on. We, on the other hand, assured her that we had been delighted by the tonic effect of Emil's efforts, and were satisfied that her Mother had in no way outraged the proprieties.

To M.H. La Guelle. 3rd August, 1940.

History is marking time. Surely the much-discussed Invasion will soon begin. We constantly think of you all; and are beset by gnawing anxiety, which we try to exchange for delightful visions of reunion. The sheer ecstasy of such a prospect is almost unbearable. Clearly, these agonising flights of fancy must be drastically curtailed in the name of sanity; though it would require the *sangfroid* of a confirmed stoic, so soon to put one's emotions into cold-storage, no matter how soothing the result.

Peter and I cycled to L'Ancresse on Sunday. Sitting on the grass overlooking the bay we ate our lunch. We could see Diana leaping from rock to rock and shrimping in every pool. Raising our cups, we drank to next year's picnics together (?) in lemonade.

In the afternoon there were Germans bathing and sunning themselves. They nodded affably as they passed. We nodded sombrely in return. They shall not call us bad losers; no matter how much we dislike the admission, the score is against us for the time being. We feel that, with the exception of the odd nigger in the woodpile, Guernsey's attitude towards them is correct.

German Officials have organised dances at St. George's Hall, and one or two civilians (whose names would not surprise you) have actually held return functions at their homes. These turncoats, I hasten to add, are being suitably ostracised. Meanwhile some barbed comments have been exchanged between the natives of Guernsey and the Mainlanders. One of the latter astonished me by the remark: "This sort of thing would never happen in England." I felt bound to retort, that the only renegades to my certain knowledge, giving these return functions, are of English origin; and at least one of them newly arrived from the Mainland. Which indeed is true, and will be widely remembered in the day of reckoning. (He is already commonly alluded to as Herr Blank). Inevitably, Guernsey will produce her own crop of traitors, they infest every sizeable community the world over. Nevertheless, we are confident of overwhelming loyalty to the British Crown. Meanwhile, the Germans, finding a dearth of dance-partners, have issued invitations to the daughters of some of our friends. Needless to say, these are declined, firmly, but not without a certain trepidation. The position is extremely precarious, since we mere civilians are supposed to feel honoured by attentions of this sort.

The weather this week has exorcised the Ghost of St. Swithin. Most of the days, though gusty, have been fine. I am sitting once more under the mulberry tree where I first began these ramblings. The mulberries are ripening, so I shall not be able to continue here much longer, as you will fully appreciate. We are eating bread made from questionable ingredients, including bran. Bread is no longer being delivered. Instead, Depôts have been set up all over the Island where we have to collect our rations. Peter is using their ex-errand boy's bicycle with large front carrier. It serves many purposes, including a carriage for Kala when we go on long journeys. We have our hectic moments when he espies a cat and leaps from the carrier to give chase. I have been lucky to find an almost new bicycle for Five Pounds; the only means of transport—for the 99% who do not fraternise with the Germans; and as delivery-vans are a thing of the past, we cycle to the Laundry and Bread Depôts and also collect our meagre rations from Town. Our salt ration is reduced to two ounces a week, and we shall soon begin clothes-rationing. New restrictions are published in the Press almost daily, becoming more rigorous as time goes on. Rumours continue to circulate, several of which were selected and categorically denied in today's Press by Mr. Sherwill. The most promising and most persistent was the alleged imminent departure of the Germans. More of Father's lorries have been commandeered for export, lending a little colour to the rumour. There is plenty aerial activity today, two Fighters flying over as I write. The air is buzzing incessantly with the noise of many planes. They seem to be for ever expecting a flare-up over here, which will not be particularly healthy for us. Many people feel that, having decided to leave us, the R.A.F. would serve us better by keeping to that policy. I have an open mind, but it is obvious that this minute chip of Britain cannot accommodate large-scale activities, or even mere dog-fights without embroiling the entire community.

Two weeks ago an alluring fable was prevalent. A talk was to be broadcast from Britain by one or more Guernsey schoolteachers. This story grew from strength to strength, until it became obvious that there must be some truth in it. The whole Island was keyed up to a crescendo of expectation. A few days later we heard a short talk in "The World Goes By" describing the Alderney Evacuation. "Why?" we cried out in our wrath, "Why broadcast on Alderney of all places?" In any case it was not a faithful account of what in fact took place there. Be that as it may (as brother Henry would say), there are only Germans in Alderney to hear it. The Alderney refugees in England (bless their hearts) knowing the real facts of their exodus, must have been as mystified as we were deflated. Alas! Just how gullible can we be? It would seem that wishful thinking has reduced us to a level of naïve credulity. Then, like thwarted children, we lay on others the blame for what we feel are 'the slings and arrows of outrageous fortune.' Shall we never learn to leave truth and rumour to do their own winnowing, and come to terms with the present instead of waiting for miracles to ease our lot? This reminds me of those occasions in our childhood, when we would pester you for some desired object, usually a second helping of food. You would bait us with: "Will you have it now? Or will you wait till you get it?" We soon learned not to say "I'll have it now." That would have been fatal. You employed a unique brand of psychology. I grant you had to be subtle in order to control your clamouring brood of seven.

So now, if we are patient, we may yet be rewarded. Perhaps the dynamic F. E. Fulford, may one day pull a string in the proper quarter, and refresh us with news of our children whom we were so strongly advised to send away.

At the moment I find it difficult to feel anything but calm resignation. The fretting ghosts of yesterday are decently interred and I am as happy as it is possible to be under these conditions. The weather is divine, the mulberry leaves are gently flapping in the breeze, the borders are ablaze with petunias, roses, antirrhinums, dahlias and other delights, the birds are making a twittering aviary of this tree; and I do feel (with apologies to Robert Browning), that if all's not well with the world, at least God's in His Heaven.

I must now come down to Earth. The meat has arrived and must be dealt with: and as I am cook this week I must go in and prepare supper. It is now 5.10 p.m. and I am going to pick some of your American blackberries. The loganberries and raspberries are finished, though they have given us many a luscious feast. It has been a good year for fruit and vegetables. A great compensation.

To M.H. La Guelle. 10th August, 1940.

Another week has passed and still no sign of Invasion. Praise be! We are so worried about you all. The air raids seem to be more widespread and there are no reports this morning of enemy planes being lost. A British plane was seen over Guernsey last Thursday. The Germans had been on pins, anticipating trouble for some days; and sure enough, we came actively into the War again last evening, exactly six weeks since the massacre at the Harbour. We now have a new 'enemy' from which to take cover. We were finishing supper at 7.45 when the planes came over. We paid no attention to them in the habitual belief that they were German. Within a few minutes we heard anti-aircraft fire, followed by loud explosions as the R.A.F. released their bombs. We deemed it time to take cover, with the exception of Peter, who gave me the vapours by insisting on being a spectator; and would listen to none of our appeals to leave the landing window. It turned out, that the R.A.F. were attacking the airport, and we believe scored direct hits; but Guernsey is so small and so heavily fortified, that one simultaneous burst from their many guns, and the whole place vibrates as though both guns and bombs are in every back garden. We hope there were no civilian casualties. A few German wounded were seen to enter the Victoria Hospital soon after the raid. There was a short sharp raid about an hour later; but that only brought forth one loud bang and a little desultory popping. We are not enthusiastic about this sort of thing; but if it helps to make Guernsey a real headache to Hitler, and more and more difficult to hold, we shall welcome these nuisance raids. Also, it is easier to feel heroic and uplifted when one is at the heart of things.

The Chief-of-Staff, Dr. Maas, has been replaced. We can hardly expect a change for the better; for, by all accounts, Dr. Maas was always approachable and, at times, even conciliatory.

Meanwhile, we live from day to day, comparing experiences and reactions with our 'fellow-prisoners'. Many people long to escape; the Jeremiahs continue to preach impending doom; a small minority think it is high time the War ended no matter who the victor; and fewer still are constant victims of the jitters. We know of one family who have slept in their basement since the first air raid, and must surely have been driven underground for the duration by yesterday's attacks.

I wonder if you are feverishly writing to us following the good news broadcast this week. What a joy to feel that the British Government have not abandoned us! If you were not listening at the time, we hope you will hear from other Channel Islanders of the B.B.C. announcement, that you may now write to us via Messrs. Thomas Cook. I expect it will take a little time to organize. Also, we are not counting our chickens this time. We are becoming a little less credulous of second-hand information.

So far I have not touched upon the nature of public opinion with regard to the Evacuation or "Panic" as the cynics will have it. It is certain that at some future date you will hear their criticisms. We want you to know right away that we dissociate ourselves with this attitude: and for this reason, I record our limited impressions. Also, the end of your exile and our isolation are not yet in sight: and, let us face it, our reunion always in the balance.

The evacuation was a moving experience in every sense of the word.

We were not at the Harbour when the boats were leaving, and dense crowds swarming the jetties; so perhaps we are not competent to judge. We do realise, however, that even a football crowd would get out of hand if the authorities failed to handle their job efficiently. For my part, I saw no panic among the groups of relatives and others as I watched them preparing to leave. Widespread bewilderment there certainly was. I was one of the bewildered. This was not surprising, since our Officials were unable to claim the attention of the whole population simultaneously.

The first official announcement in the "Press", you will remember, was the focal point upon which pivoted several other mistakes. Far from helping a harassed community, it simply spread confusion. This first manifesto (whose origin, we presume, came from official sources), stated that everyone wishing to leave the Island, must register at their local Douzaine Room by eight o'clock that evening. Since a large proportion of the population (ourselves included) did not see a copy of the paper until nearly six o'clock, confusion was inevitable, if thousands of people were to attempt registration in so short a time.

Peter went to the Vale Douzaine Room to enter our names as a precaution. He found the place surrounded by surging crowds. They had been given officially to understand, in effect, that if they failed to have their names enrolled by eight o'clock, they were automatically doomed to fall into enemy hands. When Peter saw the magnitude of the task facing the Committee, he opened a window and, clambering into the room, proceeded to help in the enrolment of names.

Some people were registering for invalids, and for others who, for various reasons, were unable to be there. One poor soul was harassed almost to borderline because her father was paralysed. There were expectant mothers, one of them weeping because she was unmarried and deserted. There were infants-in-arms and in perambulators; in short, there were people of all classes and types; but there was no pushing, yelling nor "mass hysteria" such as typify panics.

As ever, rumour was rampant, with much to feed on; and very soon, the Island was alive with so-called 'Official Statements' and 'inside information'. There were even notices printed in the "Press" for public guidance, you remember, alleged to have been issued by States Officials. These were contradicted in the paper's next edition and new ones substituted. If our minds had been visible, they would have resembled some extravagant Heath-Robinson concoction.

Propaganda played no small part in torturing the minds of an already baffled community. Certainly, the thought uppermost in the minds of the multitude was — escape at all costs. The public had heard many lurid stories of atrocities in Poland and elsewhere. I am not presuming to deny their veracity, though they seem fantastic in the light of the Germans' present conduct here. I say this with the utmost reservation, for these are early days and we are told that they usually begin by ingratiating themselves with their victims, in order to get away to a smooth start gradually giving less and less sugar with the pill.

If the neurotic members of the community panicked, surely it was the natural outcome of their particular psychological make-up; and not an exclusive characteristic of Guernsey people generally, with our traditional mulishness. It would be interesting to see how any other body of people would have behaved in similar unorganised circumstances. Imagine the War Council and all in authority under it, being rendered ineffective, through lack of means to transmit vital instructions to the whole country simultaneously. I have no desire to throw the blame on the States, for I honestly believe they did their ineffectual best in deplorably difficult circumstances.

That was the Evacuation as Peter and I saw it. Certain smug individuals here, are posing as level-headed and heroic; and are contemptuous towards those whose mentality, they consider, let them down, causing them to "run away" or "bolt" — to quote two of the most hackneyed jibes. Now that they find themselves trapped for the Duration, and further decision taken out of their hands, they hasten to forget the ignominy of having themselves squirmed and wriggled and finally, having floundered with the rest of us, while the cataclysm was at its height. I believe these sham heroes to be in a small minority. Most people have taken a more rational and intelligent view of the whole thing. Everyone had his own particular problems to solve in the way he thought best. Circumstances were not the same for everyone. There were women whose husbands were in the Services, and thousands of others with their source of income in England. Parents with children under school age, who were urged by their Doctors to take them away. There were people who stayed because they were reluctant to leave home and business. Some, whose old folks refused to leave, and could not be left here to fend for themselves. Some people went away because they thought the Germans were coming; and their opposite numbers remained because they thought the Germans would not come. For every reason one could call to mind in favour of evacuation, there was an opposite point of view equally convincing. This formed the crux of plans made and broken numerous times in a few days. Thousands of people are still uncertain why they are here at all. They belong to the category of those who packed their cases, and found it difficult to make up their minds either way. The States of Guernsey were themselves baffled by the vacillations of the British Government who, in their turn, had far graver issues at stake than our immediate salvation. They know that will naturally follow once they have rid the world of the satanic forces now threatening to destroy us all. With the storms of indecision still upon us, Peter and Stan saw masses of arms and equipment arriving in the Harbour by train-ferry, for our promised protection. A day or so later, Peter saw it all being reloaded and rebound for England. Small wonder, therefore, that we poor orphans of the storm were pained and bewildered in the face of this skirmishing in high places.

During the morning of George's wedding day, while I was catering in town for the festivities, I met Douglas McLeod in the Arcade. In a most agitated state he exploded: "I have just arrived—on leave! I had no idea that Guernsey was being evacuated." German planes flew over us as he spoke. Looking up in horror he continued: "On no account must I be caught here. I simply must get away, even if I have to steal a fishing boat." A forlorn hope indeed. The last possible boat had left Harbour during the raid the previous day, and was fortunate to get clear at all. She had pulled out in the midst of the battle with guns blazing, taking with her people who had only gone aboard to bid their last farewells to sons and daughters, and leaving on the jetty in hopeless abandonment, a husband or wife now doomed to see this thing through alone. One can understand the plight of an Officer on leave, being trapped and rendered useless to King and Country. We learned afterwards that McLeod was imprisoned with one or two others in Castle Cornet, and has since been transferred to a prisoner-of-war camp in

Germany. On whom, one may ask, lies the responsibility for sending men on leave to a place in imminent danger of invasion?

I know that Father was reluctant to go. Yet most of his income would have been frozen in England, and he would have been hard put to it, at his age, to support you all in Guernsey. Even so, I venture to say that you would still be here, had he seen the notices which were placarded all over Town a day or so after you had left. They bore the bitterest taunts: "Don't be yellow!" "Cheer up!" "Stay where you are!"

A certain gentleman of noble lineage and high office, took one of these notices and begged Mr. Hargreaves to stick it on his car, telling him in heated terms: "This degrading panic must be stopped!" The next day, he too had flown, belying his flaunted heroism. Like the chameleon his skin had changed colour overnight, judging by his own avowed precepts. Which all goes to show how unwise it was for anyone to inflict his constantly wavering plans on others. In so many instances (to coin a phrase!) it was a case of 'the blind leading the blind.'

As the days passed between your departure and the arrival of the Germans, we lulled ourselves into the comfortable illusion that they would not think it worth while occupying so small a place. The air raid of June 28th, however, awoke us abruptly to the fact that we had been living, all too briefly, in a fool's paradise.

During the next two days, German and British planes took turns to visit us. There were several dog-fights as they chased each other out to sea, while we held our breath and hoped that the right side would win. The R.A.F. came less and less, as the Germans increased and gained confidence. Like huge black monsters, they flew so perilously low, that we could clearly see the men in the cockpits. They seemed to miss trees and chimneys by inches. No doubt this was done in order to intimidate us; and, following upon the heels of the raid, I must own that this strategy had the desired effect. We began to wish they would land quickly and deliver their ultimatum, be it what it may, anything to relieve the tension. With mixed feelings of apprehension and relief, the bulk of the population received the news on Sunday afternon, June 30th, that we were indeed Occupied.

The news came to us in a most alarming manner. After an anxious day of sirens and ceaseless droning of planes; Peter, George, Felicia and I decided to take a cautious stroll in the field opposite the house where we had our last hay-picnic.

It was a beautiful evening. Not a leaf stirred. The large shimmering expanse of sea below us, strangely undisturbed by the usual week-end pleasure boats. The new young after grass had covered the field with a fine coat of green. Here and there were clumps of old dried grass missed by the mowing machine. Of the chill blast which had swept over us in the past few days not a single breath remained to remind us of its passing. The lull was complete. As though by common consent no one mentioned the aching void within us, nor our growing apprehension as we realised that we were indeed bereft, and must, from now on, stand alone.

Suddenly, the large telephone bell in the garden halted us with its harsh clanging. We hurried indoors to hear what further entertainment lay in store. As George picked up the receiver, a voice at the other end could be distinctly heard by the three of us standing beside him. In caustic tones it said: "We want a lorry at the Royal Hotel immediately." We were still unaware of the Germans' arrival; and, as you know, we are not accustomed to receive orders in that peremptory manner. George queried incredulously: "A lorry at the Royal Hotel on a Sunday evening?" There were more acid comments from the other end. I most helpfully prompted George to ask what they could possibly want with a lorry at such a time. This ingenious advice brought him a rap over the knuckles. We were amazed and horrified to hear The Voice bellow: "You'll very soon know what for if you don't come at once! The Germans are at the Royal and want a lorry immediately!"

George was too stunned to do anything but acquiesce, and putting down the receiver proceeded to obey the command. He had no stomach for the job; but, for that very reason, could not send one of the drivers, even if it were possible to find a man at such a time.

Felicia came to life instantly and stoutly refused to let George go. Feebly remonstrating, he gave the insane excuse that the lorry was needed to take some German Refugees to

Fort Houmet. He sadly underestimated Felicia's intelligence, but I fear that none of us appreciated the humour of this spontaneous irony until the Occupation was several days old, when it provided us with some much-needed hilarity.

George disappeared at once, while Peter forcibly restrained Felicia from following. Only by drumming into her the fact that her interference would make matters serious for us all, did he manage ultimately to calm her. Of course she fully expected George to be shot as soon as the Germans had done with his services, and she pictured herself a widow after a marriage of only one day. I must own, that voice on the telephone had confirmed my worst fears, and I foresaw a terrible future for us all, if any.

George was absent for about two hours, keeping his appointment with our unwelcome tourists. Peter left us for a short while to warn his family up the road of the Germans' arrival. Meanwhile, I paced the dining room and tried to say encouraging things to poor, distracted Felicia; things in which I had little or no faith myself. I doubt if she even heard my empty assurances. Gone was her gaiety of the early morning; her brave resolve to make the best of things, temporarily eclipsed. Her mother, who had been visiting relatives, soon arrived and reiterated her professed belief that all would be well.

At long last we heard the front door open, and braced ourselves for further shocks. To our amazement, George walked briskly into the room smoking a cigar. He told us that whilst having a drink at the Hotel, he had gathered various scraps of information. He had gleaned, for what it was worth, that the Germans intended to respect the people of Guernsey, and would not interfere with our Civil Administration. He had heard the German exclamations of surprise on learning that we are virtually an Independent State, with our own Coinage and Self-Government. They clearly see that we are not going to fall on their necks for freeing us from "British Tyranny."

As George approached the lorry, intending to drive home, a German soldier had barred his way, informing him that the lorry belonged thenceforth to the German Army and that he must walk home.

Whereupon, the terrible tension relaxed, we executed a ridiculous version of the Lambeth Walk, and resuscitated our already soaring spirits in conjunction with those on the sideboard. Imagine our sense of relief, even if it should prove to be but a temporary reprieve.

Thus, procrastination is ultimately responsible for our isolation; and, if by our presence here, we are able in some way to protect our Island and our homes, we hope it may yet be said of us: "They also serve who only stand and wait."

To M.H. La Guelle. 22nd August, 1940.

Nothing momentous has happened since I last wrote. The R.A.F. have been over a few times, but we learn nothing from the Germans for, naturally, we are precluded from their deliberations.

Not for years have Peter and I done so much gadding about. Being, unfortunately, relieved of family ties, we tennis at least twice a week at Elm Grove Tennis Club, with the Ginge de la Rues, the Wellingtons, Mr. and Mrs. Don Rose and a few other 'survivors'. It gives us a great thrill to go about and meet friends and acquaintances who have remained here with us. We feel less and less abandoned each time we meet and compare notes; and much closer to people with whom we have hitherto been on barely nodding terms.

Once a week we go to the cinema, and cycle as far as L'Ancresse to see Les Dunes on Thursdays and Sundays. These diversions are a great respite from boredom. Since we settled into our home at L'Ancresse in '34 with Diana and Kala for company, we have not hankered after bubble entertainment. Peter would often say that we might be in our dotage, so content were we to sit, with a book, toasting our feet in the firelight after a hearty meal; or absorbing our favourite music by wireless or gramophone. The occasional celebration, or bridge evening with friends were our only variations. We were content to vegetate indefinitely, but now we feel the need to be more gregarious; a custom never difficult in a place this size, where most of one's relatives and friends live within such a small radius.

Last Sunday we lunched with Mrs. Veal and Edna. We compared Occupation notes since we went our separate ways after George's wedding. We left them in the afternoon to do some work at Les Dunes; but, on arrival, were dismayed to find that we had left the keys at La Guelle so we spent the time gardening.

I wish you could see Diana's garden. Most of the plants you gave her are in full bloom. The stock have not yet flowered, but the marigolds, antirrhinums, lobelias, petunias and asters are a riot of colour, as though she had indiscriminately shaken a packet of seeds on the ground and walked off to amuse herself elsewhere. A proceeding typical of our offspring.

We open the door to "Paradise Lost" whenever we enter our house. Diana's room, with all her cherished possessions, remains undisturbed. There is still a goodnight message on her blackboard written by Pam when she went in and found her already asleep. I wonder if Audrey and Pam ever mention that last week-end spent with us; and whether they told you how, amid much scuffling and ribaldry, the messy creatures squirted Kolynos Toothpaste all over Peter's face as he lay in bed. This, in retaliation on finding the limbs of their pyjamas tied together in Gordion knots. Those lively week-ends seemed all set to go on for ever. Now, as we leave the old haunts, pedal our way down the drive, and back once more onto the open road, with the scent of gorse in our nostrils, vistas of unclouded years close in behind us.

To M.H. Friday, 23rd August, 1940.

We believe the R.A.F. called again during the night; but, as rumour inevitably stifles fact, we are left wondering. I hear planes now and, as conditions are ideal for a raid, I am on the qui vive. Eight German fighters are speeding towards France and, as I finish this sentence, have flown out of sight. As Peter says: "They don't exactly loiter."

At 2.30 this morning we were wakened by the drone of a plane, followed by loud explosions. We both leapt out of bed and leaned out of the window. A flare was suspended over the Football Track. There were more explosions and, as anti-aircraft guns started banging, we stepped back from the window, fearing that a bomb might fall near by. The raid was mercifully brief.

Air-raid shelters have been made available to the public at the Market and at " Boots " in High Street.

Our Curfew has been reduced an hour. We are expected to be indoors by 10 p.m. I should have said long ago, that our Time was advanced an hour when the Germans occupied Guernsey, to correspond with German Summer Time. At first it was daylight until 11 o'clock. We are not allowed out until 6 a.m., a serious deprivation (!) The Press is often plastered with " Achtungs " and " Verbotens " and, because it is expedient for our safety that we heed most of them, the Germans publish spurious claims to our loyalty.

The Civil Authorities are constantly exhorting us to observe the strictest economy in the use of electricity, water and gas. We are warned that only a few months' supply remains. We picture communal living when these essentials peter out. A bleak outlook is envisaged without our news bulletins.

Among other things now scarce, are eggs, toothpaste, biscuits and chocolate, while permits are issued for petrol. Anyone will swap a car for a bicycle, which, once acquired, must on no account be parked without padlock and chain. Razor blades are also scarce so, if the war is prolonged, all the men will be bearded.

To M.H. Amherst. 28th August, 1940.

Felicia and I are whiling away a sultry hour in our old field near Beau Séjour. I have been describing to her those rollicking hay picnics we used to revel in as children, with masses of our home-grown strawberries on cabbage leaves, your home-baked bread with lashings of our butter, and cream, and how we loved making houses with the hay, and riding on the loaded carts.

O that the idyllic scene before us now, truly reflected the serenity of the world at this moment! Only the ever-present void of separation reminds us that a deadly war is being waged, on which our whole future depends. A vague stillness, helped by the calm weather, has haunted us all the week, like the oppressive lull before an approaching storm. Far away below, between the branches of the elm trees, there gleams the quivering sea, and above us an onyx sky, almost transparent. I hear the distant popping of a fishing boat, the faint rumble of far-off guns, and nearby, the buzzing of bees, or the occasional rattle of a cow's chain as she shakes her head in an effort to rid herself of flies. This simmering heat is having a soporific effect on Felicia. She has fallen asleep.

Last night we four stood at your bedroom window watching a gigantic firework display over France. A series of flares, anti-aircraft flashes and what we imagined to be tracer-bullets, travelling through the night in all directions. What a spectacle! Every door and window in the house was shaken by the explosions. We pitied the poor souls on whom the full blast descended.

To M.H. La Guelle. 23rd September, 1940.

This correspondence is becoming spasmodic. Time and inclination do not always synchronize. I am appalled to see the date of my last entry; but there are many uneventful gaps with nothing to record, when we feel a sadly unmilitant body, waiting in the wings like actors without a rôle.

Peter is in the garden pruning arches, so I take this opportunity to keep abreast with personal happenings and sensations; the latter not to be misconstrued, for drama is not the keynote of our present existence. Our nearest approach to it, since our initial dose, came a few days ago.

Felicia and I were washing the breakfast dishes when the doorbell rang. It was just after nine o'clock. Peter answered the summons and came to tell us that three Guernseymen, accompanied by a German Officer, had called to collect clothes for French and Belgian Refugees (!) I told him to say that you always dispose of your old clothes in the Spring. But our visitors were not so easily put off.

We leapt upstairs in order to do those trivial and common tasks not usually performed under the curious eye of complete strangers. With slight palpitation and some resentment, I was covering the beds when the four men walked into your bedroom. Although I was somewhat embarrassed, it would be quite wrong and stupid to garnish the incident with an air of drama. We fully expected them to demand the opening of drawers and wardrobes; but fortunately they were more reasonable, and were content to take our contribution without question. The local men assured us that the whole proceeding was extremely distasteful to them, while the German behaved with silent courtesy. On seeing a woman in the room, he clicked heels and bowed. With studied indifference I continued my work.

Harry and Allie Marquand had spent the previous evening here at La Guelle. We had told Harry that we had seen these men leaving Mr. Cohen's house down the road laden, presumably, with linen and clothes tied up in laundry bundles. Harry had declared with ill-concealed mirth: "You are the next on the list." Naturally, when this prediction materialised, we remembered his words, and wondered if, under a smokescreen of banter he (as States Supervisor) had, in fact, lifted the veil of officialdom in order to give us a timely warning.

Later in the day, however, when the news of our visitation reached him, Harry telephoned to disclaim all previous knowledge of the affair. He apologised for any inconvenience caused and told us that our visitors were unauthorised to enter occupied premises on any pretext, and that the clothes would be returned. Needless to say, we had unearthed a humorous miscellany of garments, some of them of pre-Victorian design and obscure purpose. Certainly, in the words of a well-known comic opera: "They'd none of them be missed."

To M.H. La Guelle. 24th October, 1940.

Another whole month has elapsed since I last wrote. There never seems to be time for all the things we have to do.

Felicia and I take weekly turns with the cooking. After hours of laborious preparation, the fruits of our labours are consumed in a few minutes. Our week of cooking over, we heave a sigh of relief. We sometimes regret dismissing your Muriel, who came after you left to ask if we would keep her on. She is a nice girl, but we felt that we could easily manage on our own, the only real plagues being the fires and the clearing up after meals.

I regret every day that I allow to pass without adding something to this diary. Somehow, this task I have set myself, has forged a precious link with you all. I often wish we had not been quite such an undemonstrative family. We seldom revealed our innermost thoughts and feelings towards each other. Vocal praise or affection were taboo. Thanks for gifts received or favours rendered were grudgingly given. Yet, if ever I paid you an unexpected visit and found none of you at home, I always felt acutely disappointed. Later, I would tell you that I had called, but never hinted that I was sorry to have missed you. I suppose it was due to some innate dread of mawkishness running through our entire family relationship. We were hamstrung by an unfortunate tendency to taunt anyone found guilty of emotion in any form. I believe this "cloaking and dissembling" prevails, to some degree, in most families: each member enveloping himself in a hard crust of indifference, as an essential part of his mental equipment, an insulation against that demon—Ridicule. To resort to tears, unless universally condoned by the grievous nature of the cause, was to invite endless calumny, to be administered at the most searing moments. But, this universal approval once given, it was bestowed freely and in full measure, when the almost fortunate victim fairly glowed in the rare sunshine of filial affection. I fear that the 'patient' was barely convalescent before the limelight was smartly switched off, and he was left once more to become just another pebble on the beach.

We like to think that the mind grew up with the body; and that childish taunts gave way to healthy banter, accepted or ignored, with fewer and fewer sparks flying, according to the prevailing mood of the recipient. This calls to mind the oft-remembered day when we were celebrating a family birthday. We decided to stand at the table and sing with raised glasses: "For he's a jolly good fellow." One of our number (who shall be nameless), said it was "all damn nonsense" and, remaining seated, refused to join the chorus. Whereupon the rest of the family, on reaching the last line of the song, slowly and solemnly declaimed: "And so say all of us — except one." This, to the utter disgust of The Silent One and the hysterics of everyone else. It was a hard school. Yet, those were enchanted days, now far away and gone, it seems, for ever. For one solemnly wonders whether an entire family of such dimensions, now scattered indefinitely, can really hope once more to reassemble at the same table. The cult of the large family is over, too. No longer do parents produce hosts of unpremeditated children. A sobering thought for all late arrivals. Your thoughts I can well imagine as you read this. Believe me, as number six, you have my undying gratitude. I would not have missed it all for worlds, whatever the end may be.

Reluctantly, one returns to the present. Many changes have taken place since I last wrote. For some weeks now, shopping hours have been altered by German order. The present hours are from 10 a.m. to 12.30 p.m. and from 2 p.m. to 4 p.m. This makes shopping a mad scramble, for most people find the allotted time inadequate. As a 'concession' shopkeepers are allowed to stagger Saturday lunch-hour.

Cigarettes, cigars and tobacco are now rationed, each man receiving a weekly allocation of twenty cigarettes and half an ounce of tobacco. Women are not catered for at all. Fortunately I gave up smoking before the war, and Peter is thankful that he never acquired the habit. A day or so before rationing began there was a wild rush on all tobacconists' shops, in which many Germans took part in spite of their ample rations. Ration cards have also been issued for clothing. Each person has a yearly issue of one hundred coupons. On looking at Peter's card for instance, I see that he can buy in the course of a year:

1 pair half hose	10	coupons
1 handkerchief	5	,,
1 pair walking shoes	30	,,
1 pair flannel trousers ...	20	,,
1 shirt	20	,,
Soling one pair shoes	15	,,
	100	,,

A suit takes sixty coupons, which leaves him with forty to cover everything else for the rest of the year.

All drapery shops have been closed for compulsory stock-taking, and large quantities of clothes commandeered by the Germans. For the past month, shopkeepers have been forbidden to sell soap, and have been compelled to submit a list of their stocks. To off-set this, our supplies of flour, meat and sugar have been replenished. Tea is also scarce, and many other things are unobtainable. These include cheese, fish, marmalade, bacon and biscuits.

The shortage of fish is a blot on the names of a handful of men who escaped from Guernsey a few weeks ago. We understand they received an enthusiastic reception in England; but there may well be a very different reception awaiting them here when the war is over. For, by their action, they have deprived most of our fishermen of a living. A German edict was immediately published, ordering all owners of boats to take them to the Town Harbour by a given date. Since all boating was forbidden, this meant that many fishermen were obliged to wheel their boats several miles across country. This was no trifling feat, as you will appreciate. We met one crew near Saumarez Park, already weary and with still a long trek ahead of them. We were also warned by the Germans in the "Star" of September 28th that, should anyone else escape, all the male population might be evacuated to France by way of reprisal. That would be catastrophic for the whole Island; and we fervently pray that no one is contemplating such an unpatriotic move.

Following on the landing here of a small number of British Servicemen, another manifesto was issued about two weeks ago, commanding the immediate surrender of any members of the British Armed Forces. Two young men gave themselves up. They had been landed here by submarine which failed to collect them as planned. Their relatives and a few close friends were arrested and put through a gruelling cross-examination for a few days. Most of them have since been released and speak well of their prison treatment.

Such happenings and other known pinpricks irritating the German command here—although we care not how deep they go — have a disquieting effect on everyone. One wonders if, like Hitler, their august patience might suddenly be exhausted, and threatened reprisals begin in real earnest. There is always the risk that some fiery character might go berserk and carry out some of the things we all feel the urge to do at times. If such acts would assist our cause in particular, and the war effort in general, no doubt many attempts would have been made long ago, with the full blessing of us all. But one must be wary, even with the pen.

We have been issued with Registration Forms on which we have to fill in a detailed description of ourselves. We then have to report at any one of five depôts in order to sign the completed form in the presence of a Special Constable or Douzenier. George inadvertently entered the date of his birth as 6th September, 1940. With a raised eyebrow, Peter looked at his watch and advised Felicia that it was time to prepare George's bottle, top-and-tail him and put him to bed. Peter was in one of his facetious moods, as you will gather; for when I asked him where these depôts were to be found, he gave the following list, presumably his own idea of the appropriate places:

1. The Museum
2. The Model Yacht Pond
3. The Mental Home
4. The Public Lavatories
5. The Slaughter House.

This buffoonery reflects a universal lack of respect for impositions designed to benefit the wrong cause.

The Germans have begun to export cars, lorries and buses in large numbers. Inevitably, some amusing tales on this subject are circulating. One man had dismantled his car completely and had buried the whole thing in various parts of his garden, deluding himself that the Germans would never know he had possessed one. How wrong he was! The Germans, having the official records in their possession, simply demanded that every registered car was to be cleaned, put into perfect running order and sent to its collection depôt. With muscles and joints still aching from his exertions, our friend was obliged to re-arm himself with all the necessary tools needed to excavate and reassemble his own car for export.

One of our worst afflictions so far is the recent rationing of milk. Children of two years and over are allowed one pint of whole milk daily, and adults, half a pint of separated milk. Many invalids and old people have applied for full-cream milk, and were notified to appear before the Medical Board, but very few of them have been successful. An extraordinary thing, you will agree, for Guernsey people to be subjected to milk rationing. The Medical Board sent a note of protest to the Germans who gave the peremptory reply, that should they receive any further complaints, there would be serious trouble.

It now seems that the men who escaped to England recently, must have informed the appropriate authorities that we still have our wireless sets; for, to our delight, we heard the Channel Islands Broadcast a few evenings ago. So perhaps the fugitives have rendered us some small service after all; though I fear that the fishermen will not consider this meagre result to be sufficient expiation for the loss of their livelihood. I do hope that the B.B.C. will repeat and improve on these programmes. They wasted a lot of precious time talking about holidays in Guernsey; hotels, bays, lilies, tomatoes and other products. There was ample time for them to mention all the schools instead of just a few. However, we are grateful even for crumbs; and I suppose it must be impossible for the producers of the programme to know what it means to be isolated indefinitely from kith and kin. Could they have seen how everyone here glued his ears to the wireless, as we did, lest he miss the voice of his dear ones, or the reassurances of their safety, surely they would not have wasted vital moments regaling us with an account of our own habits and customs. But perhaps the broadcasters had little say in the matter.

Two landaus have just gone by, returning from a wedding. The coachmen's whips and carriage lamps were decorated with white ribbon. A reminder of bygone days. Presumably, the honeymoon will be spent in Guernsey.

A few days ago, Peter was cycling to business, when a brougham passed him. An arm shot out as he cycled past; and, to his intense amusement, he saw that the occupants were two Bank clerks of his acquaintance. They had been making the routine collection from their country Branch. They shared Peter's amusement at their strange turn-out. Thank Heaven for our British sense of humour! It sheds a ray of light in many dark places. May it continue also to be your first line of defence. It stands out here in stark relief against the expressionless masks of the Germans, who appear to take themselves so seriously.

The esprit-de-corps of the Guernsey people has never been more pronounced. The joy of walking through Town and seeing one friendly face after another, among the thick sprinkling of Germans, is truly comforting. We are all in it together. Words are not necessary to convey the unity of spirit in the nod, wink and smile exchanged behind the German uniform as they pass between us. In this fashion we greet and are greeted by all and sundry, as though a lifetime of detached recognition has ripened overnight into mature friendship.

I must leave this now to prepare tea. I hope that another month will not elapse before I find a chance to continue. Peter has just returned from tennis and is in the bath. Tennis! A north-easterly gale blowing, and leaden skies. I am at your bedroom window as ever; and although it is tightly shut, the cold still manages to penetrate. Nevertheless, I find it difficult to write downstairs. The only fire is in the kitchen where we have installed a settee and armchairs, they save space and also serve as dining seats. We removed the cumbersome kitchen table, and use two card-tables for meals, folding and putting them away when not in use. You would be surprised how cosy the room is with comfortable furniture and a little imagination. Unfortunately, the stifling proximity of communal life is not conducive to lucid writing. Snatches of conversation, shufflings, wireless and the like, mingle with my thoughts until my brain feels like a mental stockpot.

To M.H. La Guelle. 6th November, 1940.

So President Roosevelt is in for a Third Term. Praise be! It is to be hoped that he will forge ahead with further aid for Britain.

Yesterday we were shattered to hear Mr. Churchill speaking in terms of 1943-44. We were just wondering how much longer we were destined to endure this stagnation, when the shell burst. Felicia said: "Good Heavens!" George, who came in too late to hear Winston, thought we were joking: I blinked and gaped, while Peter, as usual, started the laughter. We were helpless! Peter taunts me with such inanities as: "Diana will have left school and be in a job before the war is over." Our ten-year-old! I refuse to believe it.

Mr. Churchill's motto: "It's a grand life if we don't weaken," strikes a lofty note, but I doubt if the first half of it applies here. However, we know that to weaken in these circumstances would be futile. Mr. Churchill delights us with his clever anecdotes and tricks of speech. Our creeping paralysis of boredom and anxiety flee at his opening words. That inflexion in his voice which we have come to know as the precursor of some new masterpiece of wit, sets us all laughing even before he can get the words out. He is better than our best news bulletins. Most of our encouragement comes to us over the air from the Land of the Free.

Often, in the stillness and beauty of the night, when the whole earth seems scarcely to breathe, Peter and I have stood together at this open window in complete silence, our thoughts doubtless running along the same channels. Sometimes a voice from the shadows whispers those comforting words spoken by the King last Christmas. More often than not I am half-way through the quotation before I realise it: "That shall be to you better than Light, and safer than a known way."

It has come to me also numerous times when strolling in the fields, on reaching the brow of the hill where we get that glorious panorama of sea and islands, that you know so well. We are always sorry to leave it, and linger on till the last vestige of light fades and dies. If only we could live in the open like the birds, instead of being cooped up between four walls.

To M.H. La Guelle. 7th November, 1940.

We are now in the midst of a turbulent spell of weather. Incessant rain and gales have swept the Island for weeks. The wind reached an alarming velocity last Wednesday night. Felicia and George were sleeping at Tom Bennett's. Stan Noel and Harry Marley were playing bridge with Peter and me until three-twenty a.m. They slept in Audrey's bedroom. The hurricane began at about ten o'clock. Large trees were blown down, numerous greenhouses were completely flattened, telephone wires and roof tiles were scattered all over the place. Never had we experienced anything like it. It stopped as abruptly as it had begun; and before we finally went to bed, not a breath of it remained. We leaned on the window-sill, looking up at a clear sky bright with stars.

I find it bitterly cold up here nowadays. I wear a dressing-gown over my clothes, a pair of Peter's socks over my stockings, warm slippers; and, wrapped round me with a hot-water bottle tucked inside it, a thick travelling rug. The results are negligible, but how worthwhile to continue this conversation with you all, however one-sided. By States injunction, our electric and gas fires have been sealed to prevent us using them. A manifestly wise, though unwelcome, move.

A really sinister event has cast a shadow over the Island since I last wrote. All those people who were imprisoned and subsequently released, in connection with the young British Servicemen who landed here recently, have been re-arrested and taken to France for trial. The parents of these boys, seeking guidance, had divulged their presence here to Mr. Sherwill and Harry Marquand. The Germans had promised a free pardon to all concerned if the British soldiers surrendered. Harry and Mr. Sherwill are among the deported, presumably as accessories, in spite of their advice to the young men to give themselves up.

Thus the Germans have violated the traditional British trust in the given word. Not satisfied with that betrayal, we are all being subjected to further reprisal. Our wireless sets are being confiscated. Lorries are being sent to collect them. They have to be in by the nineteenth of November.

We shall miss the News Bulletins. Good or bad, they were of paramount importance to us. Helpless, we stand and wait in grateful admiration while the best of Britain's manhood once again adds glorious pages to our history—written with their blood—as their fathers did before them on the fields of Flanders. No longer shall we be able to follow their exploits broadcast by the War Correspondents. Mercifully the news had recently improved. Some wishful thinkers even assume the confiscation of our wireless sets to be a good sign, indicating that the Germans resent our enjoyment of their approaching doom(!).

1941

To M.H. La Guelle. 2nd January, 1941.

What an age since my last entry!

Christmas has come and gone; and with it many sensations and experiences also. I think everyone felt a new surge of emotion on Christmas Eve and Christmas Day. No children—no stockings. Like most other people (including yourselves I have no doubt) we had our bad moments; but they had to be stoically stifled. In fact it was a much more enjoyable Christmas than we had thought possible; though many of us were keenly disappointed that no message of greeting was broadcast to us from the Mainland. We half expected to be mentioned in the King's Speech, or to have a few minutes of news from Channel Islanders in England. Some casual mention was made in an obscure programme, we believe, heard by a small number of people here. Our wireless sets had been returned on Christmas Eve, a universal boon, and we felt like prisoners set free.

On Christmas Day we invited two grass-widowers to lunch with us, Tom Bennett and Harold Le Lievre. Our menu being roast beef, brussels sprouts, baked potatoes, and Allie's Christmas Pudding, with crackers to give the festive touch. The poignant moment came when we stood and toasted the Absent Ones in Grâves; but we revived once more to the tune of *Auld Lang Syne,* though by that time, one of our little band had crept away.

Peter and I had accepted an invitation to spend part of the holiday with two more 'widowers' Stan Noel and Harry Marley at Stan's bungalow. We left Felicia, Allie and George with their friends in the afternoon and cycled to L'Ancresse where Stan and Harry were waiting to celebrate with roast chicken, cooked by Mrs. Stacey at the Farm. This was followed by one of 'Weazle's' well-matured Christmas Puddings, and a few sweetmeats and crackers which we had saved for the occasion. The toast to the Absent Ones (this time in liberal quantities of Champagne) threatened, for the second time that day, to cast a blight on the proceedings. But the moment passed; and after some inevitable reminiscings and conjectures on the future, it was in really convivial spirits that we finally settled down to one of our endless sessions of Bridge. At two o'clock in the morning we revived ourselves with coffee, and played on till four o'clock by which time we no longer remembered what were trumps, or which cards had been played. The coffee had fought a losing battle with the champagne.

When first Peter and I met our deserted men-friends, we felt truly conscious of the effect we must be having upon them; as though we had somehow broken the rules by refusing to separate; and as though the stability of our connubial state, reflected a lack of constancy in their own. Possibly this feeling existed only within ourselves, because most of our companions happened to be forsaken husbands.

Their homes sadly lack the feminine touch. Imagine Stan for example, bereft of the competent 'Weazle' upon whom he has always relied for every creature comfort. I remember her telling us one day that he had never so much as bought a packet of cigarettes for himself. It must be a novelty now for him to enter a shop and to tackle his own housekeeping. One wonders indeed how such a human dynamo can ever stay the course. He told us that as soon as Weazle and Nan reached England, Nan telephoned him, exclaiming excitedly: "Daddy, what are you waiting for? Jump in '*The Merlin*' and come!" Still he hesitated to leave home and business, convinced that the Germans would not invade Guernsey, and that they might soon be able to return. Some people did leave here in their own boats, but we have never heard of their safe arrival into freedom. A risky venture to undertake with enemy planes in attendance and (for them), uncharted seas to navigate.

As for the steadfast Harry, the separation from his adored American Martha must be a prolonged purgatory; with her slim elegance, her perfectly ordered ménage, her carefully chosen objets d'art, her frilled American curtains, her artistic floral decorations, and her delectable American dishes. At least he knows that she must be safe in America with her family for the Duration; and their reunion assured unless Fate unleashes some further lunacy upon us.

Boxing Day arrived, and after a long lie-in we emerged from our bedrooms, had breakfast, took one look at the kitchen and set about clearing the wreckage of the day before. Peter and I have always prided ourselves on our team work on these occasions. We were due at the tea-rooms for another day and night, so we took leave of our hosts and made our way across the Common.

We were delighted that Unice and Winnie had asked us to be present at their festive and most hilarious gathering. There were nine of us, including Mr. McCathie and two District Nurses. Roast beef being the Island's meat theme with or without variations (!) once more we put our blind eye to the 'Doings' and imagined we were eating the traditional turkey. We had a rousing time and refused to think of you sadly, sincerely hoping that you were doing the same. We firmly contemplate re-union for next Christmas.

I wish that you and the McCathie family could have seen Mac, Peter and me at breakfast in the tea-room on the morning after Boxing Day. Winnie had stoked the fire before retiring (at 3 a.m. we were drinking tea) and it only needed a little coaxing to revive it. After setting our breakfast, Winnie took hers on a tray and joined their other guests in their bedroom. We remarked how amazed and amused you would have been had you taken one peep into that place and seen the three of us re-living the riotous episodes of the previous night. In particular, the scene where the dignified and dour Mac, suspecting that Unice and Nurse Taylor were plotting to make him an apple-pie bed, made a dive to

lock his bedroom door in order to forestall them. He slipped on the polished floor and almost totally disappeared under a table, clutching a bottle of champagne which he had knocked over and miraculously caught as he fell. The look of astonishment on his face rendered us speechless with laughter. There he lay, leaning on an elbow, the green serge table-cover over his head and a fringe of green plush pom-poms on his forehead; still brandishing the bottle, he turned to look at us, uncertain whether to join in the laughter against himself, completely unaware that an enormous vase of flowers was literally swaying within inches of his head before mercifully righting itself. Poor Mac! He had put on an act, utterly alien to his character, guaranteed to put any piece of rehearsed slapstick in the shade.

Reluctantly we said our farewells, and the three of us cycled the five miles into Town in the raw frosty morning, feeling refreshed, though sorry, that our brief holiday was over. As we came out on to the sea front, the sun was just rising, the whole eastern sea and sky a blaze of crimson glory. It might almost have been the afterglow of many celestial bonfires commemorating the Nativity.

I should have said before, that at the end of November the Arcade shop suddenly found itself without a lady assistant. I was asked to step into the breach just for the Christmas rush and I am still there.

German summer-time has not been altered, which means that we get up and breakfast with the black-out curtains still drawn. The weather is bitterly cold. Fortunately, the shorter business hours give us more time for home duties, but life is still a rush. My chores (that ugly word!) are done before and after work, including washing and ironing, bedroom cleaning and cake making. No longer do we buy cakes, they are quite uneatable with existing materials.

We have been lucky to find a capable little maid of eighteen years, and although she meanders somewhat, she is always on the go, and eventually gets things done. By mutual consent, Felicia and I do our own breakfasts and suppers, which gives us all more freedom to come and go without being time-bound.

Our food supply has been good so far, but cannot be expected to continue indefinitely. There is a sad lack of tea, a literal headache. Thanks to your foresight, the produce of this garden and the co-operation of Lily the cow, our rations should be agreeably augmented for a year or two if need be — though Heaven forbid. If, after that time, we are still in this pickle, it will be a case of the survival of the fittest.

With the acquisition of a daily help, we are able once more to live in the dining room. I am overjoyed at being able to continue this downstairs, where there is plenty of room and an open fire. Having to economise with fuel, we let the kitchen fire out as soon as Lucy goes home. The 'others' are urging me to play Rummy, so I must adjourn. Goodnight.

To M. H. La Guelle. 7th January, 1941.

The New Year came in on a much more cheerful note.

On New Year's Eve, Allie Marquand invited us with other friends, to usher in the New Year at her house. The curfew was extended to 3 a.m. We had been officially informed that all the people previously arrested and taken to France, had now been released and were expected back in Guernsey at any moment.

As we neared Allie's house I remarked to Peter how exciting it would be if Harry had actually arrived to see the Old Year out with us. As we entered the house, his was the first voice we heard. Suddenly feeling 'de trop' and thinking that Allie might be regretting her invitation to us, we decided to respect the privacy of their re-union. We were turning away from their door when Allie came into the hall and caught sight of our retreating figures. She insisted that we join them in their rejoicing. Other guests were already being welcomed by Harry, who was eager to see everyone, and delighted at having so much company after weeks of solitary confinement; but it was obvious that he had endured great mental strain. He expounded for hours on his ordeal, giving us a moving account of his day-to-day struggle for mental and physical survival. In common with the rest of the Guernsey prisoners, he had lived on a diet of watery soup, of questionable origin, and very little else. He had kept a record of the date by making one pin-prick each day on an empty cigarette carton, happily left in his possession. He had paced his cell for endless weary hours, with, by all accounts, boredom and anxiety eating away at his powers of resistance. The familiar inquisition they had all endured, when the barbaric sounds of other prisoners being beaten up, brought home to them the vital importance of every answer coinciding with those of their compatriots, to the satisfaction of their inquisitors. This they must have succeeded in doing, for they were all mercifully spared corporal punishment. Just as their hopes of freedom were at the lowest ebb, they were suddenly released from prison, and bundled into a lorry, were driven like cattle for mile after mile across France. With grim irony, Harry recounted the details of that journey with its inevitable embarrassments. The high spirits with which they met every emergency, were utterly devoid of ribaldry, but rather that especial brand of gallantry only attained in rare moments of communal danger. We were proud of their performance, carried through 'sans peur et sans reproche', their only lament being, that their original number had been reduced by one. A day or so before their release, one man, unable to stay the course, and unaware of their imminent reprieve, had decided at the eleventh hour to end his life in his own way.

Despite Harry's obvious enjoyment of this New Year's Party, we felt that it would have been infinitely more sensible for him to have spent it quietly with his family; and so it proved, for we heard afterwards that he had spent a tense and restless night still determined, much against the dictates of body and mind, to sit up in bed and continue talking, far into the night.

With the return of these people and our precious wireless sets (on condition that no more German orders are ignored!) life has assumed a much brighter aspect, further enhanced by the ever-heartening war news.

Meanwhile, petty restrictions continue. All the pigeons in captivity have been killed because the Germans suspected, not unnaturally, that they were being used to carry messages to England. This slaughter was disastrous to pigeon-keepers, some of whom lost birds valued at £20 apiece. Peter spoke to one or two breeders who were absolutely desolate at the cold-blooded destruction of their treasured specimens.

Snow has been threatening for the past few days. The weather is icy cold and we are unable to thaw unless we sit almost in the grate. Our day begins at 8.30 a.m. (6.30 by the sun). As dawn breaks we set out for business, where I am still a square peg in a round hole. We are trying to learn a number of colloquial German phrases, mostly bearing on our work. Mr. Sigwart, who came here from Germany many years ago to work for Peter's father, has now come out of his retirement to help us, and has written a list of relevant sentences for us to memorise. Peter is much more fluent than I am, though even he flounders at times. He is also taking lessons in German with a Mrs. Tate, the German-born wife of an Englishman who settled here some years ago. Among the foreign workers in Guernsey doing forced labour for the Germans, there are many Frenchmen on whom to practise our rusty French. This sudden profusion of languages can be somewhat confusing; and occasionally I hear Peter in the middle of a German sentence saying: "Oui! Oui!" for "Ja! Ja" and the next moment he is saying: "Nein! Nein" to a Frenchman. We have only to speak one sentence in German, and the eyes of the soldiers sparkle. They say: "Gut! gut! Sprechen sie Deutsch!" No protestations from us of "Nix sprechen die Deutsch" will stem the ensuing guttural flow of words; until our shrugging shoulders and blank expression finally convince them that we are out of our depth, and have not taken in a single word. Hopefully we try out one or two of the parrot sentences which sounded so polished at home: but nothing we have memorised seems to have the slightest bearing on the present subject. Inevitably, it ends with a miming-match until one side or the other sees the light. We heave a sigh of relief as they click heels, Heil Hitler and depart. Then, as they are leaving, to our dismay a number of their comrades arrive in their place, when the whole charade commences all over again.

We resort in the course of a day, to so much grimacing and gesticulation, attempting thus to convey what our linguistic efforts fail to do, that we frequently find ourselves punctuating our conversation with these foreign gestures at home.

O that we might be "far from (this) madding crowd's ignoble strife!"

To M.H. La Guelle. 19th January, 1941.

Yesterday, the first time for nearly thirty years, I failed to send a birthday present and greetings to Flo. Also I shall have to forgo her reciprocations next month. I wonder if she is still in Surrey with Ted and Rosemary. So many friends are scattered far and wide, and all is conjecture between Red Cross messages.

Meanwhile we keep the home fire burning. As I write, the wind, whistling and moaning around the house and thundering in the chimney, mingles with the hissing of pine logs in the grate. Peter and George are playing draughts, Allie is sitting beside me with the " Press ", Felicia is pottering upstairs, her knitting lying on the seat of her chair, while Kala lies curled up at my feet. Snow has fallen this week, which, with the abating of the easterly winds, has risen the temperature a degree or so. This Arctic winter has given me a crop of chilblains on hands and feet, the first since childhood.

I wish you were here to enjoy this old familiar scene. Living in the old home and writing to you, my thoughts inevitably turn to far-off Sunday afternoons when we were very young. Everyone absorbed with some favourite hobby. Some of us reading, others drawing and painting; Henry, as likely as not, scribbling some of the doggerel to which he was addicted, preferably and ironically about Kaiser Bill and Little Willie. You and Father would be half-dozing in your fireside chairs with the newspapers; your pince-nez threatening to fall into your lap. I can see Father now, with patriarchal beard, his watch chain looped across his waistcoat, and the drifting incense of his cigar, all combining to set him, in our eyes, upon that awesome pinnacle from which Victorian fathers were wont to govern their dependants. Not, I hasten to add, that Father was always unapproachable to his children. He would have deeply resented any odious comparison with Mr. Barrett of Wimpole Street. I freely own that I spent more time on the paternal knee than anyone else. Nevertheless, I came to it with due reverence, waiting for him to thaw when he saw fit. Then, he could tease and be delightfully playful. But woe betide anyone who, given an inch, presumed to take a yard!

To this day, on any turbulent wintry afternoon, I have only to close my eyes and listen to the wind moaning through some ill-fitting door or window, and I smell those hissing pine logs and Father's smouldering cigar. Perhaps this feeling is stronger in me because Peter and I are non-smokers, and this memory has not been vitiated by the usual fug of tobacco smoke which hangs about the average house.

These recollections will always be green in your memory as with all of us and, since the future is unpredictable and the present unpalatable, one tends more and more to escape into the sheltered past. It is always there for our refreshment. Inviolable. Neither men, nor systems, can steal one little gem of it. Fortified, we return to the present.

> " What is to come we know not. But we know
> That what has been was good.
> We are the masters of the days that were.
> Shall we not take the ebb, who had the flow? "

To M.H. La Guelle. 30th January, 1941.

Life just pursues its humdrum course. We pass these days in a coma of boredom. An enervating malady. We begin to realise a little of the frustration endured by the prisoners-of-war in barbed-wire confiniement. Here we remain, captives in our own country, while the German grip continues to tighten; and warnings continue to appear in the " Press ". There is now a nine o'clock curfew.

All Men's Clubs have been closed. Even the Salvation Army Citadel, of all harmless places, has not escaped this veto. Apparently the Germans regard any gathering of men as a potential underground threat.

We are still most anxious about you all, and only hope that you are not in danger zones. Like yourselves we long for the end of hostilities; but we are prepared, as doubtless you are, to wait indefinitely for the war to end the right way.

Meanwhile, we seek to fill our leisure time with every available diversion. Tomorrow night we shall have the company of Stan and Harry (Marley), when we look forward to one of our bridge marathons, a few hours of real refreshment. Felicia and George will be at Louis Béghin's house. On Saturday, Harry Broughton is expecting us to a similar bridge session at his place, Bert Williams who lives with Harry will make the fourth. On these occasions the guests set out equipped with pyjamas, toothbrush and food-ration; for it has become the custom to spend the night wherever we go, in order to defeat this juvenile curfew.

We wonder incessantly if the Invasion will be launched. Various opinions on the subject are freely expressed, but we are still in the dark together. Meanwhile, the lull continues.

Peter still contrives to read in bed at night, but I usually feel too pre-occupied. I just lie beside him, listening to the solitary German plane — known to us all as "Minnie the Moocher" — on her nightly reconnaissance, droning and droning above us, hour after hour, mingling insidiously with the maze of thoughts which dominate all our waking hours. Each one of you has a place in this labyrinth of conjecture, with Diana high on the list. When sleep comes I invariably meet some of you in the Wonderland of Reunion, ecstatic while it lasts, though it means a crude awakening.

To M.H. La Guelle. 7th February, 1941.

Thank Heaven for the cheering African news! It is the one bright spot in to-day's bulletins.

Life in Guernsey at present would be extremely difficult for you all if you had stayed, without a car to take you about, and the weather too awful for you to go far on foot.

A number of people are receiving messages from relatives in England. They are notified by post when a message arrives at Elizabeth College, where it may be read on request. Most of these messages are not worth the journey. Allie, for example, set out full of hope in answer to a summons, only to find the typewritten name and address of her sister in London and the date July 30th, 1940. Not only was this several months late, but it only told her that her sister was making enquiries about her on that day.

We are still passing through a phase of mental drifting; vaguely and anxiously feeling our way, uncertain what the next day will bring. Will the pessimists prove correct with their macabre prophecies? It is possible at times to generate large doses of optimism, and to feel confident that, come what may, nothing will reduce us to the morbid state of the local Jeremiahs. Then suddenly a depressing news bulletin, or a particularly sinister German threat, descends upon us like a pall; and it becomes all too clear how narrow is the towpath, how deep and swift the torrent on either side.

If there is any truth in the old adage: "The hand that rocks the cradle rules the world" — then Somebody's Mother did seriously bungle her job. How many men of letters have subscribed to this view I know not, but I know that Emerson was on their side with his version: "Men are what their mothers made them." A shattering thought for the mothers of the world, who, by pandering to the tantrums of their sons, might be guilty of nourishing a potential despot, capable of plunging the whole world into total war, from which mankind can only be saved by the combined sacrifice of many nations: when all that was needed at the outset was the back of a hairbrush applied to a juvenile behind.

Poor Diana! This was the punishment which she endured (though delivered by hand), on the few occasions when she committed the cardinal sin of answering rudely if thwarted in some way. I hope that she and her foster-parents are reaping the benefits now. Incivility was also a crime in your eyes, deserving of severe punishment, your well-known maxim being: "I don't mind a joke but I hate impertinence."

I well remember one occasion when, at the age of seven, Diana incurred this dreaded penalty. This time Peter was the outraged parent. He took the rash course of giving her the choice between two punishments; either to go across his knee, or to give up a precious afternoon gardening with him. Poor Peter! He might have guessed she would choose the spanking. She was upstairs and we were down when she made her choice. Peter looked at me as a drowning man at a floating straw and said: "You had better do it. I feel like a murderer." But I was not to be coerced into inflicting a punishment devised by someone else. Meanwhile, the miscreant, impatient to have the affair settled, leaned over the banisters, and in a loud tearful voice called: " Come on, Dad! " Our eyes met for an agonised moment, before he slunk up the stairs, as though he were the victim of the wrath to come, regardless of the fact that he might indeed be about to clip the wings of a budding female despot. Peter's suffering was even more acute than Diana's smarting seat, and she rubbed salt into his wounds by hugging him fiercely, rushing out into the garden, and calling him to make haste and join her. Never again did he give her the choice of weapons.

My birthday yesterday I spent in bed, where, in fact, I have malingered for several days with a chill. Never have I endured such cold as in the Arcade this winter. Peter, who had bought some oranges and lemons of golf-ball dimensions, had set his heart on making marmalade. He carried knives, basins and all necessary paraphernalia to my bedside, where we peeled and cut up the fruit until 4 o'clock, when I dressed and came downstairs to cook it. We made four pounds of marmalade, a birthday present in itself.

We have remembered all your anniversaries in turn, yours comes next. We toasted Marie first, then Audrey, Doris, Bill and Pa. Diana will be the last in May.

For the first time in my life, no parcel arrived from Aunt Mabel, though a more conscientious Godmother it would be impossible to find. Of all Father's five sisters, I think she was the prettiest. The most vivid memories of her are set in our childhood, for we were all very young when she married and went to live in Melton Mowbray.

One disastrous episode connected with her, stands out from all her less eventful visits. It was a Sunday afternoon, I was only about five years old, when she came to say good-bye before returning to England after a Guernsey holiday. She drove Grandpa's black pony and chaise down Foote's Lane, with Teddy the collie in attendance. I can see her now, peering over her pince-nez from which hung a long black ribbon; her tightly buckled waistband between her long flowing skirt and her stylish blouse with boned neck-band of lace, her fob-watch resting on her shapely bosom; her whole person dominated, as in the manner of the day, by a huge straw hat, abundantly garnished with the fruits of the earth, her hands busy with reins and whip, one foot imperiously pressed on the bell announcing her arrival. One almost expected to see an escort of outriders flanking the equipage.

Disaster, you will remember, came within seconds of her departure. As the sound of the carriage wheels and the clip-clopping of Bobbie's hooves died away down the lane, we all turned in a body to stampede into the house. I was in front of Bill, who, in a fever to get past, gave me a mighty push which sent me crashing into the sharp edge of the gable. In a few moments the front of my new white silk frock was dyed red. Dr. Conrad Carey was urgently summoned from his afternoon nap, and I remember that he gave me a fivepenny piece for being brave while he stitched my forehead. The mark remains, the only indelible souvenir of a by-no-means scatheless childhood. A clinical examination of the whole family would doubtless put me in the shade. But one obviously remembers best the lurid details of one's own disasters.

Poor Bill! He was panic-stricken and cried aloud: "I've killed her. I've killed Kitty! Will the policeman come and take me away?" Without waiting for reassurance, already in his infant way he felt the mark of Cain was upon him.

Mercifully Aunt Mabel was well on her way, blissfully unaware of the pandemonium she had left behind. I wonder where she is now, and hope that she and her family have left London: though, with her public-spirited nature and deep religious convictions, I can well imagine that she would consider it a moral obligation as the widow of a militant evangelist, to stay around in order to minister to those whose duty it is to remain at their posts. The rest of the community we hear constantly being urged by wireless, to leave London and so spare the Wardens unnecessary labour and hazards.

To M.H. La Guelle. 28th February, 1941.

At last news of Diana! Cards have been received by Elsie, from Winnie and Bubbles. We feel truly grateful to them for mentioning Diana, though no doubt they little knew that none of your messages has reached us. Naturally we were both overwhelmed. This is one of the advantages of having numerous relatives on both sides of the family.

There must be many messages drifting somewhere between us, and our turn must come soon, since hundreds of them arrive in the Island every day.

In the eyes of the world, I am, once again, a lady of leisure, having renounced ' City life ' after my chill. Business is almost at a standstill now that the Christmas rush is over; and that was due to the fact that our goods are not rationed. There is still much activity in our repair rooms, but that did not concern me. This decision to retire was precipitated by my sudden collapse in the stairs one freezing morning after cycling into town. As Dick would have said: " I was built for nourishment, not punishment."

We are now with Winnie and Unice at the Tearooms enjoying the happiest days since you left. The brief week-ends spent here during these trying months have given us new life. Everything would have been so much more difficult without the hospitality of these good friends.

There are usually eight of us here at the weekends, including Unice's parents, Mr. McCathie and Nurse (Jane) Taylor.

The clearing up is a communal effort, and sometimes of a riotous nature, with Mac, Unice and Jane splashing each other and skylarking generally. Then follows a long session of Rummy, with Unice and Jane openly peeping into adjacent hands, and warnings from Mac to: " Keep your cards close, where Cunning Kate and Slippery Anne can't see them."

When we leave here on Monday mornings, Unice and Winnie stand at the door waving again and again. Having pushed our bicycles over the Common and up to the brow of the hill, we turn for a final wave of the hand, knowing full well that our next visit will be as welcome as the last and, by us, as eagerly awaited.

George and Felicia's bungalow is nearing completion, and they will move in as soon as possible. We dare not leave La Guelle empty, lest it suffer the fate of all large houses, and be occupied by the Germans. It was a problem to know what to do for the best. We have discussed this fully in family conclave. It would be useless to put all your furniture and other effects into a depository, and let the house to suitable tenants; for the Germans are raiding the depositories and carting away the contents for their own use.

Certain it is, that we and the Georges could not find room for half your possessions in our small houses, already replete with our own things. Therefore we have decided to stay at La Guelle for the time being and to pay frequent visits to Les Dunes until we see what Fate has in store.

Nothing is certain in these circumstances, and we live from day to day, taking each fence as we come to it.

To M.H. La Guelle. 8th March, 1941.

Many Happier Returns of the Day. We drank your health at lunch — in coffee. A delicious brew it was, made from a surprise packet, happily unearthed by George from the bottom of a kitchen cupboard during a shattering mouse-hunt with Kala.

We remarked how full of flowers this room would be if you were here. Faithful to tradition, I roamed the garden in search of an assorted bouquet, the sole reminder of the usual family tokens in your honour. It stands beside your photograph on the mantelpiece here in the dining room, a credit to your March garden. Blue hyacinths, wallflowers, primula, stock, daffodils and tiny blue iris (whose botanical name escapes me), all laden with wafted memories.

It would have been appropriate to have received a Red-Cross Card from you to-day: and better still for one of ours to reach you. We sometimes wonder if any direct message from you will ever come our way. Some people have received as many as six messages at once. Mrs. Philemon Dorey telephoned one evening saying that she had heard from Marie; and asking if we would like to send a reply through her. We naturally took advantage of her kind offer in case our other messages have gone astray.

At the beginning of each week our meat ration provides us with a couple of square meals; but by Wednesday we resort to vegetables only. On Thursday a 'friend' arrived with a small piece of bacon. We suspected that it was *bien mal acquit* but the still small voice of conscience was no match for the clamourings of little Mary. One-course meals are now the order of the day, and we have made it a crime to open a tin without the full consent of a quorum.

To M.H. La Guelle. 29th March, 1941.

We still have a nine o'clock Curfew even with these lighter evenings; and now we are forbidden to use electricity after 11 p.m. More than nine months have passed and still no word from you. We can only imagine where you are, and what you are doing. How irksome must be this exile for you and Father. Only on rare occasions could he be persuaded to have a meal anywhere but in his own house. He always had a fund of excuses ready for emergencies, if only to attend to Lily the Cow. And now, he must be wondering if he will ever again sit at his own table. Such thoughts are dangerous and must not prevail; though even my ebullient Peter was downcast for an unguarded moment yesterday, a prey to the prowling troops of Midian, but they were soon repulsed and his mercurial spirits restored.

Food seems to be the foremost topic of conversation at present, and we are really beginning to see the wisdom of sending Diana away. This garden has been a boon, and Allie has kept us supplied with eggs, enabling us to conserve what remains of your far-sighted store. Yet, I regret that large part of it which you returned, against your better judgment, after reading in the Press the pious homily of some misguided pundit, as to the unpatriotism of hoarders; and this, against the advice of the Official who advocated the buying of all available supplies that the shops might be replenished before we were cut off from the Mainland.

And when I survey our little store-room with its sadly depleted contents, and remember the sugar, flour, tinned meats and tins of coffee which you returned in a fever of patriotism, I cannot but feel that you were ill advised after all, for these comestibles in particular are now at a very low ebb.

Those who kept their children here must be very worried indeed. An egg, to most people, is more precious than gold, the milk ration lamentably low, fish seldom seen; and the bread ration now reduced to 5 lbs. a week for men, 4 lbs. for women, and 3½ lbs. for children. Fruit is as scarce as fish and oatmeal a thing of the past.

We eagerly await the middle of May, when Lily is due to function and will be producing milk again. Skimmed milk is an apology as well as a punishment to farming folk, it looks like chalk and water and is quite tasteless. We ran out of tea and cocoa weeks ago and would joyfully part with the family plate for one pound of tea, regardless of post-war recriminations(?). The difficulty, I assure you, would be to find someone stupid enough to make the exchange. A Barter Column appears in the "Press" daily. Some of the items are pathetically amusing, and many quite impossible. One from last evening's Edition reads: "Apples exchanged for golden syrup, sugar, soapflakes or paraffin: Write 'Apples', Press Office". *Quel optimisme*! Another reads: "Tea exchanged for flour". O that we had flour! This may sound odd, but at times we crave a stimulant above all else.

Whenever a German regiment leaves here, they take all their equipment: guns, telephone wires and endless other trappings. Rumour travels round the Island that the Germans are pulling out altogether. Just as our spirits are tentatively rising, a hundred or so Germans leave here, only to be replaced by several times the number, bringing with them another mass of equipment. They install themselves in unoccupied houses, until there are very few left; turning people out of house and home at a few hours' notice, sometimes forbidding them to remove any of the contents. Will our turn come? is the thought in every mind. It is always a possibility, and we should be particularly put out now that we have jointly put money on labour and produce for this year's crops. Peter and George have done good work and results should be rewarding in the next few months. Every commodity is scarce, Grocery shops are almost empty, and what little remains is rationed.

The States reviewed the situation last week. Electricity we read, will cease after April, and gas only promised for a few more months. The setting up of Communal Kitchens is being contemplated. The future looms far from picturesque but, like Mr. Micawber we refuse to be morbid.

To M.H. La Guelle. March 31st. 1941.

On Sunday, at the King's request, Peter and I attended St. John's Church, our first appearance there since our marriage in '28.

This is a strange War. In 1914 the men were missing from the choir-stalls: whereas this time, the small boys were absent, and their places taken by young girls in surplices and mortar-boards.

As we left our pew, I was reminded how, in the old days, the organist was wont to irritate us, and really provoke Marie's wrath in particular, by his method of dismissing us from the Church.

The Blessing over, the Choir would leave their seats in the Chancel, hands decorously folded before them in solemn procession; the tremulous voice of the Organ quivering through the aisles its own soothing benediction. Then hey presto! The moment the vestry door closed upon Clergy and Choir, the Organist pulled out all the stops; and, as though the Hounds of Hell were suddenly unleashed at his heels, proceeded to attack the noble instrument with an almost blasphemous gusto; so that, instead of leaving the Church engulfed in an odour of sanctity, we were driven forth as a legion of devils, that the Organist might with all speed get home to the Sunday Roast.

Yes, I was certainly engulfed in a flood of memories at St. John's on Sunday. How could it be otherwise? With the ghosts of numerous Heads overflowing our pew; and the muffled mirth of an overflowing pew of simmering Arnolds behind us, relishing together the trivial inanities, magnified out of all proportion, at which adolescents are wont to giggle at the most inappropriate moments, whilst attempting to dodge the censure of the parental eye. Such oddities as the Verger's boots, squeaking like the rusty hinges on some ancient oak door (or so it seemed amid the silence of the Place), were sufficient to set us going. Numerous incidents were evoked within me after all these years, a happy respite from the morbid absorptions of the present.

The Violin and Organ recitals given in Unison by Marie and Mr. Davies, the Lay Reader, about twenty years ago, however, echoed and re-echoed in my ears, and that was not such a useful vehicle of escape. They revived " thoughts that do often lie too deep for tears ". You will remember how the Puritans objected to " Les Marionnettes " as being too frivolous to be performed in Church, and how Mr. Tabor dismissed their objections by asserting that, to his knowledge, the Almighty had revealed no predilection for purely solemn compositions. Handel's "Largo" and Goddard's "Berceuse de Jocelyn" which Marie played, with Organ accompaniment in many of the Island Churches about that time, made a terrific impact upon my adolescent mind: always transporting me, as I suspect it did many others, into heights of discernment and vision far beyond our natural endowment. A paradise not to be regained in retrospect even at the best of times.

These excerpts, you will remember, were usually played as a kind of entr'acte at Mr. Tabor's lantern services during Lent, when every pew was packed, every available vestry chair and form, jammed into the aisles. The solemn chanting by that packed assembly of "The Story of the Cross" also made an impact on young and old alike, the voices of the multitude rising and falling in slow rhythmic waves, as verse after verse unfolded the Story to its pitiful conclusion.

What sermons that man preached! The congregation would settle itself as he waited with studied calm, until the lights were dimmed, the last spectacle case had snapped shut, the last nose had been blown and the last pair of feet had come to rest. Only then would the arrows begin to fly, as the words of his mouth and the meditations of many hearts, became acceptable or unacceptable in the sight of the Deity, whom he had called upon to bear witness. Certain it was that he never let up until the last arrow had found its squirming victim. Not even the senile fell asleep. His oratory, for he was a born orator, was by turn, moving, vitriolic, pleading and always controversial. At times, I fear, he rent the air with the most uncanonical broadsides, providing his parishioners with much of their Sunday table-talk. It seems to me as I look back, that he stressed overmuch the "Thou-shalt-nots".

Surely a demarcation line should be drawn, lest some over-zealous Preacher, with "fire and brimstone" technique, should see fit to extend the list; and thus acquaint the uninitiated with the more alluring vices; evils with which they might never have been confronted. I know that many of my adolescent illusions suffered dethronement about this time. Perhaps that was inevitable, and might easily be explained by Freudian argument. However, this is no place to embark on polemics, even supposing that I were mentally equipped for such an exploration.

There were unmistakable signs that Mr. Tabor was a woman-hater. We suspected a jilting somewhere in the past. One day he took the perilous step of asking Bill what he would say, if he told him that he (Mr. T.) had never kissed a woman. Needless to say, the answer came straight from the horse's mouth: "I'd say" said Bill "that you were either a liar or a fool!" This brought forth a bellow of laughter from the Vicar who, in all fairness, could take as good as he gave. He freely admitted that from such a forthright specimen as our William, he might have expected just such a spirited retort. And once, on opening a door in our house he beheld some female gathering, he exclaimed: "The Chamber of Horrors!" and beat a hasty retreat as though fully expecting to be pursued by a volley of missiles.

His uncanny skill at Palmistry became almost a ritual, into which each new guest at our supper table, would be initiated on Saturday nights after Tennis. How amused we all were, you remember, when he told Dorice Bachmann that she would remarry and produce twins (which she did!). I was destined, he said on another occasion, to marry a well-known local athlete of outstanding build with the letters A and C in his name, and Peter (christened Albert), at Boarding school at the time, was unknown to anyone present, including Mr. Tabor or myself.

Our experiences with the Vicar's various 'locum tenens,' to whom he hoped we would extend our hospitality during his annual vacations, would make a tome in themselves.

There was the elegant daughter of one Parson, whom we privately labelled 'Venus', by virtue of her statuesque bearing: the constant adulation of whose parents only added to our secret mirth. We would arrive at the Vicarage for coffee, to behold 'Venus' drifting through the drawing-room in a trailing sheath gown of gold lamé and hair piled high, in striking contrast to the rest of her family and ourselves, attired as we were in less formal fashion: thus setting off the Greek goddess to perfection. In countering their party piece that 'Venus' had been presented at Court (her dumpy sister of course had not); we thought Father a trifle harsh when, as we sipped our coffee, he casually revealed that Marie had played the Violin before the King and Queen, withholding the fact, that while this was true, Marie was only a member of the Island Orchestra on the occasion of their Majesties' visit to Guernsey in 1921. On being chided later by the embarrassed Marie for his rather obvious gibe, Father defended himself by saying that he could take no more of their eulogies, as though 'Venus' were a Prize Exhibit at a Flower Show. Albeit, so immersed were they with the performance of their Combined Effort, that I doubt whether Father's thinly veiled innuendo even registered. The mechanism of the limelight had mercifully jammed.

The Oswald Family who followed them, were an entirely different proposition. Two of the girls of my age were thrilled to be visiting the homeland of Phyllis de la Condamine, Head Girl of their (Cheltenham) College, on whom their current bout of Hero-worship was fixed. The Oswald boys read the Lessons in Church most beautifully, I used to try to imitate one of them, the other one not being so easy to copy. They certainly caught and held the attention of the congregation.

The whole family were as mad on Tennis as we were, and made an equal number of playing members as ourselves. You will remember that we put all the names in a hat and drew for partners, resulting in whole day battles-royal, with only short intervals for refreshment, plentifully supplied by you; with lashings of strawberries and cream, homemade bread and Guernsey Gâche.

One gruelling Final stands out from the rest, when Father and the eldest daughter were engaged in almost mortal combat against Mr. Oswald and myself. The panting Paters left the Court with bald heads steaming, while all four of us resembled boiled lobsters. I still have the fading snapshots of the Teams.

Such was the pattern of our lives over a number of glorious years, which alas, it now appears we took too much for granted, and shall almost certainly never see again.

Following the Day of National Prayer, the week began on a livelier note. Yugo-Slavia has joined the Allies. It may even be the beginning of the end. They may inspire other countries to make a stand over a wide area of Europe. "Hope springs eternal"—however naïve.

I am finishing this now to the edifying strains of a Beethoven Violin Concerto, and trying not to think how much we shall miss this link with Freedom now that the loss of electricity is threatened. Fortunately the news is improving, as we hope it continues to do, during the next few weeks, leaving us with high hopes when the news bulletins will be scrappy and uncertain, and hard to come by.

To M.H. Les Dunes, L'Ancresse. 30th April, 1941.

What an incredible time since I last wrote! Even at this eleventh hour I must add a few lines as April passes. You may well suppose that a month's respite was needed for me to recover from writer's cramp, mental and physical, after my last effort; but the real reason is, that time and the mood do not always synchronize.

As you see, we are now living at Les Dunes, and having some meals at the Tearooms, while George's bungalow is being completed. Your message to Felicia with the news that Diana spent Christmas with you, caused us great excitement and a tremendous feeling of gratitude. We were also relieved, for your sake, that Jerry has left us in possession of La Guelle.

This must be brief. I am due at the Tearooms for supper. In a few moments I shall stroll across the Common, now covered with daisies, buttercups and full-blown gorse; whose intoxicating scent mingled with the familiar tang of the rising tide, will help, for a few dizzy moments, to oust such thoughts as air-raids, shipping losses, African set-backs, Greek failures and other pressing torments; whilst the gradual entry of America into the War, and now this crazy landing of Hess in Scotland, all tend to keep our emotional mercury ever on the move.

To M.H. Les Dunes, L'Ancresse. 14th May, 1941.

A new incident has added yet another anxiety to an already full programme.

German soldiers had stolen a number of articles from certain shops in Town. Some days ago they decided to give Peter a turn. When, by methods well known to the Trade, he saw a couple of Jerries about to leave the shop with two diamond rings, he challenged them: "What about the two rings which were on this pad?" The chief crook spread out his empty hands as proof of his innocence: but Peter accused him of slipping them into his pocket. Whereupon both Jerries became abusive. One burly specimen sidled round the counter, definitely showing a strong inclination to fight. As they were armed, things began to look ugly. Peter stood firm, and threatened to telephone the Feldgendarmerie, if the rings were not instantly restored.

Although the soldiers are known to dread the fury of the German Police, in this case, the warning seemed to have lost its magic: for, leaning insolently against the counter, the soldiers urged Peter to carry out his threat; obviously believing that he would not dare to call their bluff. However, Peter knew that to weaken now would be fatal: and, making for the telephone urgently summoned the Feldgendarmerie. As he replaced the receiver, the shop door was opened by a local customer. The thieves, having lost their bravado, seized their opportunity, dashed out of the shop and up the street, with Peter in hot pursuit. He caught up and grappled with the accomplice, but was unable to hold him: and decided to return to the shop in order to safeguard the rest of its contents, and to await the Feldgendarmerie, who might or might not believe one word of his story.

Within minutes they were on the scene. Cursing Peter for not holding on to his man, they ordered him to close the shop, hustled him into their car, and set off once more in the direction taken by the fugitives, in full view of the general public. It never occurred to Peter, until I mentioned it later, that passers-by might be nudging each other and saying: "There goes another collaborator!"

Needless to say the thieves had made good their escape, but not before Peter had made a mental note of their epaulettes and cap badges. He was told to report that evening at Headquarters (Grange Lodge Hotel), where four car loads of Officers, Military Police and one monocled Personage, were waiting to take him to Les Beaucamps Arsenal for an Identification Parade.

Approximately 400 soldiers were lined up before Peter and Mr. Sigwart, who had had a similar experience of theft at our Arcade Branch. "We were stunned" Peter said "at the sight of all those blighters who, at first glance, were as indistinguishable one from the other, as the blasted mugs on the canteen shelves!" Although the chevrons on the uniform tallied with those of the accused, they sensed with some trepidation, what the reaction would be, should they fail to identify the offenders.

As luck would have it, the "two Beauties" (as Peter called them), were within the first half dozen. They looked straight through and beyond him as though he were not there at all. As previously instructed by an Officer, Peter tapped them on the shoulder. Whereupon, the Officer bellowed a command at them in real Teutonic style, rasping enough to delight even the most flamboyant Hollywood Film Producer. The two unfortunates stepped forward, heads erect and with completely expressionless faces. Meanwhile, Peter, having gained confidence by his success, proceeded down the line in the hope of identifying yet another man whom he had, some days previously, suspected of shoplifting. He hesitated before one of them; but, not being certain in his mind, returned through the ranks as though satisfied with his inspection. He was asked by the Officer why he had hesitated before a third man. When deciding to give him the benefit of the doubt, Peter had underrated the filter mind of the Régime, to which no detail is too minute for sifting. At that moment Mr. Sigwart, who had completed his tour of inspection, stood before the accused and set the seal on the fate of the third suspect. This poor fellow was subjected to the same pulverizing treatment as his fellows as he stepped from the ranks to complete the unhappy trio.

Police were despatched to inspect their belongings, returning with a biscuit tin full of loot, purloined from various shops in Town.

For the first time Peter felt a certain compassion for his now sweating quarry, so ruthlessly run to earth, and due for equally ruthless punishment. No such qualms, however, beset their superiors. They clasped Peter's hand as though he had just pulled off a major victory for the Fuhrer, and thanked him profusely for his invaluable help. To Mr. Sigwart and Peter, this seemed a most ironical conclusion: for, until that moment, they had been unaware of their assistance to anyone but themselves, and possibly to other business people in Guernsey.

The Germans fixed the trial to take place in Jersey; and told Peter that he must be prepared to go there at short notice in order to give his evidence. His protestations that he could not leave his Business, were curtly dismissed; and, after all, the sole object of this whole affair being the restoration of the merchandise; if the trip to Jersey promises to attain that end, then to Jersey he must go. A prospect which delights me not at all.

The call came this morning. Peter telephoned from Town to say goodbye. The boat is due to leave at 4 o'clock this afternoon: and the trial scheduled for to-morrow.

During the past few days, other Beaucamp soldiers have told Peter that the accused men had Police records before the War, and that it would not be surprising if one of them, a hardened criminal, were given the death penalty. As a reprisal, ever since the arrests were made, the whole Camp has had an early Curfew, with lights out at 10 o'clock. The Occupied Countries have reason to be thankful for this iron discipline: a further confirmation of Nevile Henderson's impressions in his book: " Failure of a Mission ".

At Unice and Winnie's kind invitation, I am staying at the Tearooms during Peter's absence. Your absence has been tough enough to bear Heaven knows: but would have been far worse without this Oasis.

It has illuminated all the dark places—and there have been many—during the past weary months, further aggravated by a deterioration in my health. I cannot rid myself of the belief that a number of Doctors have boobed over my appendix: but one cannot thrust the appropriate weapons into unwilling or indeterminate hands. Time will tell. Though in my case it does not exactly 'fugit': this grumbling having been intermittent for so many years, as well you know.

I began this entry while Kala's dinner was cooking. The poor little blighter is clinging to life, as his present diet of limpets did before we prised them off the rocks. I have just shelled a bowlful of the smelly things; and, as I write, am regaled by the briny tang which penetrates the whole house.

Winnie is expecting me for 4 o'clock tea, and as it lacks but a few minutes to, I must adjourn.

I stroll over here across the Common to Les Dunes every day, to air the place and to enjoy the solitude, which I have shared with you this past hour. I think constantly of you all and the joys of reunion.

To M.H. Les Dunes, L'Ancresse. 26th May, 1941.

A few days ago Peter returned from Jersey without warning. He walked into the Tearoom just as tea was being served. As you may imagine it was a merry meal, and such a relief to see him safe and sound. He described the trip to Jersey as a rather ludicrous affair, not without a spice of danger. He travelled in the custody of a German Corporal, on a barge covered from end to end with looted Guernsey cars. In fact, so jammed were they, that there was no seating accommodation. They crossed the Big Russel sitting in one of the cars, the German sprawled across the back seat, loudly snoring all the way; while his prisoner kept an anxious eye on their escort of R.A.F. Fighters, luckily not in fighting mood; but probably on routine reconnaissance, for they soon disappeared without incident.

The return journey was uneventful. As expected, the accused soldiers were given prison sentences of two to two-and-a-half years.

Presently we shall stroll back to the Tearooms in time to hear a Channel Islands Broadcast, a long-awaited treat. I spent most of this afternoon turning out drawers and cupboards, so things will be fairly shipshape when we return for ever.

I shall not dwell on Diana's birthday on the 17th of this month. Suffice to say she was not forgotten by us; and we are confident that you all remembered. A pity it falls in Term-time when she is away from you all.

To M.H. Les Dunes, L'Ancresse. 4th June, 1941.

We need not have hurried back for that Broadcast. From Guernsey's point of view it was a travesty. It really is most provoking, that each time anything 'Guernsey' is Broadcast, we are portrayed as a nation of nitwits. Ancient Guernsey-French songs are dragged from the archives in the sacred name of tradition. Songs, which none but the oldest inhabitant can remember, depicting us as some backward race still in native dress, poke-bonnets, shawls, elastic-sided boots and all, astride our donkeys on the way to market. We wait to hear a few well known Guernsey voices giving us up-to-the-minute news of our kith and kin. The only song universally recognised to-day was our Signor Santangelo's " Sarnia Chérie " (almost our National Anthem). It struck chords perhaps a trifle too evocative for our good, if we are to tackle the job in hand in philosophical manner.

Meanwhile, we remain at Les Dunes until George and Felicia move into their bungalow. They little thought the builders would have taken so long to finish the job: having been given a verbal promise for the end of April. They were taken in by the oldest Fairy Tale in the world. It never fails to procure a customer, like the spider and the fly, and equally deceptive.

We anticipate the return to La Guelle with scant enthusiasm; as though we are entering a family vault, empty even of ghosts.

O dear! One misses the towpath at one's peril, capitulation to despair can only lead to spiritual impotence, and that was not the basic idea when we tossed the coin less than a year ago. At times we still toy with the idea of letting La Guelle to reliable civilians, and of coming home to roost before this house falls to the Germans or to their Organisation Todt. It has been burgled a few times. If only it would hold all your furniture and effects as well as our own. Alternatively, we do know that La Guelle will hold the contents of both houses should the need arise. And so we continue to do what seems best, while keeping this place under our protection as far as possible, and ready for our speedy return should the Germans decide to commandeer your house at short notice. The neighbours are very kind, and phone us whenever prowlers appear to take more than a cursory interest.

There is nothing very encouraging in the War News, except our help from America. Meanwhile, many people here are joining the S.S. (Skeleton Society). Inevitably, the plump ones show the most dramatic reductions, some are really gaunt. What can we expect on a sixpenny meat ration (weekly of course): a small daily dose of skimmed milk: a weekly ration of 4½ to 5 lbs. of so-called bread: and a dearth of all other basic necessities?

Periodically, we indulge in drooling flights of fancy, recalling past orgies of roast beef, pork or lamb all with the appropriate accompaniments, including roast potatoes, sizzling hot from the oven. Then, back to earth and the meatless, fatless present, from which there is no escape. We should do well to embrace frugality as a virtue, and thus defeat it before it subdues us, keeping us in a permanent state of aggravation. But I fear we have studied our à Kempis too late. The enterprise already lacks our voluntary adoption, and we begin the exercise at an advanced stage, with already empty, protesting stomachs.

To M.H. Les Dunes. 9th June, 1941.

Eleven o'clock and all is ready for our return to La Guelle. Lovell's are due at any moment to collect our luggage and as many of our possessions as possible.

Now that we leave L'Ancresse, the recent appalling weather has given way to brilliant summer. Our garden is a joy to see after Peter's final effort yesterday. I love the heady scent of these privet hedges, a plant much despised by many a zealous gardener: as though Nature seduced by some mongrel element, while pleasantly inebriated with the joys of Spring, had conceived one of her so-called freaks. Rather a presumptuous view I feel. For my part, at this moment of nostalgia, I would not exchange its perfume for any other. Perhaps the humble privet appeals to my plebeian streak.

We have stuck on this window a notice which reads: "This House is Occupied." A thing not strictly permitted unless we are permanently domiciled. But risk forms part of our daily diet: and if this one deters the Germans from installing themselves, it will suffice "advienne que pourra" as the College motto so aptly puts it.

There is a certain amount of Spring-cleaning to be done at La Guelle and, as George and Felicia have moved into their bungalow at last, we dare not leave your house empty any longer, the Germans being more partial to large houses.

And now, Lovell's have come and gone. Apparently, pantechnicons are a thing of the past, for a one-horse van arrived, already half-filled with other furniture. This entailed much weeding-out of our own cargo, not an easy task, considering we may never again set eyes on the stuff we leave behind. But we have much to be thankful for, and far more urgent matters now occupy our minds, of which more anon.

It only remains for me to call on dear old Mrs. " Beesh ", and ask her to collect our refuse; then on to the Tearooms for lunch. Nurse Taylor will drive me back to Town, as my health continues somewhat truculent. Hence, my bicycle travels on top of the load, while I take one last nostalgic look around Les Dunes, wondering how long before Peace comes and we return for ever. Inevitably, the ghosts of the past beckon, and I am lost for a moment in all our yesterdays: but Hope is firmly astride her sphere to-day and there is no time for yearning. The news may suddenly become tremendous. The Free French are asserting themselves to good effect and, coupled, with American aid, may work wonders for the morale.

To M.H. La Guelle. Aug. 13th, 1941.

What an age since my last effort! More than two months since our return to Town, and nothing seems to have happened to hasten or affect the War. Apathy and frustration prevail for days on end. One day we long to push the Allies on to greater efforts, and on the morrow we rejoice at their gigantic strides. Every ear is strained to news bulletins from every available source. On these depend our swift changes of mood.

The difference between the news displayed in our German-censored Press, and that broadcast by the Allies, is quite ludicrous: but we know that the Army here must be fed on the diet chosen by their propagandists. Naturally, we assume our bulletins to be nearer the mark for, after all, we do receive liberal doses of good and bad: whereas the German versions in our Press are always flattering to themselves; a point which can hardly escape even the most gullible of the species.

Guernsey is now swarming with Germans, most of them it seems, marching this way every day with stacks of ammunition, including lorries, tanks, guns and other trappings of war.

Mr. Cohen's house has been 'taken', and soldiers are also billeting themselves on reluctant civilians in ever-increasing numbers. We have our bad moments, but so far our luck has held and Les Dunes remains free.

Save for one solitary message from Doris to Felicia, received some months ago dated December 8th, the line between us is dead. Now we cannot imagine that you are deliberately neglecting us. One solution strikes me, that with your usual direct approach, you are writing things uncomplimentary to the enemy in our midst: a laudable pastime, placed as you are in a free Country, but censors are touchy beings, and it could be that they prefer adulation thickly spread. So that, if your messages are to reach us at all, they will have to be more cunningly cryptic and less obviously septic; for, in the words of the old song: "They're so mercenary Mary that you have to be mercenary too." (I do believe this is the first time ever that I have addressed you by your Christian name!).

You will no doubt be delighted to receive George's message announcing the birth of his son George on July 2nd. It was a treat to have something to celebrate, and with his love of parties, George was in his element. As an old hand (with my brood of one!), I was called in next door a day or so before the event to state whether, in my opinion, it was time to call the Doctor, Hospital or Ambulance. Assuming the calm air of one who might actually have delivered hundreds of babies, I advised a call to the Hospital, not that Felicia betrayed signs of panic.

I trust that I acquitted myself a trifle better than the charlady who 'did' for us when Diana was in the offing. On seeing me about to hang out clothes, this worthy exclaimed: "Don't overstretch me dear. You don't mind me telling you, I 'ope, but I oughter know, I've had ten o' me own and buried seven." Peter's reaction? "Not exactly a good average."

Young George weighed but 5½ lbs. at birth, and seems destined to be of small build. He cries often at night and, against Doctor's orders, Allie may be found in the small hours, furtively augmenting his diet with the connivance of Lily the cow.

Someone suggested that George might have an hourglass tummy, and should be fed every two hours: but Dr. Sutcliffe, with a flash of clinical sadism, suggests that he be put out of earshot and forgotten.

We returned from Les Dunes to an orgy of spring-cleaning, which Felicia was in no condition to do after moving into their bungalow. My own chances of survival were threatened even with maximum support from Peter. The rescuable contents of Les Dunes are stacked in your drawing room, the other rooms being virtually unused. We live in your bedroom, miles from the kitchen of course, but this view is quite irresistible.

By a great stroke of luck, my old help from Diana's infancy is with me again. On meeting Peter in town recently, she said: "A few nights ago I dreamt that I was back in your house working for Mrs. B." With unconcealed alacrity he offered her the chance to make her dream come true, and felt suitably gratified when she declared: " Mind you, I wouldn't do it for anyone else."

How often are things put down to Luck which should be ascribed to Providence. Truly, life has its compensations, for if we had remained at L'Ancresse, May could not have done the six-mile journey. Albeit, I fear that our pleasant reunion will be all too brief. May's husband brings her along each morning on the back of his bicycle; but the Germans are threatening to prohibit this form of transport and, unfortunately, May is too nervous to cycle alone. On existing rations, one can fully appreciate her reluctance to walk every day from and to Les Ruettes Brayes.

To M.H. The Emergency Hospital,
Câtel. Sept. 29th, 1941.

This, after more than five weeks at the above address.

Peter-John, scheduled to arrive to-day, was born to us on August 26th, exactly twenty-four hours after Dr. Sutcliffe had removed my perforated appendix and, with it, my dog-eared label of hypochondria.

This upheaval created a further anxiety for Peter, somewhat of a facer for Dr. S. (who functioned in the nick of time), and a personal ordeal, whose sole comforts were the existence of our son, and the total eclipse of all previous woes including wars and invasions. " Great are the Uses of Adversity ", was the subject of an essay set us at school in what now seems another era. However, if pain and oblivion rendered me some service, they only saddled Peter with a heavier yoke, chafing most at those times, when it seemed likely that I might be absent from the family reunion. Of his full torment I only learned days later when my brain resumed its normal function.

Faithfully he has cycled out here each day to cheer me on: and back to La Guelle at night, there to write inspiring letters as he sat up in bed, his supper-tray beside him. One of many lyrical phrases runs: "As I write these words, I see the full moon delicately poised on the rim of Herm." And one morning, after a particularly tortuous night, during which I had allowed the current to bear me downstream in a state of limp submission, a letter arrived from Peter, bearing within its folds the very fillip needed to rescue me from the lethal snare of self-pity. He had written: "As I leave you each night, and cycle down the hill, I look up at the lighted window through which all our hopes for the future are fused."

How could I not make rapid strides spurred on by such a Champion? Repelled by my own weakness, I lay for some time physically immobile, while doing mental contortions, till finally the waters of contrition had done their job.

By the aid of Providence, skilful treatment, and just the right mixture of ward-mates, my recovery is assured, despite complications and set-backs too tedious for these pages. Suffice it to say that in answer to one of my lamentations, Sister Collas remarked: "You must admit that you're interesting!" to which I retorted: "If this torture must be endured in order to be interesting, then I would prefer to be as dull as ditch-water."

There have been turbulent nights when the R.A.F. have flown over Guernsey to bomb Brest and other French Ports. At times they have bombed our Airport, Harbour and various gun-emplacements dotted about the Island. Protected by the huge Red Cross on this roof, the four big guns, subtly and ignobly placed around the Hospital, set up a furious barrage. The verandah beds were wheeled into the Wards as shrapnel fell through the glass. All windows were flung open as on previous days, when the Germans issued warnings before they indulged in artillery practice. Although reasonably confident of the R.A.F.'s ability to avoid the Hospital, the danger that a loaded bomber might be shot down, was not to be ruled out.

This anxiety added to the confusion, as ringing bells and cries of 'Bedpan!' sent nurses scampering to and from the sluice. Death and destruction seemed imminent as we lay with trussed-up bodies, waiting for the bomb which must surely be pin-pointed at our specific bed.

Long after the uproar had died away, Nurses were still complaining that their men-patients refused to settle. They chatted and smoked regardless of rules. Sleep had deserted everyone, and it scarcely seemed worth trying to recapture, before the Ablution Brigade would be rousing us for flannel and toothbrush drill.

The atmosphere in this place, though not exactly given over to joyous abandon, has been anything but dull, and there has been humour in plenty. Indeed, on one of her rounds, Matron Hall pronounced ours to be the noisiest ward in the whole place: but, as I told Dr. S., what could they expect, when one of my three ward-mates (a Mrs. Allain) literally does not know that she is comic, and is virtually the original innocent abroad. Her every word and action creases her audience almost to danger point.

On one occasion, Mrs. Wyatt (next to me) implored her on my behalf to be less talkative, as my medical embroidery (a collector's piece), threatened to give at the seams. I was obliged to laugh backwards, in order to avoid excessive pain and probable disaster.

At one time, I was also obliged to ask that Nurses Ozanne and Lucas be put off making my bed. They knew that laughing caused me acute discomfort and, as they were humorous types, they had only to approach the bed with poker faces, obviously determined to be solemn, for the fun to start. All three of us would studiously avoid exchanging glances. The air was electric and, before anyone could say a single word, we were helpless. The fault was mutual and I begged that no word of censure be meted out. I missed them after the embargo on bed-making, though they often came to attend me after I lost my stitches when, naturally, the occasion for convulsive laughter never arose. The bed-making episode had served to forge a link between us however, and, whenever possible, they would stop for a few words at my bedside and sometimes help me dispose of the perishable fruits of my locker.

Then, there was the day the meat was brought in, tough as cowhide. On this occasion, Mrs. Allain had us all in metaphorical as well as medical stitches. Her Operation? The extraction of all her teeth! She sat up in bed, a piece of meat impaled on her fork, inviting suggestions for eating the same. Impelled as much by our guffaws as by the continuous ringing of Mrs. A's bell, Nurse hurried into the Ward, anticipating some emergency dreamed-up by a spiteful Fate, to bedevil and accelerate the usual lunch-hour panic. She revealed no sign of relief when it became obvious that the laugh was on herself. One could almost pardon the ungracious manner in which she snatched the offending plate of meat from the Toothless One, and flounced off to unearth a mincer capable of dealing with leather.

Mrs. Allain wore a permanent air of surprise, and was quite bemused by the laughter she engendered. Because of my infant, I was allocated an unlimited supply of milk, being often exhorted to take more than I felt able to consume. Whenever a glass was set beside me, Mrs. A. would ask for one also, while Mrs. Wyatt would chide her for being greedy: telling her, in response to her query as to why I should be given priority: " Surely you realise that Mrs. B. needs the milk for her baby! " " Do you mean to say that's all her baby lives on? " our ingénue would exclaim.

Poor Mrs. A. had much to endure. Apparently the bad state of her teeth had caused blood-poisoning and she had been very ill. All her skin had flaked off bit by bit, while she suffered torments of itching. She would sit up in bed, scratching all reachable parts of her person chimpanzee-fashion, one stray curl bobbing about on her forehead, her mouth and chin like Popeye the Sailor Man, as she muttered diabolical incantations into the carbolic atmosphere.

Drs. Sutcliffe, Rose and Fox came to and fro on motorcycles in order to conserve their petrol. Dr. " Bill " Fox, being resident Physician, we would hear him in the dewy hours leaving the Hospital to go fishing. With sagging spirits we would surely know that yet once more, mackerel would be on the lunch menu, pallid, tepid and almost certainly accompanied by turnip nicely chilled on the way to the Wards. This would be followed by a grey sludge masquerading as milk-pudding, made with barley-flour in place of the once-despised rice or semolina for which we now yearned. But real tea never failed during my incarceration, and proved a panacea for most torments. Nurse Le Page has my undying gratitude for bringing me a cup from the staff teapot at 4 o'clock one morning when sleep had finally deserted me.

Dr. S. bestrode his motor-cycle attired in jodhpurs, much to Mrs. Allain's disgust. One day, as he left the Ward, she called across to me: "Is that your Doctor? Huh! He looks more like a Vet to me. My Doctor is the best and the most expensive." Well, jodhpurs notwithstanding, my 'Vet' saved my life and no mistake. I only wish we had met in time to avert the "parlous state" in which we found ourselves a few weeks ago; and I guarantee those were his sentiments also. I must admit his present garb to be a far cry from the sartorial elegance adopted by the Profession in our youth. It might have been yesterday, that Dr. Robinson strode down the garden path in top hat and gloves, his overcoat flapping about his heels. On one occasion, hat, gloves and coat were missing from the hall-stand, for Brother Henry had seen fit to stage an outdoor mannequin parade. Blindfolded by the topper and tripping over the surplus yards of coat, he strolled calmly about the garden, while Dr. Robinson sat upstairs tuned-in to the pleural crepitations of the latest invalid.

I see you now, haring about the garden to capture and divest the delinquent of his status symbol, just in time to save his medical eminence from an apoplectic spasm.

To M.H. La Guelle. October 14th, 1941.

La Guelle at last! Peter-John and I returned by Ambulance on September 30th. Peter, George, Felicia and Nurse Le Cheminant were at the gate to greet us. Your bedroom was decked with flowers sent by friends and relations. I should have felt like Titania in her bower; but the freshly painted Ambulance had upset my delicate mechanism, thus robbing the occasion of all romance. I arrived in a state of collapse. Also, our journey had been diverted to restore another patient to the bosom of her family. As I lay waiting on the narrow stretcher the infant precariously balanced on top of me, the Ambulance began to rotate like a planet in outer space. Nurse, returning with the stretcher-bearers, gave me one look and thrust an enamel bowl under my chin. Mercifully it was not required, for, with a clinging infant and a thrombosis leg (now in its fifth week of torment), any convulsive use of the bowl would almost certainly have added a hernia to my already lurid list of accomplishments. Nurse Le Cheminant told us later that her first reactions were of acute alarm, that anyone in her profession could have been so dim as to discharge a patient in a coma. However, she ceased her denigration of the Hospital Top Brass when, after the administration of brandy and smelling-salts, I sat up to a hearty and hilarious tea, scrounged for me from Heaven knows where.

What a cosy homecoming! A fire in your bedroom, which is now the living room, constant companionship with Nurse and Peter, good old May coping downstairs with those endless chores and, above all, our sleeping son blissfully unaware of his dramatic début into this demented world. I feel an awful fraud, basking in undeserved limelight and thinking of poor Mrs. Wyatt, my boon companion for the past weeks of adversity. She looked so envious as I left the Ward.

Thirty minutes later. Dr. S. has just ripped off the leg-plaster, a hair-raising procedure in both senses of the word. When I came down from the ceiling, I recalled how amused he had been at the Hospital when he saw that I had feverishly shaved off every leg-whisker within reach, before he put on the plaster. I had thought this a shrewd piece of self-defence after long and bitter experience of skin-raising tummy-plasters, until he gleefully dashed my hopes by warning me that hair thrives under adhesive tape. How right the sadist proved to be! I swear he sprinkled fertiliser on the plaster before he applied it.

Hospital life is not in my line, and I am certain it would prove insupportable to you if only for its many indignities. I remember your utter refusal to enter The Victoria Hospital only a few years back, when Dr. Montague advised an examination. You were adamant, and exploded: "Do you think that I'm going to submit to being washed by those little bits of girls? Not likely!" Dr. M. called you a prude. and allowed you to remain at home, only after a qualified

Nurse had been installed. I shudder now in restrospect at the heinous offence committed with the connivance of a certain much-bemedalled Nurse, a personal friend of the family who shall be nameless. You conspired with her to be in attendance whenever Dr. M. called. Resplendent in her uniform, she dutifully took his instructions, saw him off the premises, removed her uniform and, after lunching with us all, allowed herself to be driven home in Father's car. This highly inflammable routine, just to save you from "Doing time" in Hospital. How the poor soul must have quailed and quaked each time the Doctor's car stopped outside the house, and his bounding footsteps sounded on the stairs.

I wrote to Mrs. Wyatt soon after my homecoming and reminded her of the night she had us all with thumbs pressed on bells, as she feebly moaned: "I'm slipping away! O dear! I'm passing away!" Night Sister flew up the Ward at breakneck speed on the highly polished floor, only to find a deeply embarrassed patient striving to disappear under the bedclothes. "I'm terribly sorry!" she blurted, "I dreamt I was dying, without a single relative to hold my hand and say goodbye." I fear we failed to give this confession its due solemnity.

The idea that a cup of tea would restore the patient's calm, and recapture for us all our shattered sleep left Sister unimpressed as we feared it would.

Mrs. Wyatt had entered Hospital fulminating against Hitler. Owing to the gas-shortage (engineered of course by the Third Reich), she and her husband had installed in a kitchen alcove, a solid-fuel cooker which the workmen had failed to connect to the water-system. Midway through lunch the cylinder had exploded hurling fragments of burning metal about the kitchen, some of them striking Mrs. Wyatt about the face, arms and legs, causing extensive burns. The rest of the family miraculously escaped injury.

The inevitable intimacies of life in the raw at close quarters, crudely shattered any need for formal introduction; and we soon formed a mutual-commiseration bond.

Mrs. W's first reactions to Hospital life were identical with mine. That we should die of NOISE was never in doubt, the gravity of our ailments being purely incidental. Her first conscious comments were: "Dear me! How awful! Is it possible? Good Heavens! " She was convinced that the very clock in the Ward had been chosen for its loud tick. One could not have conceived it possible that, when people were ill, some of them 'in extremis', and trying to slip into sweet oblivion, that everyone would go about as though they were at a fun-fair on a Bank Holiday. The banging of doors and dishes, the barking of dogs (whose for Pity's sake?), the dragging of screens, to say nothing of those enamel teatrays being thrown about the kitchen, whose open door gave on to the Wards: all these have to be experienced as a patient, to be believed. Until a more rational appraisal of the situation percolated into our consciousness, it seemed obvious that the Nurses were utterly regardless of the helpless victims to whose creature comforts they were dedicated to administer, and whose sufferings they were pledged to alleviate.

Our Ward was situated over the Staff sitting-room, through whose open window a wireless blared incessantly. One tune in particular reverberated mercilessly even through our brief snatches of sleep: "Mother must I keep on dancing? Yes my darling daughter."

One day Dr. S. stopped at my bedside and ordered Sister to go and switch the Thing off. "This is ludicrous! " he snapped. Sister returned to report that the wireless was on at full throttle, playing to an empty room.

Mrs. Wyatt had a cradle over her legs (to match my own): When, on one of his visits, her husband placed a large bouquet of flowers on her cradle, she cried out: "For Heaven's sake take them off, it looks like a coffin! " The universal reaction of those present was far from funereal.

Hospital life with its gamut of emotions lying between ecstasy and despair, provides a copious stream of anecdotes to the raconteur. Much of the wit engendered there is permanently stored in the memory, obscuring the doldrums which are best forgotten. Adversity, however, was seen to have its uses; and the same fears, pains, ironies, and even dramas such as beset the few of us in that Ward alone in divers ways, will befall its future occupants as part of the inevitable pattern of life. Those who survive, and a few did not even during our tenancy, will come away enriched or impoverished according to their congenital stuffing. There are those who contrive to live in idyllic ignorance of the seamy side: where smells are always aromas and blood remains decently confined to invisible veins. But hospital life removes the blinkers, and any ethereal ideas of the stork's function, or of dwelling on a different plane from one's fellows, are promptly dismissed. For my part, I soon discovered that, despite all former viscissitudes, I had entered those portals in many respects a raw recruit in the Battle of Life. There, everyone is reduced to a common denominator, and there the busy world is never hushed, the Fever of Life goes relentlessly on, literally from the cradle to the grave; from the newly-minted specimens in the maternity ward to the 'rigor mortis' types who make way for them.

Stoicism in the face of Adversity is often regarded as the bovine acceptance of a feeble intellect; but that sounds like the facile excuse of the weak in spirit. I read somewhere that "all martyrdoms looked mean when they were suffered."

Any analogy here between the martyr and the stoic, can be left to the eager Platos of the world who ruminate in the complex fields of human behaviour. Being neither martyr nor stoic and certainly no philosopher, I am content to graze and gambol in leaner pastures, an occasional peep over the fence will suffice, with no desire to trespass.

To M.H. La Guelle. 6th November, 1941.

We had been living in hopes that the War would be over by Christmas, but time is running out. Meanwhile, the future threatens to be even more uncomfortable.

Numerous people have, at short notice, been evicted from the houses they stayed here to protect. The Germans have enquired of George how many we are in family, and how many rooms we have in this house. George stressed the point that I am in bed, and that we have a nurse and infant. Nothing further has evolved.

Last week a Form (one of hundreds!) appeared in the Press, to be filled in by every householder, stating the number of their rooms, sanitation, lighting and so forth. This lends credence to the rumour that mass-billeting may be imminent, many Officers having already foisted themselves upon reluctant hosts.

Recently, a Mr. and Mrs. Brouard were obliged to house an Officer whose bedroom was situated above their drawing room.

One evening, the German was cleaning his revolver, when the thing went off. The shot penetrated the ceiling of the room below, killing Mr. Brouard as he sat with his wife at their fireside. As in the early days of the Occupation, when all Guernsey was drawn to intimate friendship by sudden contact with the common foe; so all hearts went out to Mrs. Brouard as though her loss were our own, and this, regardless of the fact that she does not figure in the local *Who's Who* and so, like ourselves, is personally unknown to most of the population. Quertier Le Pelley presided at the Inquest and absolved the Officer of all blame!

We are told that potato-rationing is in the offing, the weekly allocation to be 5 lbs. per capita; a meagre allowance for the many who live mainly on vegetables. Thanks to your foresight and the produce of this garden, we may see the winter through without the need to tighten our belts to the last eyelet-hole. Many will be less fortunate.

On Tuesday, Peter John attained the ripe old age of ten weeks, and now weighs 11 lbs. whilst all around him shrink visibly. The weighing ceremony is intriguing. Nurse places the nude wriggler in a miniature fishing net suspended by a hook on a steelyard, while blobs of pink infant protrude through the holes like tinted ping-pong balls. Scrutinising the needle at eye-level she waits for it to settle before proudly announcing the weight of her 'catch'. Last week, on surveying his son's cherubic contours, and drawing himself up to his full height like the Monarch of the Glen, Peter declared pompously: "Michael Angelo lived before his time." In terms of importance, I felt this statement bore some vague analogy to Mahommet and the Mountain. Anyway, I cannot imagine the Great Man being inspired at the sight of the embossed creature which eventually emerges from the net, by the time all minute fingers and toes have been unravelled from its meshes. Nor yet by the soggy bundle of noise and hunger clamouring for attention when, "in the dead vast and middle of the night" his deserving elders are wrapped in heavy sleep. Before the weighing ceremony, however, all freshly bathed and powdered, it is less difficult, with parental eyes, to imagine him drifting among his cocherubs with others of the heavenly host beneath the dome of the Sistine Chapel.

The christening must take place before the Mighty Atom outgrows the family robe, created by a long departed ancestor for your own baptism and all of ours; but my convalescence has been so lazy, that I fear the ever-swelling child will have to be eased into the garment with extreme caution, as his agile limbs are in perpetual motion.

We give thanks for the German Army discipline, especially in view of the mounting tension about us. Among the morass of rumour, one hears that 6,000 S.S. troops are due to arrive: also, that the Harbour is to be much enlarged. Guernsey is very heavily fortified and, on reliable information, we hear that the Army is to reach 20,000 strong. Naturally, our milk ration will be correspondingly reduced. Like all generously upholstered people, Peter has already discovered bones hitherto concealed, and insists that he is the better for it, but I cannot help feeling that the reduction is too sudden.

Our mainly vegetable diet is occasionally transformed by a longnose or mackerel. A very rare soup-bone or pig's trotter will provide a hot-pot feast. We drink bramble-leaf tea as a matter of course; but have abstained from carrot-tea and parsnip-coffee, neither of which is enthused over by the initiated. The kitchen Front recipes keeps us "au courant" with your diet and, although it falls far short of pre-war fare, we rejoice that cheese, oranges, oatmeal, cake and real bread are still on your menu, with restaurants open to fill the aching void. Even so, they are a poor substitute for indefinite exile. How you must long for home! With all the pros and cons in your possession I still think you might prefer our lot. *Néanmoins,* Time may prove this preference to be a rash one.

We do indeed have our morbid moments, but there are many gleams of hope, with Mr. Churchill the brilliant light amid the encircling gloom. We have come to hang on his every word, since he gives us the good and the bad, and has said: "The goal is in sight." At his opening words, we are instantly and hilariously borne upwards to the crest of the wave. So stirring are they that, be he grave or gay, he leaves us with the feeling of unbounded elation and equal once again to any emergency. One cannot over-stress how profoundly is this impression shared by the numerous British subjects here in Guernsey, our compatriots and fellow-prisoners.

Still unable to walk unaided, I spend most of the time in bed. Sometimes I sit in an armchair for tea, or walk about your bedroom, helped by pieces of furniture judiciously placed. It is heavy going and I long to be back at the helm. A few days ago, Nurse told Doctor Sutcliffe that I am tired of lying about useless. She returned with his comforting message: "Tell her from me that she is lucky not to be lying down permanently."

Peter has many chores to do as well as the family scrounging for the odd egg or piece of fish. He makes quite palatable cakes with barley-flour and grapes, the latter dried in the Triplex. An occasional over-ripe Camembert from France sends him into raptures; but I shall have to be a skeleton before I change my view that it should be eaten in the backyard, if not relegated to the dust-bin. He scoops out the less decomposed portions and, mixing these with a little milk, he heats the repulsive concoction in a saucepan to kill off the more tenacious bugs. This he spreads on our so-called bread and relishes it as though it might be caviar.

To M.H. La Guelle. November 14th, 1941.

From my bed I hear the daily tramp of jackboots coming up the road to the swelling strains of the German songs. The soldiers are often followed by an assortment of small boys who, like everyone else, know the tunes by heart, and add some of the more familiar words as they goose-step in their wake. One wonders if the soldiers suspect that they are being ridiculed by these children, or if, with their complete lack of humour, they suppose that they are converting our youth to be good little Nazis.

Once again I am reminded of those pre-1914 summers when the German Band toured these Islands with their fiddles and 'cellos. They would set themselves up at street corners and in front of houses, resin their bows, tune their instruments and launch their familiar tunes into the drowsy summer air. Inevitably, "Chant sans Paroles," "Traumeri,"

"The Skater's Waltz" and "In the Shadows" would form part of their repertoire.

At the sound of their crunching footsteps on the gravel path, your psychic streak would take over and force us to duck behind the nearest piece of furniture; so resolved were you not to drop a single coin into the proffered hat. "Mark my words" you would mutter from your crouched position, "one of these days, they'll be waging war against us." How right you were! For after thirty years or more we find ourselves living in the shadow of the Swastika.

Nevertheless, those youthful summers of family outings, with you driving the donkey-trap: when water-carts were driven about the Island in order to keep down the dust: a heat-haze quivered everywhere, and picnics could be arranged weeks ahead, are so coveted now in retrospect, that those tunes surge through one's very soul like the fleeting perfume of the last rose of summer.

Our travels with a sometimes reluctant donkey, having to be cajoled up hills with carrots held before her nose, would by today's standards, be regarded as a test of endurance for all concerned. The end of the journey in sight, we were all agog for the coveted first glimpse of the sea.

I savour once again, even as I write, the salty tang which met our eager nostrils, and the smell of burning furze and vraic* wafted from the chimneys of the old white-washed cottages. Once again I feel the coarse grass beneath my feet as we tumbled out of the trap and romped with childish glee; while the donkey, freed from shafts and harness, rolled over and over to match our joyous abandon, her shrill braying adding to the general pandemonium.

Those days passed all too quickly, spent mostly in the breakers, floating idly on the surface of the water, or lying prone in the shallows, the wavelets spilling over us on to the warm sand, the seagulls planing overhead in a cloudless sky.

I well remember waiting my opportunity to slip away unnoticed and, making for the farthest promontory I would bask in rapturous solitude, while the shimmering sea rose and fell up and down the gully where I was lodged. Gently swelling and receding like the deep breathing of a placid

* Vraic — seaweed.

sleeping monster, the blue-green water rose and fell and, on it, fronds of many-coloured seaweed floated to and fro: rare lichens would be gently covered and uncovered with ceaseless regularity, while tiny finned creatures darted in and out of their secret crevices. Sometimes I would vary my childish meditations with snatches of song, as I sat swaying dreamily, my feet dangling in the water. I well recall one haunting lullaby I never could resist, even though it might be high noon:

> "Night sinks on the wave,
> Hallowed gusts are sighing.
> Sea-birds to their caves
> Through the gloom are flying."

Alas! since those halcyon childhood days, one global war has been fought and won and another now furiously rages.

Many cargoes have been sunk, and numerous brave men sent to a watery grave. Submarines are wreaking havoc in the green swirling vaults beneath the oceans of the world, to carry out the evil machinations of despotic rulers bent on the destruction of all who stand between them and their ambitions.

We mourn with those lamenting their loved ones who, for our sakes, inhabit for ever the sea's silent grottoes, and feel our undying gratitude to be a puny reward for their sacrifice.

If events deteriorate no further we shall consider ourselves lucky: but we realise that we live on the edge of a volcano which may erupt at any moment. The very air we breathe seems not our own, and we have constantly to remind ourselves that, now the situation is irrevocable, the choice was our own and that we must stand or fall by it whatever the outcome.

The R.A.F. continue to visit us from time to time. I once enjoyed their excursions, but now I see things from a different angle. I sit up here by your bedroom fire (one smouldering log), your trusty stay-laces fixed to the mantelpiece to air Peter-John's washing and, when the big guns begin to crackle as though they are on our doorstep, I realise with taut nerves, my inability to dash for cover should the need arise. Sometimes during these bombardments, passers-by come in to shelter from flying shrapnel, or the more hazardous chance that a plane-load of bombs may be shot down. When, to my shame, Peter's attempts to reassure me fail, he carries me to the top of the stairs from whence I wend my way down to the hall on my seat, where I suffer silent tortures of fear on the baby's behalf; knowing full well that Peter would emphatically draw the line at disturbing his slumbers. Peter is most tactful and patient with my weakness, but I sense the hidden smile and we keep our laughter for the return journey. I fervently hope that my present wave of cowardice is only attributable to my convalescence and not inherent in my constitution. I am comforted on recalling my normal interest in these raids when I was hale and hearty.

The Island is being shorn of many of its trees, which are being used for fuel. The row of tall elms in Mr. Cohen's field are being felled this week. It will give you a much more extensive view from this window. It includes the Vale Castle, and an almost uninterrupted sea view around to the Vale Church. True, another gasometer presents itself in the middle distance: but I think it is more than offset by the general result. You will now see the traffic in the far distance along Les Banques, including Belgrave Bay as far as Richmond Corner.

We are sending you another Red Cross message this week, with the forlorn hope that you might receive it for Christmas. We omitted seasonal greetings in order to save the precious twenty-five words for news. I wonder if one of your messages is among the new batch of cards which arrived yesterday.

To M.H. La Guelle. 22nd November, 1941.

Allah be praised! George received two messages from Father yesterday, and the day before our first one arrived from Doris. The Hargreaves received one from Bill and telephoned its contents. We are truly grateful to hear such good news of Diana, and we can imagine how she enjoys donkey-rides. Your messages make us feel nearer to Peace. May they reach avalanche proportions.

Nurse is still with us and unlikely to leave until I am able to walk steadily enough to carry the baby in safety. How lucky I have been to have such a splendid Nurse to take full responsibility. Peter feels this blessing also in full measure.

Guernsey is far from being a pleasant place. They tell me that the Town is alive with Germans and various mixed races brought here to work for them. On Armistice Day they paraded the Town arm-in-arm, singing the Marseillaise and trying to rope in our population. They met with little response, for they were half-drunk and of a most unwholesome species. Our people are more nervous of them than of the German soldiers whose conduct is beyond reproach. But they are not our rulers, and being mere pawns in the game, they have no dominion over us except as their masters, our real oppressors, dictate. Herein lies our constant anxiety and potential threat, for we have ample reason to believe that, no matter how vicious their orders might become, they will be executed to the letter, the pawns being pre-absolved of all guilt in the name of the "Most High" (*e.g.*).

The story goes that a certain family who entertained the Germans, have a small son, who found favour with a German guest. The soldier would dandle the child on his knee and make a great show of affection. One day, the father tested the German thus: "If you were ordered by the Führer to destroy this child, would you do so?" The German replied promptly: "I would have no choice but to obey!" This frightful admission of weakness so shocked the parent that he ordered the soldier to leave his house forthwith and never to return.

One day last week, three Officers came to see our vacant bedrooms, and were told that Audrey's room is occupied by Nurse and infant. Apparently this pronouncement did not make its intended sacrosanct impact, for the next day, Gwenyth Wiltshire who was visiting me kindly interviewed another officer on my behalf. He refused the back-rooms as we had feared he would, and waving aside all protestations on behalf of its occupants, deposited his belongings in Audrey's room. So now, Peter-John and Nurse are installed in George's old bedroom. We had named it "Tom's Room" when George and Felicia lived with us, as they often invited Tom Bennett to supper and to spend the night. I wonder if you might be in contact with his wife and children.

"Rudolph" sleeps in Audrey's bed! His Eagled hat and medalled uniform hang in her wardrobe, his suitcases are stowed under her bed. It seems only yesterday that we were listening to their approach across France never dreaming that it would come to this. It is difficult to become inured to the heavy German tread on stairs and landing. The first night I was restless. The atmosphere was not conducive to sleep. Our 'guest' was noisy over his unpacking, and kept up a solo of alternate humming and whistling. The sight of his shaving tackle and other toilet requisites on the bathroom shelf beside Peter's is ludicrous.

Nurse's reactions are vastly amusing. The first morning of what promises to be a protracted stay, she burst into my room exclaiming angrily: "What do you think? He's used our Lav.!" I pointed out with a shrug and raised eyebrows that after all it was the orthodox place. Nurse was about to flounce out of the room in disgust, when the funny side of the situation dawned upon her and she exploded in a fit of uncontrolled laughter.

Now I might add that Nurse is coming up to eleven stone and is rather short, with her avoirdupois nicely balanced both fore and aft: so that when she really laughs it becomes a full-scale operation, usually involving everyone in her vicinity. Should Peter be present during one of her outbursts, he will dash around her in mock attempts to rescue ornaments, dishes, or any light pieces of precarious bric-à-brac which may threaten to fall during the convulsion. This in turn brings forth fresh paroxysms from the exhausted victim, much to Peter's delight. A chance remark at mealtimes is enough to start one of these bouts of hysteria. Nurse throws her table-napkin over her face and head and sits back like a shaking bag of jelly, emitting no sound, but just quivering through the 'attack' until we also succumb to the infection, and all three of us have the tears running down our cheeks. How we shall rear this son of ours to good table manners if we are together much longer, I cannot imagine, but I know that each convulsion is worth ten battalions in the field to us at present.

One must own that 'Rudolph's' conduct is correct. So far, he has avoided their nauseating habit of foisting friendship upon us; though he indulges in their absurd practice of using strong scent. There are those who suspect it is because they find it difficult to live with their natural aroma.

The whole set-up is incongruous. We lie in bed listening to the news bulletins on the wireless beside us, and let our National Anthem out at full blast, while 'Rudolph' lies in the next room presumably sleeping or sweating through it. We sleep under the same roof, trying to acclimatize ourselves to a strange and dignified mixture of reluctant hospitality and mutual aloofness.

We have to agree that it is preferable to billet an officer or so rather than to be turned out of house and home. His batman comes each morning to waken him and to clean his boots. On the first morning, he proceeded to polish them on the carpet outside Audrey's door. 'Rudolph' came up from the bathroom in the middle of shaving and sent him into the garden to do all future polishing. This was a decent gesture which you will no doubt appreciate. I forgot to mention that 'Rudolph' is just the nickname by which we allude to our lodger. It is extremely unlikely that our acquaintance will blossom into a formal introduction. The initials on his suitcase being H.L., Nurse has christened him 'Henry Lenfestey'.

To M.H. La Guelle. November 26th, 1941.

On Saturday evening Peter left me for the first time to play bridge with Dr. Sutcliffe, Bert Williams and Harry Broughton. I was glad that Peter was able to have an evening off duty. Being Nurse's half-day, Elsie came to sit with me and, as I had a streaming cold (bestowed on me by a generous visitor), I felt very guilty on her behalf. Peter had refused to leave me in the house alone despite my assurance that nothing ghastly could befall me, and the Curfew would ensure his return before the baby's feeding-time.

The news which started so magnificently on Sunday, seems to have become highly involved. Heaven bless the Allied efforts, or our prestige will plummet yet again. We seem to have made such trumpetings about the start of this African campaign. The Moscow situation being tense, a great change in the War outlook seems likely. We only hope and pray that another set-back is not in store.

The Barter Column in the Press contains some peculiar items. People are willing to barter almost anything for food, including cigarettes, roller skates, gramophone records, vases, fur coats, besides all sorts of clothes and oddments ferreted out of drawers and cupboards, from whence, but for this emergency, they might never have seen the light of day.

On Sunday Peter took me out in an invalid chair. For some time he had threatened to do this, but I vowed that I should never come to such a pass. Now, I feel that it was rather unkind, as Peter so obviously enjoyed taking me around the old haunts, and, I must own, that it was quite a change to be out in the fresh air. Naturally I felt The Complete Idiot, but we came home with a good appetite for tea. We made the round of Beau Séjour and called at Garrivoe to see Emil and Elsie and Peter's old people. His Ma kept muttering tearfully: " It's a resurrection! " while Dad held my hand and made enquiries about his new grandson. Since then I have had several offers of perambulation. Mrs. Wynne and Gwenyth took me out to-day. We made a tour of Cambridge Park and Les Côtils, little Hugh-John sitting at my feet on the way home.

To M.H. La Guelle. Thursday, Nov. 27th, 1941.

We are sitting in bed listening to the news which is still very involved. The announcer is telling us that the Germans are willing to pay any price to get Moscow. Heaven forbid! The Japanese are still trying to be difficult, and events are moving rapidly in Libya. " Eb Doodah " (not marked on our map, and with apologies to the announcer) was taken by our troops to-day. I must arouse my sleeping husband, for he wants to hear the War Commentary and the News Review from Boston.

The wireless still mentions German atrocities in other Occupied Countries. We wonder if these reports are causing you grave concern, or if our family code word (which must remain anonymous here) has had the desired effect. I know that it has reached Flo, for she has replied suitably and will no doubt have passed it on to you. Mercifully, no extreme horrors have befallen us.

To-night, Miss Millbourne telephoned to say that "Les Dunes" has, for the third time, been forcibly entered. Fortunately, Peter has removed most of our smaller possessions, but I do wish that we could find a reliable tenant before it is taken over by some of our unsavoury immigrants.

To M.H. La Guelle. December 2nd, 1941.

Supper over, Peter has gone downstairs to warm my milk. He has started a week of holiday and really needs it. I wish I were not such a handicap to him, as I told him a few days ago when he carried me along to the bathroom, where he helps Nurse slide me into the bath. He managed as usual, to give the answer most likely to put me at my ease: "Forget it. You have given me the son I never gave up waiting for."

As the news improves, the face of Guernsey becomes ever more desolate. The Germans continue to dig themselves in, the Island is slowly but surely being absorbed into their War Machine. Buildings of all shapes and sizes, gun-emplacements, ammunition dumps and other horrors are creeping up everywhere: while new houses and bungalows literally disappear overnight, presumably to supply the Germans with a variety of materials.

Rows of new houses are occupied by soldiers. Peter took me in the chair through the Coutanchez this afternoon. The sight of all those little homes so sadly changed has haunted me ever since. The tables seemed to have been turned and we were the foreigners among a different race of people. The sort of bizarre situation prevailed, of which dreams are made.

"Rudolph" has left us! He rushed in yesterday, announcing that his regiment was being transferred. Albeit, Nurse saw him this afternoon and was saluted as she went by. I can imagine her turning up a disdainful nose as she passed. Possibly he has found a more congenial host and hostess. Although he gave little trouble we shall not grieve for him. His air of rigid dignity was at times too much for our depraved sense of humour. He loved to trip spritely down the stairs without relaxing for one moment his attitude of egotism. Should he pass us on the way, he would swagger by, his wide-lapelled coat flapping about his ankles, and leaving in his wake the sickening odour of strong scent, whilst only acknowledging our existence by his studied air of indifference. Like his Master, he would never have risen to such an exalted rank under the Prussians.

So we live from day to day. We see friends and exchange rumours grave and comical, credible and bizarre. We seldom reveal our innermost thoughts, but we know just as surely as though exchanged by word of mouth, that the next person's feelings are identical with our own, thought for thought. What a mess we are in! How will it end? And the inaudible cry goes up: "How long?" Will the Germans become more oppressive as time goes on? Will any of the horrors we hear broadcast really fall upon us? Will the Jeremiahs around us prove to be right when they say: "The Germans will leave us only our eyes to weep with?"

To M.H. La Guelle. December 16th, 1941.

So Japan is in it after all. *Quelle Horreur*! This gives the final answer to the American Isolationists. Yet, the rest of the news is encouraging and your messages, now arriving in larger numbers, help us to see the brighter side. Pessimism, no matter how justified by events, could only aggravate our difficulties.

Peter-John was christened at St. John's Church on Sunday, the 7th of December. Having dressed himself for the event, Peter made a ceremonial entry into the dining room and announced himself as Lord Halifax. Until that moment we had not realised how gaunt he had become. His suit, not recently worn, hung on him as though made for a man twice his size: whilst his trilby totally eclipsed his eyes, nose and ears in the most comical fashion. He was obliged to wear Father's trilby which, before the war (on those occasions when they would exchange hats in order to amuse the family), looked like a snail on a pumpkin. Incidentally, far be it from me to suggest that the British Ambassador to Washington is a sartorial oddity.

You should have seen the christening procession. It resembled yet another ridiculous dream, in keeping with much of our present way of life.

Nurse and Peter walked side by side, the former pushing the perambulator and the latter my invalid chair. Down La Rouge Rue with Emil and Elsie, George, Felicia, Allie and Baby George bringing up the rear, the quaint assembly wound its way. We were all in lively mood owing to the crazy circumstances of the affair, and the motley crew we must have appeared in the eyes of the public. The Rev. Kilshaw had forgotten the important function and, as Peter had roused him from his Sunday nap, he was inclined to be irate. He mumbled sleepily: "Someone had better call at the Verger's house and bring him along while I prepare for the Service." I think Nurse considered him too drowsy to clasp her precious charge to his bosom, for she kept giving him anxious glances. Suddenly he came to life and appeared to shower a cataract of water over the shuddering infant, so turning the event into more of a launching than a christening which, on reflection, and in all solemnity, is surely what Baptism is meant to symbolise.

Emil took his place as Godfather with all due reverence, whilst Nurse stood proxy for Doris as Godmother.

We returned up the hill in festive mood, the two perambulators and the invalid chair, causing many a backward glance as you may imagine. After snapshots had been taken in the front garden for the family album, we sat down to an almost pre-war tea, with real cakes made from carefully hoarded ingredients and a cup of real tea. Naturally, no one probed into the source of these luxuries. For a while we forgot the war.

To M.H. La Guelle. December 19th, 1941.

Christmas is almost upon us for the second time and still no sign of a German collapse, despite the persistent tactics of the Russians. Trouble now seems to be brewing in Spain, and one wonders which way Turkey will jump under further pressure. For our insignificant part, we pray that the end may come before the face of Guernsey is changed beyond redemption.

The story goes that the Germans plan to construct two diagonal roads across the Island: one from Jerbourg to Grandes Rocques and the other from Bordeaux to Pleinmont, both of them to be sixty feet wide. Everything in the way will be demolished.

On a recent visit to L'Ancresse, Peter was amazed to see the beginnings of a new road leading from Fort Le Marchant, and cutting across the lovely stretch of Common towards Les Fontenelles. He calls it: "The Crowning Horror." We might be living in B.C. times when the Romans busied themselves in building roadways in Britain. Imagine the havoc if this present threat becomes a reality. Peter is now at Les Dunes fitting the third set of locks on the doors, which is almost a waste of time except for the faint hope of compensation against house-breaking or burglary.

Nurse now sleeps at her house at Bordeaux, which saves her a long cycle-ride back here at nights after preparing her husband's dinner. Happily, the need for expert night-duty is extremely remote. She is off-duty most of to-day, so I lunch in rare solitude, on potatoes, carrots, marrow and fish-cakes! Yesterday, Peter went hunting in the Markets and there, for the modest price of one shilling, was a conger's head waiting for him on a slab and not a queue in sight: "As you can imagine" he said: "I didn't bother to haggle." Nurse cooked it with bay leaves and stuffing made from our ersatz bread and herbs from the garden. We feasted off this yesterday, I am having another feed to-day and there is still enough for us all to-morrow. This sounds like the cruse of oil. I wish you were here to share it.

One hears over the wireless that the B.B.C. deplores the activities of the Black Marketeers. The system here is known as the G.U.T. (Guernsey's Underground Traffic). The victims are not British, therefore the principle is not the same, as you will readily appreciate. Practised here it is a far more hazardous, not to say, heroic procedure.

To M.H. La Guelle. December 24th, 1941.

The afternoon of Christmas Eve. With very mixed feelings I write these lines. In some ways this is the worst day of our separation. To-morrow we join our few remaining relatives and contrive to banish the blues which threaten to submerge me at this moment. I sit here alone, steeped in the past and dwell on former Christmas Eves of great excitement spent in this house with you all. Immersed in an atmosphere of suspended animation, remotely I hear some of the family moving about the house. I sense the mysterious rustle of gifts being stealthily concealed, parcels of Christmas fare arriving at the door, and the postman delivering belated cards. Surely this is reality, and the other, only a nightmare from which I have just been spared. O sweet illusion! Must it pass?

There is someone at the door and there are footsteps on the stairs: But Alas! the approaching voices are not those I long to hear, and I have but a few moments in which to conceive and deliver an ecstatic welcome.

Gwenyth and Hugh-John have come and gone having blown away the past and restored the unwelcome present: but the welcome I showed to them was genuine, for I did appreciate the kind thought behind their visit. They have brought presents for P.-J. in his absence (for he was out with Nurse), a tin of dried food and a bar of barley sugar from Hugh-John's ration, firmly pressed into my hands regardless of all protestations. A most generous gift!

Nurse left us officially on Monday and we were all sad at parting. She tells us that it was like a bereavement, and that she cycled blind all the way to Bordeaux. Personally, my anchor gone, I felt cast adrift and all-too-conscious of my limitations and unequal to the task of starting from scratch. Mercifully, the slippery eel survived his first bath at my hands without our hovering Nurse: which achievement gave both infant and mother some measure of confidence. The menace draws her like a magnet, and to-day they are in town shopping for sleeping-suits.

Everyone has been most kind since Nurse left us. Besides Gwenyth, Jean Martin and a friend, also Pat Hargreaves call in turn to wheel the baby around the Park or through the Water Lanes. I am very grateful to them all, for it saves my game leg and my energy for the trivial round.

On Monday we asked Dr. Sutcliffe to write his signature in Peter-John's log-book. He took a dim view of the fact that we could not produce a gold pen for the deed.

To M.H. La Guelle. Tuesday, December 30th, 1941.

We spent Christmas with Emil and Elsie at Garrivoe, P.J. doing his best to swell the sadly depleted ranks. We hung up a forlorn stocking for him, chiefly because we felt that Diana would be imagining him delving into it with chortles of delight; though far too young to register the meaning of it all. We had little heart for gaiety, but we visualised Diana unwrapping her own parcels. How Audrey will have enjoyed that with her flair for making Christmas really festive. Her zest for living and pronounced sense of occasion will accompany her throughout her life, and guard her secret of perpetual youth. Those people are rare and usually at the centre of things.

The boisterous hilarity of last Christmas, now only a memory, makes striking contrast to the one just over. Does this foreshadow what further deterioration may attend each successive Christmas with the Germans? We dare not think so far.

Though scarcely a rhapsody, we have lived eighteen months under German Rule and survived. There were forebodings in plenty, not always justified by results, but Hope never deserted us. The coming year will doubtless be fraught with many problems; it would be naïve to imagine otherwise, but we shall have to play it as it comes. As I wrote at the beginning, it is as well that the distant scene is wrapped in obscurity.

1942

To M.H. La Guelle. January 26th, 1942.

Nearly a month has elapsed, a month with nothing of note to record. Prosaic events pursue each other as day succeeds day, with sickening repetition. Your message dated on Father's birthday, October 7th, arrived last week, and did much to cheer us with its carefully chosen words: " Keep your sunny sides up! Soon be eating ormers." Your vigorous high spirits did as much to refresh us as did the message itself.

Peter is reading, and minor, reinstated in Audrey's room after the departure of Rudolph, is sound asleep: a condition I envy at this moment. My brain is in a state of atrophy due to fatigue. Our maid, after ailing for some time, has now taken to her bed with pleurisy and may not return to us. Indeed Dr. S. does not advise it, since it transpires that she lost a brother with T.B. and Nurse is suspicious of her own case: especially since I visited her and found her condition rather alarming. It looks as though we shall have to find another maid.

To-day, while Pat Hargreaves walked out with P.J. I seized the opportunity to sweep the landing and stairs. I felt like Anne Boleyn in the Tower. In the words of the popular song: "Along the dusty corridors for miles and miles I went" and understood what you meant by the long trek between kitchen and dining room. Tomorrow, I expect my protesting limbs to remind me of this marathon effort.

Pat took P.J. to be weighed, and I wince to record that at five months he tipped the scales at nineteen pounds four ounces. A few days ago I mentioned his size to Dr. S. comparing him to his Cousin George next door. I was fobbed off with the remark: "Are you afraid that he will become another Fat Boy of Peckham? Anyway, how can George expect to produce the same size offspring as Peter with his peace-time sixteen stone?" The second remark we felt contained a crumb of comfort: the first we decided to ignore!

The Libyan Campaign seems to be developing into a mammoth game of Nuts-in-May. Each time our Forces are driven back, our spirits reach subterranean depths, " Successful Attacks " and " Strategic Withdrawals " repeat themselves in quick succession, until we feel much the same as those fowls which our neighbour's boys used to hold head down in a pail of water, until they had apparently reached their last gasp: when they were quickly restored to full breathing and put through their ordeal over and over again. The grandmother told me how she caught them in the act, lambasted the little devils and packed them off to bed. So our spirits rise and fall with our troops' changing fortunes. We pray each night for our fighting men everywhere, and for the families who suffer the terrible strain of waiting for news.

Our war effort seems to consist of holding down a couple of German Divisions and, by our presence here, to prevent the R.A.F. blasting Guernsey to pieces in order to annihilate our enemies. We remain tethered here with a sizeable slice of the German Army, all fellow-prisoners, they in exile and we in isolation.

Should Britain recapture these Islands, she would be obliged to feed, clothe and reluctantly defend well over one hundred thousand Germans and Channel-Islanders at great personal risk: to say nothing of the teeming cosmopolitan thousands who make up the Organisation Todt.

May I say how comforting it is to be indirectly useful to the War Effort even in a microscopic way, and in a fuller sense to be the preservers of our Beloved Guernsey. We take no credit for none is due, it became Hobson's Choice from the moment we decided to remain and take the consequences.

The R.A.F. pass over us whenever they visit Brest to bomb the German battleships the *Scharnhorst,* the *Gneisenau* and the *Prince Eugen.* The ear-splitting barrage of German guns sends people scuttling for shelter from falling shrapnel, or the possibility of a British Bomber coming down with a full load.

The return from Brest usually coincides with P.J.'s feeding-time when I am unable to journey downstairs. I only hope that our son does not grow up to be a dithering idiot. I have begged Peter to climb into the loft and discover if it is floored or merely joisted: as though our very lives depended on inch boarding. Otherwise, such is the state of my nerves, that I shall go on feeling every night as though I am sitting out in open country at the mercy of a violent thunderstorm. O to be back on two sound legs when I hope once again to enjoy the visits of our heroes!

Last week, in broad daylight, the R.A.F. carried out a very daring low-level attack on the Harbour. I was at your bedroom window when the three Beauforts arrived. From my vantage-point they were quite close in as they passed the gas-works and came on over Belgrave Bay. They flew level with the hedge at the end of the field opposite this house, streaking across the sea in front of the Royal Hotel. Many casualties were reported, one local man having both legs blown off. Two horses were in a crane-crate in mid-air when the delayed-action bombs exploded: no trace of them has been found. Another bomb exploded in the hold of a large German cargo-ship which was sunk and not refloated for some days when the Germans deemed it safe to begin salvage operations.

The audacious raiders were well away before the German guns could be brought into action. It was a very neat performance, despite the tragic results for some local families.

To M.H. La Guelle. Sunday, February 1, 1942.

Last night the R.A.F. carried out another series of raids on Brest, and we came in for our usual blasting. The zooming of planes and barrage of guns lasted from eight o'clock until midnight, with only brief intervals of a few minutes. Consequently we overslept this morning until eight o'clock, and still the infant slept.

We are now having a goodly ration of spaghetti, and occasionally we are blessed with a chunk of Dutch cheese. P.J. and I have also received two rations of 'Chocolat Menier' two small bars for me (as a nursing Mother) and a six-inch slab for the baby. This, we have put away for his future enjoyment.

Last week, two German 'engineers' came to inquire if we had spare bedrooms. Reluctantly, we introduced them to those of George and Doris, which they condescended to accept. Gladys from Havelet came to help me spring-clean the rooms in readiness. We divided all the personal contents between the landing and the baby's room. The following day, these men returned and said that the rooms were not for them but for their superiors. As they seemed to be of a superior type themselves, it set us wondering what Elite were about to honour us with their presence. The German habit is to keep us on the 'qui vive', so we are quite prepared for these arrangements to come to naught. These men, by the way, were civilians sportingly attired in plus-fours.

The news is like the Parson's egg, good and bad in parts. Libya and the Far East are the dingiest spots on an ever-expanding war-map. Thank heaven for the Russians whatever their ideologies! Are they the Devil's tools turned against himself?

As I write, Peter is reading, while a nightdress airs for our son. We still live in your bedroom, for not only is it more pleasant but I, for one, cannot abide the downstairs rooms without you all. Whenever I enter one of them the starkness of separation is emphasised. One dismal glance at the empty chairs, and the general air of mustiness, and I retreat with a shudder as though closing the door on a vault, full of ghosts. This irrevocable feeling of desertion is still the most chilling aspect of this existence, and the most difficult to overcome. This must be almost the only sensation which Peter and I do not share, for his family is nearly intact. I feel sure he understands this, though it is never mentioned outside these pages. To reiterate upon the irrevocable is only "to aggravate the worm that dieth not", and so, with the closing of those doors, I must close my mind or become a crashing bore to my fellows.

It is now nine o'clock of a damp quiet evening, the sort of muggy weather when wet clothes can hang about indefinitely. Fortunately, we no longer have nappies to air, for Mrs. Wynne kindly offered to have them all in her airing-cupboard. Peter takes them in the morning (clean of course!) on his way to business, and collects them on the way home in the afternoons.

The Wynnes are now living in the Gruts' house in Upland Road, their own bungalow at L'Ancresse having been overrun, from the first, with those of their neighbours. Unfortunately, someone had cleaned out the Gruts' store of food before the Wynnes moved in. A thousand pities!

To M.H. La Guelle. February 16th, 1942.

The news is grim! Japan appears to be more formidable than was expected. We shudder when Mr. Churchill mentions, as a matter of course, War Plans for 1943.

The lack of food presents an awesome problem for many people. Adults, including invalids and old people, now receive a quarter of a pint of skimmed milk daily. You may imagine the consequent hardship in mid-winter. The Germans are ever more demanding of provisions: and also, many useful fields have been commandeered for military use, including ammunition dumps, sheds, kitchens and even railways. Our precious field opposite is staked out with pegs for some military purpose. In answer to George's inquiry as to their intentions an engineer replied tersely: "Workmen's huts!" This promises to be the end of Lily, 'Little Mary's so-useful ally!' (as I mentioned in a cryptic message to you earlier on). We fervently hope that these same huts will not be sleeping quarters for the rabble of humanity with which the Island is now overrun. Lest you think that I am seriously lacking in Christian Charity, may I assuage your darkened opinion, by telling you that local benevolence towards these poor unfortunates, has sometimes been rewarded with villainy.

The story goes, that an elderly woman living a few doors away from us, was visited a few days ago by two of these people. While she answered one of them at her front door, the other one sidled round to the back door, entered the house, and made off with her handbag. They may have been the same two who called here, one at the front door and the other at the back. If a similar fate was intended for me, their little scheme was foiled, for I always keep the front door locked, and I only answered the knock on the back door. The innocent victims of forced labour, these poor half-starved slaves roam the streets in a ragged and filthy condition, bereft of human rights and of human dignity. One provides a couple of them with a bowl of soup one day, only to find on the morrow a dozen on the doorstep: when charity has to cease for lack of provisions. It is heart-breaking to have to send them slouching away empty, and to know that they will meet with a similar fate from house to house.

To M.H. La Guelle. February 18th, 1942.

A few lines in waiting for Peter to join me for supper. Tomorrow he will cycle to Les Dunes, where some vagrant immigrants have now definitely installed themselves. He will attempt to rescue the lawn-mower and other garden tools, rather from local marauders than from our new tenants, whose sole purpose in life is self-preservation as opposed to gardening. The remaining contents of the house we have to regard as a total loss. This blow was not unexpected, but we feel rather sick in contemplation of the squalor we are destined to find when they depart.

Mr. McCathie has been sorely tried in this direction. His front garden is a network of clothes-lines strung from his sun-balcony and windows to trees and paling, from which bits and pieces of washing incessantly flap in the breeze. The interior of his house will need fumigating and resurrecting generally.

After the first batch of soldiers left his house, Mac discovered his four-poster bed slung out in the back garden, together with other unwanted goods and chattels. He also found himself in possession of mattresses and wireless sets, stolen from other Guernsey houses. His present tenants are slave-workers who take over places which the soldiers leave when they can no longer bear to live under the conditions which they themselves have created.

It is now a common occurrence for people to discover, first thing in the morning, their gardens strewn with the heads of their fowls, the rabbit-hutches bereft of their occupants and clothes-lines stripped of washing. Nurse tells us that her neighbours' only hope of saving their washing, is for them to hang it up and sit beside it with a book or knitting, while the clothes are drying.

Guernsey is becoming another Gibraltar with its labyrinth of tunnels. One of these is in embryo at the bottom of our old quarry at Rouge Rue, a sad demise for our tennis-courts. It will have its exit somewhere in Arculon Lane. The houses hereabouts are frequently shaken by the blasting.

Father's garage is now inhabited by a pair of horses. They come to the pump on the lawn several times a day for water, and often waken our sleeping son lying in his perambulator. I was cutting some greens for lunch a few days ago, accompanied by a singing German who was grooming his horse. Peter appeared and, pressing his finger to his lips, indicated the sleeping child. The soldier, on seeing this familiar sign in any language, promptly stifled his vocal talent, and graciously allowed the infant slumbers to continue. The Germans are exceedingly fond of children. One of them stopped Nurse in the street one day and craved permission to see the baby. Even her extreme loathing of the whole teutonic race was powerless to deny adulation for her precious charge, though she tried to flounce it off as an unavoidable circumstance. I think that Peter's teasing made her regret having told us of the incident. We did point out that the poor blighter had probably left an infant of his own, to go and fight for what he believed to be a just cause.

Miraculously, a Red Cross message from Diana arrived for me on my Birthday, it was sent on September the 13th. What a coincidence for one to arrive on the very day of celebration, four and a half months after despatch.

So Pam is an Ambulance driver, a natural flair I would think for this forthright and dynamic character. Peter goes with great eagerness to collect your messages, and thrills me when he says they are in your own handwriting. I dare not ask him on oath if this be true, for I want to believe it and he could not violate our code-word if I asked for it. If he is merely trying to please me, then we are both happy. Only once have I been into Town since P.J.'s birth, as I am still lame and remain on the Doctor's visiting list.

To M.H. La Guelle. Sunday, March 8th, 1942.

Many Happier Returns of this your Birthday. We hope that you are well and enjoying the same beautiful weather now prevailing here. Last year we promised ourselves to be reunited for this Anniversary. With reluctance, we hereby transfer this covenant to March, 1943.

To M.H. La Guelle. Wednesday, March 18th, 1942.

The weather is foul! The beautiful spell was short-lived, and to-day, Peter-John has chosen Jean Martin to escort him on one of their many assignations. My gratitude is unbounded.

There is more Allied talk of launching an Offensive, which is once again encouraging, for, as the years drag on, any sign of activity is like an oasis in the desert.

Our grimy immigrants become ever more squalid: now using streets and lamp-posts like dogs with arborial inclinations: and having no objection to a public audience day and night. Stories of their activities are brought to me by Nurse and Peter, and often augmented by George and Felicia. Several dwellings have been set alight, sewage runs in gutters and down the walls of flat-roofed houses. This depressing situation will bring with it the hazard of disease when the hot weather arrives. Perhaps the Germans will be compelled to take action for their own sakes. Despite the general *malaise* of poor little Guernsey, we are lucky, if we regard ourselves as prisoners-of-war.

The R.A.F. continue to visit us, and it seems fairly certain that a German Bomber was shot down over the airport on Sunday. According to the Press of March the Third, with regard to the escape from Brest of the battleships, *Scharnhorst, Gneisenau* and *Eugen,* the German version says: " In this connection, the official figures, which have been issued by the British Authorities, are interesting. According to these, the R.A.F. made 229 attacks on these ships in Brest, dropped 4,000 tons of bombs and, as a result, have lost 43 machines." On reading this statement, one can almost hear the repulsive voice of Lord Haw-Haw. By virtue of their origin, and the impossibility of verification, these figures cannot be swallowed whole: but they are feasible to us who were unforgettably in direct line between Britain and Brest, when wailing syrens drove passers-by to seek the shelter of this house. Sad though we were at the news of this great prize escaping in mist through the Channel, under the very noses of the British, we must own that it was a boon to be delivered from the ear-splitting commotion of zooming planes and anti-aircraft fire which had assailed us night after night for several weeks.

To M.H. La Guelle. Thursday, March 19th, 1942.

Yesterday, two men were sent by Mr. Hunkin to investigate the dripping of water through the ceiling on the landing. On climbing into the loft, they discovered a large piece of granite lodged in the roof after it had smashed four tiles. You can imagine the blasting force required for a sizeable rock to be flung so far from the Rouge Rue quarry.

Two Red Cross messages arrived today, one with belated congratulations from Mrs. Luxon on the birth of Peter-John: and one from Flo (again the code-word used), with assurances of our early liberation. It savoured of a get-well card for a speedy recovery to someone with a fatal illness. However, it answered its kind purpose, reminded us that we are not forgotten, and produced from us a few humorous remarks. Our exiled friends seem unaware that we listen to dear old Winston's forecasts, and that we lost our illusions long ago. We have ceased to carp at the stings of Fate. Anxiety and boredom we have in abundance: but they leave no room for bitterness. It rejoices me that I can write these words with calm resignation and not as a victim of apathy. That this benign acceptance will endure to the end, remains to be seen: and that it may be the mood of the moment I am well aware: but it will be a sorry day for each and every one of us if it is dispelled. For the first time I walked to and from town to collect these messages, and was somewhat exhausted by the effort. Peter thought I had been rash. Supper over, he said: "These windows are disgusting! I'm going to clean them. Don't stop me." (As though I would). They are so lofty that he barely finished one of them before stopping of his own accord. He decided to send a man from town to deal with them in the morning. He had had enough of the circus act on the waving ladder. We have inserted a notice in the Press for a strong-maid to do full-time work: my present help only sparing me enough time for a few captain's pulls, which are far from adequate: most of my time being absorbed by baby-chores and cooking. With regard to the latter, Gladys says: "It's not so much the cookin' gets me down, it's the Pelmanisin'! "

Peter's Father died on the third of March. Dear old Pop. He never recovered from the attack of dysentery which he contracted last summer: and, coupled with his long-standing diabetes, he just wasted away. He was a model of endurance, and would just sit with his head in his hands, running his fingers through his white hair, only once admitting that his head ached. I saw him two or three days before he died, and it happened to be during one of his more lucid moments. His last words to me were so much in character: "Is that you Little One? Have you come to read to me?" If ever there was a time when I wanted to gratify his wish, it was at that moment, and I regretted those times in the past when I had not always been as enthusiastic as I should. But now, I was obliged to return almost at once for Peter-John's supper. I comforted myself with the knowledge that his mind could not have borne the strain of concentrating on a story, and also, that at any moment he would lapse into his twilight world, from whence he would return quite unaware that I had been present that day. Peter had spent many hours at his bedside during those past days, groping for and holding his hand under the bedclothes. He tells me that he would give his hand a gentle squeeze, and be rewarded with a feeble response, just sufficient to let him know that his presence was appreciated: they had always been very close. Peter saw his Father go with sorrow, certainly: but without a trace of filial remorse: a comforting thought, which always assuages grief.

On the morning of the funeral, Peter took with him a posy of Spring flowers from Peter-John. It contained sixteen species of blooms, most of them kindly collected by Mrs. Hargreaves. Peter's Ma was deeply touched, and asked for them to be placed upon the coffin before it was lowered. We had attached a card bearing the words: "To Dear Grandpa—The Oldest, from Peter-John—The Youngest." The family tribute was the only other adornment. Peter, Emil, Mr. Brice and Jim Bell occupied the only carriage: and the Staff of The Jewellers and Silversmiths were the only people present at the private funeral. Ma seems to have taken her bereavement very philosophically, and Elsie could not have been kinder to them both.

For the past month P.J. has been plagued with eczema all over his face and forehead. This has been an added burden to everyone, but most of all to the victim. He is so patient, just rolling his head from side to side, in mute submission. At night, his arms are encased in corrugated paper, tied at both ends like a Christmas cracker: and by day his hands are tied to a leather strap around his middle. It hurts us terribly to see him afflicted with this added torture, and to see him struggle to use his hands and arms. I bath him before Peter leaves in the morning, so that he can hold his little hands, so eager to scratch the horrible rash and headsore. We give him a few minutes' freedom after his bath, as he lies on our bed under our vigilant eyes, lest he be led into temptation. Then he is tied up again until bed-time, when his arms return to their corrugated prison.

As I close this letter, I hear a plane and pause for the gunfire. It must have been a German plane for silence reigns as the zooming recedes.

To M.H. La Guelle. April 15th, 1942.

An incredible age since I last wrote and, the baby being at Bordeaux with Nurse for the past three weeks, I had expected to do so much. He will return tomorrow to celebrate with us our fourteenth Wedding Anniversary.

When last I wrote, he was feeling decidedly off colour. It turned out to be the only case of measles known to Dr. S. It would be! Fortunately it was a very mild attack, possibly owing to extreme youth, although his back and front were generously peppered. Nurse has done a stalwart job on his eczema, which, she declares, has almost left him.

It was a great thrill to receive a reply message from you last week: and two straight messages from Diana and Doris: whilst three more have come from Flo in the past three weeks. We were amused by Diana's sophisticated: "Dearest Congratulations." This, on the birth of her brother (what an age to arrive!), instead of the expected "Thrilled with baby brother." She expresses the hope of returning for his birthday. What a forlorn hope it is for poor Diana!

To M.H. La Guelle. April 16th, 1942.

Our second Wedding Anniversary without you.

Yesterday's letter was cut short, and I felt this Diary to be doomed. I had just got into my stride, when Harry

Broughton called to use the telephone. He sat up here with me afterwards until Peter came, sampled a piece of my 'Gateau de Blitz' and pronounced it to be good. If I gave you the recipe here, I doubt if you would use the ingredients when you return.

At long last, the desecration of the field opposite has begun. Yesterday, as I wrote, a conglomeration of machinery was dragged across this green and pleasant acre, despite Lily's distracted protests, delivered loud and clear. Men began to drive what appears to be an airshaft into the ground leading to the tunnel which runs from the Rouge Rue quarry to a point under the field, and branching from there towards the gas-works.

We are at a loss to understand all this seemingly useless activity. The Germans are said to have a rooted notion that America means to attempt our Liberation. The grapevine came up with the pleasant rumour that all these foreign workers are about to leave the Island, and return to France to work on some scheme at Bordeaux. But, no doubt, the grapes on the vine, as always, need drastic pruning.

This afternoon, Peter will cycle to Bordeaux for P.J.'s luggage: and return with Nurse, also cycling with His Majesty on her carrier. My hair always stands on end, when I see Nurse astride the bicycle, with one foot on the road and the other on a pedal, before hoisting her wobbling eleven stone up on to the saddle, while the front wheel decides upon its fluctuating course of action: with P.J.'s hand eagerly clutching for a grip on her belt. I always mentally mop my brow when the wheel finally straightens and they are safely launched. Especially since it is a standing joke that Nurse is accident prone, and an expert at dropping things.

For some time now, Nurse has been 'Nan' throughout all private discourse with her charge: whose only replies are toothless grins and loud chortles. You will hereafter see that we have adopted this less formal soubriquet. It saves confusion for P.J. later on, and also, Nan is thereby firmly installed as a friend of the family. She had already asked that she might be allowed half-shares in the infant! Fate has dealt her a cruel blow in that direction. In a meagre attempt at consolation, I told her that she was destined to deliver and to mother hundreds of babies: but the real thing would have been her life's fulfilment. She has now taken on a case of nursing an old lady of eighty-five years. She vows that it will take a lot of concentrating, after so long with a baby, if she is to resist patting the old lady's bottom, and kissing her knees and toes!

Now 2 p.m. and I hear Peter playing hymns on the old family piano, prematurely bequeathed to him by his Ma, who has a rooted idea that her days are numbered.

Lunch to-day consisted of cauliflower, fried seed potatoes, and the rest of a tin of tomatoes, mixed with the mortal remains of a meatless brawn, left over from yesterday. Should you need the brawn recipe at some future date, it consists of: one cup of barley-flour, one large grated carrot, three small grated potatoes (of similar ilk to the above), one chopped onion, parsley and thyme, a few ersatz breadcrumbs and seasoning: mixed with water, put into a greased basin and steamed for two hours. Our pudding consisted of the same basic ingredients, with the seasoning, herbs and onion replaced by a little sugar, a knob of butter and a little cocoa essence, steamed for three hours. This cocoa comes from France to be used as a beverage: but it is slightly more revolting than bramble-tea. Nevertheless, we thoroughly enjoyed our lunch.

We spent the Easter week-end on Stan's farm at Les Nicolles in the Forest Parish. It was a treat to have a week-end of Bridge with Stan, Harry Marley and Pat Hargreaves.

The Farm, though somewhat primitive, is quite picturesque, and I adored the familiar farmyard odours and activities.

P. J. and Nan revelled in each others' company, along with her husband at Bordeaux.

The Guernsey Dramatic Club staged a good play last week, entitled "George and Margaret." It was beautifully done. A vaudeville group of local talent is also running at The Lyric Theatre under the name of "The Crazy Gang," and a better title it would be difficult to find. One always imagined that all the best gags were imported from Britain: but this cast quickly dispelled that idea. The write-up in yesterday's Press bore the title: "Crazy Doings at the Lyric."

Produced by Peter Campbell, the cast includes — Cyd Gardner, Fred Leeder and Tony Chubb as chief comedians.

Their antics cause roars of laughter. The Brache sisters render a selection of songs. Frank Martel plays on the accordion. Pearl White Smith delights everyone with the song: "Out in the cold, cold snow." While the well-known monologue: "Albert and the Lion" is presented in up-to-date fashion by Tony Chubb. The tap-dancing is well done and well applauded. The Bill next week is entitled: "April Frolics," featuring "Rufus and Sambo" described as "Irresponsible Coons."

The front page of the same Press is best ignored, with its headline of an "American Convoy damaged in Home Waters" and "175 Enemy Tanks destroyed on Eastern Front." These do not even scratch the surface of our morale, for they are all taken with the proverbial salt, and we leave the substance unread.

So you see the British Spirit is still in the ascendancy, aided and abetted by one short evening at The Lyric, where years of anxiety roll away and leave us with renewed vigour to face the inevitable trials which loom ahead.

After this long effort, bedevilled by many interruptions, I bid you Adieu.

To M.H. Caledonia Nursery. April 26th, 1942.

The eczema looks much better; though it flares up if we relax treatment, which consists of washing "the affected parts" with warm olive oil (for which many thanks) and after wiping away the surplus, applying an ointment called "Pini". Eight months old to-day, P.J. still has his arms tethered to prevent scratching. His patience seems unlimited for which we are truly thankful. A screaming fractious infant would be the last straw in a chain of unhappy events. So, another blessing is added to our list. Our rambles in this familiar neighbourhood help him to forget his torment.

These old haunts of our childhood we now re-visit with our son: though Peter's recollections of this place are somewhat different from mine: for somehow, we never met here in our youth, where we now forget awhile the chain of circumstances which brought us to these parts together, after all these years.

Copious springs of memory refresh us in these beautiful grounds. Rare plants and semi-tropical trees have seen us pass this way before. On Sunday afternoons in the dim past, Marie, Doris and I, attired in all our Sabbath finery, with buttoned boots, shantung suits and gaily-flowered hats, would stroll among roses of every hue and intoxicating perfume: a veritable "Walk in a Paradise Garden," where peacocks spread their gorgeous fanlike plumage. Here, Peter and I now find solace from the seething world outside. Nothing has changed.

The ancient Japanese Magnolia still lifts its head towards the sky. Busy little streams enter and leave the large pond whereon the same old tree-trunk rests, its roots still clinging to the mossy bank: a temptation to us as children to run across its length, and dare the peril of falling into the muddy water. Here, our sleeping child in his carriage beside us, Peter and I heave grateful sighs, as we listen to the almost tangible silence, accentuated rather than disturbed by the occasional cry of a bird far above us in the eucalyptus tree. With the absence of any other sound, we might be on an uninhabited island, savouring in blessed solitude, "One Moment in Annihilation's Waste, One Moment of the Well of Life to taste."

A zooming plane shatters the silence and, as receding memory ceases to evoke, our thoughts return unwilling, to the stern realities of Life.

And stern they are, with the, apparently, dire humiliation now thrust upon us by the local Police, who have been tried in the Royal Court under the German Flag, for thefts of foodstuffs, not only from the German stores, but from our Local Commodities.

All this is reported in the Press of April 23rd and 24th. The sentences on seventeen of the Police-Sergeants and Constables, vary from four weeks to four-and-a-half years at hard labour. One Sergeant was named as "The Managing Director". Of the eighteen accused only P.C. Pill was acquitted. Mr. Ambrose Sherwill was Counsel for the Defence, while the rest of the Court consisted of German Officials.

That the case was judged in a completely impartial manner, that full justice has been done, and not under military pressure, I am not qualified to say. So much of the printed matter in our censored Press cannot be taken literally, that I have refrained from mentioning by name any of those sentenced. The whole case is fully reported in the Occupation Newspapers in my possession, and is no doubt recorded in the Island Archives, possibly for all time. I leave this subject with an open mind for it is always difficult in the circumstances to sort fact from fiction.

Heaven help any of those who may be wrongfully sentenced, despite their detailed confessions, which may, or may not be freely made.

To M.H. Sunday, May 10th, 1942.

A day of much-needed steady rain, Peter is reading by the fire, which he glimpses behind the everlasting washing, while the Cherub sleeps in his room, allowing me to relax and add a few lines to this spasmodic journal.

A steady flow of Messages, chiefly from Diana, now that our need is greater, atone for the dearth of news at the start of the Occupation. Her Messages have a more adult tone, and her school news seems encouraging. We passed on her embraces to her brother. Two messages arrived from Audrey, one sent in November and the other in March. Her reference to Mrs. Hubbard rejoiced us on your behalf, since your biscuits and cakes are not rationed, and you are still able to buy chocolate.

There are many things which could be recorded if caution were not the constant watchword. The subjects exempted from these pages reduce the rest to trivialities. Life is not too untenable at the moment, although we are both losing weight.

This is a meatless week, and we have consumed so many vegetable rissoles of late, that we expect to sprout tubers at any moment.

As I write, two Germans are leading their horses to the stalls in the garden garage, Lily is aimlessly chewing the cud in the field, and the rain pursues its steady course down the window-panes. Not an exhilarating prospect, as we await news of the Spring Offensive. Perhaps Winston will be more optimistic tonight. We hope so, for everyone is suffering from mental and physical lethargy, which only the Great Man can remedy.

Infant sounds from the next room have galvanised Peter, to prevent the baby from rubbing his head on his bed; which becomes easier to do as he grows more active. A little freedom of arms will follow, while Peter is here to guard him from self-inflicted damage; during which I prepare supper. The dread ritual of olive oil, ointment and fetters will be followed by the little captive drowning his sorrows with one-and-a-half bottles of milk, and so to bed.

The rain, having stopped, Peter and Kala will brave the elements at Beau Séjour after all, to wind up the day.

To M.H. La Guelle. May 17th, 1942.

Diana's twelfth birthday. Speed the day when we shall set eyes on our Firstborn!

After supper we reminisced with Audrey's gramophone records, played on Ted's borrowed gramophone. Peter lived in the past with Diana, while I romanced on our future together. It was not difficult, with Grieg's Piano Concerto, and the New World Symphony to match both our moods, which we hope to synchronize later on with Schumann's Concerto in A. We shall conclude with the little Intermezzo which ran through the last film I saw with Audrey, on the Saturday before the crisis of evacuation.

I was at A. J. Barber's in the morning for a tooth extraction, when he asked if I had seen the film "Escape to Happiness" and insisted that I go to that afternoon's matinée, as the Grieg Concerto was the theme music running through the whole film. When I arrived at La Guelle for lunch, Audrey insisted, in her turn, that we should go together. The main stars were Leslie Howard and Ingrid Bergmann.

On the following Tuesday afternoon, I asked A.J.B. why he had not mentioned the Intermezzo to me. He said the tune was so elusive that he had 'lost' it, and thought it had escaped him for ever. I hummed a few bars, which electrified the ebullient gentleman, so that he rummaged for pencil and paper with which he drew the lines of the stave, promptly forgot the reason for my visit, and craved my indulgence while he ran down to his drawing-room to recapture the plaintive air on his piano. An amazing man, he returned and put me right on part of the tune which had escaped me, by saying that a certain note was a tenth of a tone out in my interpretation: or words to that effect, for I am unversed in the theory of music.

I remember one occasion when he was trying to recall a certain phrase in the New World Symphony. My memory clicked in time for him to commit that also to paper, while I lay back in his chair, my mouth plugged with a drainage tube and wads of cotton-wool. Yet, he was so dynamic and efficient that he got through a prodigious amount of work, despite these distractions, which included his vivid interest in every craft entering or leaving the Harbour below his windows.

His last words to me were: "Goodbye. I shall be in the R.A.M.C. by the end of the week." I felt that I had seen the last of a whirlwind.

Such was the delightfully even tenor of our lives, before those in high places (unbecoming to their origin or qualifications), chose to turn the World upside-down.

On reliable information, we believe that thousands of troops left us last week. For the first time, this news, so-longed-for, bears unwelcome overtones. Our new anxiety being that the entire army may evacuate and leave us at the mercy of thousands of foreign labourers who, having served their purpose, are now redundant. This would plunge us from the frying-pan into the fire and no mistake. One dare not dwell on the consequences in such an event.

The Scriptures moveth us in sundry places. Two weeks ago, we went to a Service at St. James's. The place was like a mausoleum: for the dirge-like singing and prayers numbed rather than inspired the sparse congregation. The Sermon lacked the verve of the Vicar's reputed oratory, as though he had ceased to fan the dying embers of the Celestial Fire. Perhaps he has succumbed to the general apathy through hunger and the discouragement of empty pews. The people seem no longer to look to the Church for inspiration and guidance. The choir consisted of three small soundless boys. No one dared sing above a whisper for fear of being heard. And so, we ambled pianissimo through that dead hour: when we longed to burst into song and startle the rest into action.

If something drastic is not done to enliven these services, one foresees the day when the Churches will be defunct for lack of enthusiastic guidance. It is a gravely disturbing thought, that the prophecy may yet come true, "it being foretold that when Christ cometh, He shall not find Faith upon the Earth."

The sparkling Good News of the Gospel is so often reduced to a palsied rambling, so that even The Almighty must, at times, be hard put to it to understand much of the lumber meted out to His sheep from divers pulpits throughout Christendom. Feeble attempts are made, to drive home some point that never existed, or was obvious even to the Village Idiot, or was too complex to penetrate the most agile minds in the congregation. Many Sermons labour on to an inconclusive finale, bearing no relationship to the text, the gist having long been lost in the jungle.

Peter and I have often agreed that every Church should be equipped with a first-rate radiogram, fed with the great works of the Masters. Handel's "Messiah" or his beautiful "Largo" or Saint-Saëns "Rondo Capriccioso", excerpts from the "St. Matthew Passion" or Elgar's "Enigma Variations" for example, would fill the churches with adoring congregations from Sunday to Sunday. Imagine the mellow voice of Clara Butt echoing through the aisles: her miraculous rendering of "Abide with Me" leading the people beside the Waters of Comfort, in spontaneous homage to the Donor of this Holy Art.

Apathy would be no more: for the Parishioners could send individual requests of records for each Service: these could replace the Anthem, and be an added benediction between the Blessing and the Recessional Hymn. Musical appreciation would be painlessly distilled into the ear of the less initiated. A shorter Service and an even shorter Sermon would not come amiss, to make way for the rich eloquence of music which proves so moving to the multitudes who attend the Promenade Concerts throughout the Summer Season.

How right Henry was, when he wrote in one of his many epistles from America, that too often do parents of the least gifted of a family say, one to the other: " I don't know what's to become of Little Oswald. I suppose we shall have to put him in the Ministry."

Can anyone imagine the vast multitudes of Biblical Times, listening spellbound to Our Lord, if He had spoken in sepulchral tones, with the deadpan countenance of some of to-day's clergy, who plunge their dejected parishioners into the Slough of Despond? And who feed the comedians with endless material for their stage caricatures?

An intensive course of elocution, not histrionic, but with verve and variety of tone, should surely be a pre-requisite for any man training for the Propagation of the Gospel: for without this attribute, his congregation will surely dwindle, whilst he alone will fail to comprehend the reason for the empty pews. All other qualifications for this high office are set at naught, if a man cannot hold the interest of his flock, so that they come again and again to hear his words.

We all remember how old Grandpa Head refused, on one occasion, to put his collection in the plate, as he had dozed off and not heard half the Sermon. All I can say to this piece of apparent heresy is, that the Sermon was not preached by a J. C. Tabor or J. A. F. Ozanne. I think they would have renounced their job if even the most senile had fallen asleep during their discourses. Surely this could be a good yardstick for all Parsons.

On the other hand, there are those who keep their congregation awake, by thumping the pulpit and, with bursting jugular veins shouting dire recriminations at the Faithful Few there present Sunday after Sunday: as though they are responsible for the empty pews, and other sins of omission committed by the sheep who have gone astray.

This always affects me (as I suspect it does many others with my degraded sense of humour), in one of two ways: either to hide my mirth, at this total surrender of clerical dignity, behind the largest hat in the pew in front, or to sit and stifle the urge to get up and walk out in disgust.

Righteous anger on the part of Our Lord, cleared the Church of thieves and money-changers, whose presence there was eminently undesirable anyway: He did not crack the whip in order to gather his straying sheep into the fold.

The clerical hierarchy might denounce the opinions here expressed, as heresy, and the work of rebels, but rebels have been known to change the whole course of history, as did a certain Carpenter, who rebelled against the teachings of the Scribes and Pharisees and the whole Sanhedrin of Ancient Times. That the present Establishment will not be moved an iota by one very insignificant voice in a very large Wilderness, I am well aware. With even a few pews still occupied, the same old tired procedure will be adhered to: while the masses continue on their 'unlawful' occasions as Sabbath succeeds Sabbath, too apathetic in their Wilderness, to add a voice in protest against the wet-blanket presentation of the Inspiring Message and Shining Light which really does exist in the Ancient and Modern Book of Hymn and Prayer.

No Business, School or other Establishment can flourish under a flabby Staff of ineffectuals: and no wringing of hands, and lamentations can boost the dwindling profits: The Management must do their homework, examine their shortcomings, and come up smartly with an antidote for their anaesthesia, before it is too late.

Peter, having returned on the stroke of Curfew, I must close. May Diana return to us before her thirteenth birthday.

To M.H. La Guelle. Whit-Monday, May 25th, 1942.

Your three January messages arrived this week-end. As you long to see me, so you must realise how we long for Diana, with filial longings reciprocated all round.

The weather is positively foul! This afternoon we sat and froze under the verandah at Beau Séjour; with P.J. asleep beside us. Last night, the first time for nearly four months, we put him to bed with his arms free. Our prayers for his safety were duly answered: for, this morning, he had neither scratched nor rubbed his face and head. He has now been free all day and, having no idea what to do with his hands and arms, he flings them about and gives his face the most violent backhands. He drops a lip when he inflicts pain upon himself. It will not be long before he finds this an unprofitable pastime. Meanwhile, it is rather pathetic to see the look of hurt indignation on his face, as though he suspects us of being amused by his actions, if not actually being in league against him. At the risk of appearing sadistic, I must own that his reactions have somewhat taxed our self-control.

Felicia and George are now walking up the road, on their way to the Essential Commodities Dance at the Ladies' College. A welcome respite from daily stagnation. Peter is treating us to another musical programme, while I sit by the fire surrounded by airing laundry. The interminable rain continues.

Meanwhile, the Soviet Offensive seems to have lost some of its impetus, while we await the outcome with bated breath.

At times we feel the impossibility of existing through another Occupied Winter: but we have been sustained through all the bad moments of the past, and we feel that the news may soon improve by leaps and bounds. So you see our spirits fall, only to rise again as Mind holds sway over Matter.

Although not entirely without food, we are ever hungry, and many people are definitely starving. Cerebral activity appears to absorb the calories, and the changes of mood are exhausting. Your Messages are an enormous help.

Peter-John will be nine months old to-morrow. A thousand pities that Diana cannot enjoy his infancy: but we never wish her to be here in these circumstances. Our dual ration would still not satisfy her appetite.

The news is on, and my feeble brain cannot function in competition with Frederick Allen.

To M.H. La Guelle. Friday, June 12th, 1942.

Once again we find ourselves childless. Nurse 'invited' P.J. to stay with her for a few days, and I know she will not be the one to suggest his return.

Joyce and I have indulged in spasmodic bursts of Spring-cleaning, which last just as long as our bursts of energy.

On Wednesday, I took tea with our wandering son at Bordeaux: only to find myself taken very much for granted, Peter had cycled from Town into the upper Parishes armed with a few ounces of tobacco to pull off a barter for eggs, which we are pickling for P.J. for the Winter.

Yesterday, we played tennis with the de la Rues at King's Road. I felt twenty years older than when I last played. We had a rousing time. The rain, intervening at eight games all, Kath and Ginge asked us to finish the day playing Bridge at their house. We lost the first rubber to the tune of eight-hundred and ninety points, and won the second by exactly the same margin. So ended the day, definitely all-square in every department.

We swapped Occupation Stories with them, and were vastly amused by Ginge's recital of a recent nocturnal experience: when he was deprived of sleep by gnawing hunger.

Creeping silently out of bed, he began to grope his way to the bedroom door by the aid of a lighted match. This he dropped as it was about to burn his fingers. Stubbing his big toe and stepping on to the still-burning match, he let out a furious "Blast!" Kath shot straight up in bed, and demanded what on earth he thought he was doing.

"I'm off to the kitchen to find some food," was the reply.

"I suppose you realise," said Kath, "that it will automatically reduce your breakfast ration?"

"I'm hungry NOW!" retorted poor Ginge, and, taking no thought for the morrow (Matthew 6, v. 34) he betook himself to the kitchen, where he hoped to appease the inner man and defeat insomnia.

Inevitably, their combined version of this episode, garnished with the usual marital interruptions and contradictions, was infinitely more amusing in the telling, than by repetition here.

Torrents of rain and gales have swept across the Island: and we are due to play tennis again this evening in calm, sunny weather at last. We are invited to supper at the Stacey's Farm to-morrow. Sunday will be spent at the Tea-room with Unice and Winnie, as in days of yore. On Monday I am Bridging with Elsie at Bob Hargreaves, and we shall take Gwenyth to the play at the Lyric in the evening. "Quiet Wedding" played by Mary Toms, Ida Santangelo, Mrs. Sherwill and Alan Mackay in the cast, promises to be most entertaining. They put things over so well, and have been a boon to the sagging population of Guernsey.

It is with much regret that I record the passing of Tom Bennett, after only a week in Hospital. His remaining kidney refused to function, and would not respond to treatment. He is one of the people who should have left Guernsey in 1940: and might certainly have survived under better conditions. A dreadful blow is on the way to "Freddie" stranded with her tiny children. One wonders how long the Message will take to reach her: and all the while she will be sending Messages to him. He just became more and more gaunt and lethargic week by week. He would have done better to sacrifice his home, which he refused to leave, and to go into the Royal Hotel with Mr. Luxon and be properly cared for, regardless of expense.

Meanwhile, Guernsey becomes ever more chaotic. Railways run through gardens and hay-crops, and the Germans are said to be reviving the Stone Industry.

It has been stated in Parliament that an agreement has at last been reached with Russia, regarding a Western Offensive. As a precaution, all Occupied Countries are having their wireless sets confiscated, which will prove too frustrating now that the News promises to be interesting.

Rumours will multiply accordingly, if such is possible and much pruning will have to be done to get at the truth.

To M.H. La Guelle. June 28th, 1942.

Felicia and George will celebrate their second Wedding Anniversary tomorrow, and the Occupation will be two years old the day after. Another landmark in Guernsey's History.

Meanwhile, the trivial round and common task, while not furnishing all we need to ask, keep the body mobilized, while the brain, in constant ferment, flits from one subject to another. Food, Baby, War, Tennis, "Les Dunes," Local Chaos, Play-going, the renewed risk of losing La Guelle, or further billeting of soldiers, Loss of Wireless and the growing catalogue of rumours, afflict our already cluttered minds. A spell of amnesia would be of enormous therapeutic value every few months: for us to re-visit our Fool's Paradise and "sport with Amaryllis in the shade" ere we return to "Live laborious days."

Your Paradise Garden promises much in the way of nectarines and peaches. The Strawberries and Blackcurrants are putting in a meagre and tardy appearance, and the birds are making off with the loganberries as fast as they ripen, or so our equestrian Germans in the garage would have us believe.

I forgot to mention earlier that the Wolseley has been commandeered. George had jacked it up, and long after most of the better cars had been taken, a General sent for it and that was that. We expected that it might have especial treatment, since it was to be chauffeur-driven; but the General returned to Paris, and the car went with him. A German told George that when last seen it was stranded about twenty miles outside Paris with a broken axle, and we thought we had seen the last of it. However, Stan tells us it is back in Guernsey and not too badly damaged.

Summer marches on and still no sign of a Second Front. We wonder what took Winston to America, and hope it was not through a divergence of views. For, with many people at starvation level, a prolonged war would be disastrous.

Even the better fed are always hungry. Ironically, I remember the terrible crisis of having for the first time to do without marmalade for breakfast!

Perhaps we are stupid to play tennis, but we put very little effort into it, and gather at the Club chiefly to meet and exchange views with old friends. All tennis is played at King's Road, for the Germans have taken over the courts at Elm Grove and Amherst, the latter being used for equestrian purposes.

Peter has arrived with supper. Nan procured for us a scrumptious "chancre"* and two pounds of luscious strawberries: while to round off this saturnalia, Peter bartered some scrounged tobacco for three-quarters-of-a-pound of tea. The twenty-third psalm having been duly sung, we felt that we had indeed been anointed with oil and our cup was running over.

* "Chancre" — the well-known flat-backed crab.

To M.H. La Guelle. July 13th, 1942.

Exactly two years since I began these ramblings and your return hoves not in sight. The past, with all its changing scenes, needs no summing-up, since much of it has been recorded in these memoirs for your perusal. If the future holds nothing more disastrous for us than the trials of the past, we shall have no cause for complaint: and our decision to remain here will be justified. The operative word is a big 'IF'.

Meanwhile, Jerry continues to burrow in his labyrinth of tunnels, a process which threatens to blast us out of house and home.

I played Bridge with "Bob" Hargreaves and Tilly Guilbert at Allie Marquand's this afternoon. Allie and Harry found Pam's last Message somewhat involved. They wondered what could have caused Pam's threatened baldness. Her news of Audrey's health rather disturbed me, and I just pray that her heart condition will not deteriorate. We have so much wasted time to make up, and years to reminisce upon. Absolutely nothing must prevent our joyous reunion.

An appalling accident occurred to-day. Mr. Le Tissier of "Le Pouquelah" was gored by a neighbour's bull, and died a short while after admittance to hospital. A terrifying experience, and a shattering blow for his wife and family.

Yesterday, we took P.J. on the beach for the first time. Near the Half-Way, we settled him down attired in a linen hat, a liberty bodice and vest. Gwenyth and Hugh-John joined us for a while, and P.J. tried out his four teeth on every pebble within reach. He now dines on carrots, peas, potatoes and tomatoes, and has rusks and cakes made from his cream of barley flour for tea. He now does Pat-a-Cake 'sans paroles' and joins in the applause for his performance.

Lily having at last functioned, Peter has just joined me with a cup of bartered cocoa, which we are about to sip before this open window from which, through the binoculars, we glimpse Les Dunes inhabited still by foreign workers. We pray for its preservation, count our blessings, sparing many a thought for the countless millions whose privations and horrors diminish our own tribulations to mere trifles.

To M.H. La Guelle. July 27th, 1942.

Audrey's third Birthday in exile. Knowing the weak state of her heart, she is never long out of my thoughts, and I have to persuade myself that Pam's allusion to her condition was not a gentle warning of impending disaster. It is unthinkable!

The desecration of our "Sarnia Chérie" continues its relentless course, and one wonders if she can ever return to her natural beauty. The concrete fortifications, known as "bunkers", are grotesque and so deeply embedded, that they seem to be as lasting as the pyramids: built to defy any known explosive.

A few days ago, I heard two children in the region of six years of age, discussing food. A mother on the beach was giving them cooked cold potatoes and raw carrots for their tea; because their bread ration was exhausted until the following day.

The weekly ration of four-and-a-half pounds of bread for adults: babies one-and-a-half pounds: older children with enormous appetites three-and-a-half pounds, means that the parents' rations are much reduced to satisfy their young: cakes and biscuits having disappeared for the Duration. Our weekly grocery bill amounts to three shillings: while the meat ration is sixpence each. Anything else, which means mainly vegetables, has to be scrounged for or bartered. Many people, especially the aged and infirm, are quite unable to compete. Few people, with all the will in the world, can help them. We should have been hard-pressed but for the good start you gave us, and the fact that Peter has managed to pull off a few lucky barters with tobacco. Even so, they are only flashes in the pan though very useful as boosters. No doubt the Founder Members of The Guernsey Skeleton Society have, by now, passed on: a state of affairs much lamented by everyone.

As I finish these lines, the throb of engines in the quarry is the only sound heard in this still summer evening, to be continued throughout the night. Those poor tunnelling slaves!

And now, as St. John's strikes the hour of ten, a few Germans stroll back to their billets, the only tangible reminder that the outside world is not at Peace. The intangible reminders are ever with us and are far more eloquent.

To M.H. La Guelle. August 15th, 1942.

Nine days ago we received the dreadful news of Audrey. When I last wrote, this disaster was nearly two months old. No doubt you are still receiving our messages to her. I do so hope that a few words of hers are on the way to me: painful but treasured souvenirs.

Emil telephoned the news to Peter on Wednesday evening of last week. He had arranged a game of Tennis for the following day, and, realising that he must make a rapid check in case of error regarding the sad news, lest anyone might allude to it at tennis:, he knew that he must go at once to see the Messages received by Mrs. McAlpine and the Giraud family, expressing regret at Audrey's death.

Naturally, I protested at his leaving home just fifteen minutes before Curfew: for I knew that he would spend the night in prison if caught on the streets after ten o'clock. He assured me that he only had to discuss a point of business with Mr. Brice, who was leaving for Jersey in the morning: a fabrication which completely fooled me by its earnestness. He failed to convince me that he would be certain to beat the Curfew, but he made it.

I played tennis as planned on Thursday (in blessed oblivion!), Peter having staved off the evil day by twenty-four hours, when he broke the news on our return.

My first reaction was to go out with him into the field and breathe the fresh air: for I was consumed by a fearful claustrophobia. Curfew or no curfew, the four walls of this house were no longer bearable to me. Eventually, Peter persuaded me to return, and I made myself enter her bedroom alone. I examined it in minutest detail in search of some magic opiate to relieve the suffocating burden of grief. I opened wardrobe and drawers in a ferment of searching, and finally discovered her snap-album. I devoured each well-known likeness of her as though seeing it for the first time, still seeking some hidden word from her: until, stuck on the inside of the stiff back cover, I did find my first crumb of comfort. Almost as though she had led me to it herself, I saw for the first time a biblical coloured picture of a young man standing in a Roman chariot, drawn by two prancing horses with flying manes: the one, a beautiful snow-white animal, and the other jet-black with shining flanks, travelling at terrific speed. The young man is clad in purple with a crimson cloak, flying like the horses' manes in the wind created by their rapid flight. At the young man's shoulder stands the white-clad figure of Christ, one hand on the young man's back and the other outstretched, pointing the way to his destination. The title of the picture is "The Chariot

Race of Life." But it was in the biblical caption that I found the crumb of comfort, it reads:

> "Forgetting the things that are behind . . . I press on toward the goal unto the prize of the high calling of God in Christ Jesus."

Stunned by my first grim acquaintance with grief, I stood for some time soaking in both the picture and its message, until I knew, just as surely as if Audrey were at my side, and stressing the words of the message, that there was, in all truth, nothing for it but to press on, until this acute phase of bereavement might be assuaged by the merciful passage of time.

My mind was all too eager to believe that this picture which had hitherto escaped my notice, had been hurriedly pasted there before she left Guernsey, for me to find at this, the real moment of our parting. What other medium than her guiding power had led me to search for this opiate and for Peter to leave me alone to make the search? Like all of us, Peter had felt a warm affection for Audrey, and will deeply feel the awful gap in the family reunion.

Mercilessly, the next day dawned. A day of brain-washed exhaustion. Even the longing to die in order to be with her, failed to recur to fan the fires of grief. I felt that I had "loved her in life too little" and now "loved her in death too well." I wish I could have shared these last two years with you all. I am much consoled when I think that Peter John would not now be in existence.

Many telephone calls and letters came to me from sympathetic friends. Marion Collas sent a beautiful bouquet of gladioli and fern. "Biff" Roussel came with a few spoonfuls of tea (a great sacrifice on her part, though she would have none of it), "in case you have a headache" she said, with touching prescience. Whereat, we both sat on the edge of my bed and succumbed together. I still get wild ideas that it might even yet be rumour: but my hopes are fast dwindling. Meanwhile we await your own personal messages, which may not arrive for months, if at all.

I know only too well how easy it is for those bereaved to canonize their Dear Departed: but it really was impossible to find a chink in her armour. One cannot recall one mean or unworthy act throughout her life. She was quite incapable of artifice or flattery, being as sincere as she was fair to look upon. Seldom did she refer to her ill-health.

Once, when she walked with me up the hospital hill, she stopped and said, with a smile: "If you want to walk at that rate, you'll have to wait for me at the top." On another occasion as we sat alone in your Sark bungalow, on hearing a throbbing sound, I remarked, "The dynamos are working late tonight." Her laugh puzzled me until the light dawned, and I exclaimed: "Surely it's not your heart beating like that!" Still smiling, she replied: "The noise is always with me. I've grown accustomed to it."

We all knew that her days were numbered, but we still hoped that, with care, she might be with us for many years. Her zest for life was so pronounced, as though she sensed its brevity. Father was always on call to take her out, or to fetch her from bridge gatherings or other social occasions. You lavished expensive clothes on her, which she wore like a model, but with never a thought of posing for effect. I remember her saying: "If anyone asks after my health, I'm fine! I cannot bear to be regarded as an invalid."

So passes a treasured era of our life, and I must learn to accept the burden. Those reminiscences we were to share, will not now take place, and I must learn to press on in very truth for, as Dr. Sutcliffe said a few days ago: "She had a wicked heart, and you wouldn't have her continue to suffer. You know, all grief is selfish." I could have slain him for that, though I knew the truth of it and that it was not meant to hit below the belt.

To M.H. La Guelle. September 1st, 1942.

It was a great relief last week to receive your message of June 12th, chiefly because you were once more sufficiently interested in life to send one at all, and also, the tone was promising. It was a great relief to me: though it confirmed what had, until then, been only indirect reports of Audrey's death. I knew that my hopes were flimsy, and had resigned myself to abandon false optimism.

I now resume this entry in bed. I left off to cook supper, which must always be done before the gas is cut off at eight o'clock. Peter is reading beside me, while a glass of hot milk awaits me on father's bedside table, and the baby sleeps in what will always be known as Audrey's room. He has just returned from another stay at Bordeaux: Nan having taken him while Peter was on holiday. Yesterday, we took him to be photographed at Grut's, and on to Boots to have him weighed, now that Nan's 'fishing net' can no longer contain him. He nearly broke the scales at Boots: weighing at a year old 29 lbs. 4 oz. He was at Bordeaux for his birthday. Diana's candles having been lost or mislaid, I decorated the cake with a Christmas-tree candle stuck on a golf tee. Nan gave him a plate decorated with nursery rhymes, Cousin George (his contemporary) gave him three eggs, Mrs. Wynne and Gwenyth gloves, Marion Collas — a coat, sandals from me, a cheque for his bank from Peter, money from Emil and Grandma Bachmann and five shillings from Felicia's mother. So he did very well. His head is covered with fair curls and he now has six teeth.

And so life goes on, another summer fading and another winter not far away. It would be comforting to hibernate, and to begin my next letter with the words: "Autumn came and went, and winter gave way to spring," as in books of fiction, but the coming months have to be lived through, day by dreary day, through many war bulletins and over many hurdles: in the presence of our field-grey "pestilence that walketh in the noonday" and stalketh by night to trap the unwary. But we have developed a sixth sense for self-preservation, and we are not afraid, though often bored and anxious about the manner of our release.

To M.H. La Guelle. November 2nd, 1942.

Another year drawing to a close, and still no sign of a Second Front. One cannot reasonably expect it, now that winter approaches. Scraps of news circulate, although our wireless sets were re-confiscated three months ago. Since I last wrote, many more families have been evicted from certain houses in Brock Road, Queen's Road, Doyle Road,

Amherst; and now the residents of Upland Road are being threatened. Among the latest victims are Mr. and Mrs. W. J. Cuming, the senior de la Rues, Drs. Sutcliffe and Rose and Mrs. Ninnim, to name but a few. Mercifully "La Guelle" remains unmolested but the 'bailiffs' may cast a baleful eye at any moment. We are tempted (but dare not succumb!) to take the perilous hint of a certain friend (who must be nameless) and rename the house "Stalingrad" because it has not been taken. But he says he has reserved the name for his own use.

Meanwhile, we grasp at every diversion offered us in this otherwise stagnant life. I belong to a bridge four, and we have joined a dancing class. These are the opiates which sharpen our dying faculties, and help us to jump once more into the saddle. Jessie Shayer teaches us the dance-steps for an hour on Tuesday evenings, until the 'Band' arrives, a two-man affair, but most effective. From then on it becomes a social dance.

Among the members are the 'Ginge' de la Rues, Irene de la Rue, Harry Broughton, Mr. Fletcher of Les Landes (husband of Loveday Hichens), 'Biff' and Charles Roussel, Peter and Verity Wellington, Alan Mackay, Dr. and Mrs. Cambridge, Kathleen Johnson-Smith, with occasionally, Dr. Sutcliffe and one or two others, to make up the number. The Curfew being at the infantile hour of nine o'clock the class opens at six-thirty p.m. and disperses at eight-thirty. Occasionally Felicia and George accompany us, and we step out down Amherst on the way home with linked arms singing: "She'll be sailing down the Russel when she comes . . . she'll be sailing down the Russel, all her sails a-bustle, she'll be sailing down the Russel when she comes!" I assure you, this to the 'occupied' is as stimulating as one of Churchill's speeches.

Now that Nan no longer sleeps at La Guelle, Gwenyth is our sitter-in, and we reciprocate when she visits her friends. Nan returns on those evenings when we take Gwenyth to the Vaudeville Shows at the Lyric.

It is difficult to tear Gwenyth away from her son for she is rather an over-indulgent parent with an over-demanding child. All the while Gwenyth must have Gordon and her parents on her mind. She is a sensitive girl and we are both fond of her.

Peter crawls about the floor with the two children astride his back, or sits with one on each knee, telling them stories about Red Indian Chiefs on big white horses: or some little boy climbing up a "big-big-big-big-big high mountain." The adjectives have to be mostly simple and highly dramatized partly because Peter John is only fifteen months old. Even then it is probably only the tone of the voice which holds his rapt attention, but Hugh-John sits wide-eyed, lapping up every word and asking for more.

The shops in town are almost empty. Last week I tried unsuccessfully to buy a winter coat for Peter John. I asked if I could have one made if I supplied the material but was told that no promise could be made before Christmas. Now, I have found a dressmaker who, for some merciful reason, seems to be inconspicuous and therefore not over-busy.

I have committed the heinous crime of ripping Father's tennis-flannels. I know you would not have your grandson perish with pneumonia. The work will be done this week.

A few nondescript garments adorn the window of 'Delas' while most shops sell second-hand clothes at astronomical prices. Of course, all new clothes come from France. The quality is appalling and the prices exorbitant. A camel-hair coat, wildly expensive at two pounds is priced at twenty-one pounds. Stockings at nineteen and eleven would be dear at one and seven. Not a baby's dressing gown is available, nor elastic, nor cotton wool.

The Red Cross is reputed to be sending a consignment of medical goods to Jersey for Channel Islands. Fruit is scarce apart from a few small figs and the remnants of tomatoes. Growers keep their fruit for bartering or sell it to a notorious grower who, in turn, sells it to the Germans at outrageous prices: while the population goes hungry.

We are now in danger of losing our precious Lily. It has been the custom for farmers to retain from their milk supplies one pint a day per person per household, the remainder has to be taken to the States Dairy, to be distributed according to permitted rations. Since the arrival of young George and Peter John our combined households have risen to seven adults (including Nan and our current maid Joyce), Gwenyth and Hugh-John. As you will know, after catering for us all, very little indeed was left to justify George cycling twice a day to the dairy, and so we have shared their residue. After all, Lily is a 'pet' cow! And not one of a recognised herd for the purpose of augmenting the Island's milk supply: she never was anyway. However, the tongue of some kind friend or neighbour must have been busy for P.C. Pill arrived this week to 'institute' enquiries. On hearing my version of the circumstances, he agreed with us that it was merely a case of 'splitting hairs' or a storm in the proverbial teacup. But he left me with the knell of Lily's doom tolling in my brain by saying that Mr. Sherwill is willing to drop the case against us on condition that Lily is sold to, presumably, a 'reputable' farmer, who will donate all Lily's yield to the dairy. George had already spoken to Farmer Sarchet down the road, who affirms his desire to buy what was, to us, far more than a family pet but a great comfort to Little Mary as we mentioned in a Red Cross message some time ago. I hope this ode, epitaph or obituary will do her justice:

ODE TO A COW

Farewell to thee blythe Lily
Bull thou'lt never be
Tho' thou capsized poor Peter
As he sat under thee.

Thou didst not know the reverence
With which he plied his skill:
Thou wouldst have shown more deference
And let him work at will.

Alas! How we shall mourn thee!
With thy so urgent yield,
Which oftimes banished ennui,
And hunger pains hath healed.

Thou art lost and gone for ever,
Thy nectar to the Law revealed,
Adieu fair Lily of La Guelle
The pride of yonder field.

We now have an agreement with Gwenyth, whereby we take over the care of the two children every other Sunday afternoon. Our free Sunday yesterday, we cycled down to the L'Ancresse Tearooms to see the 'girls'. As always, we took our rations and they provided us with cups of real tea. To our delight, and after our few seemly protestations, they persuaded us to stay for supper, a rare treat anywhere nowadays. The orgy began with fried potatoes and long-nose, followed by a boiled apple-pudding and real coffee. We thought the war was over. On our return, Gwenyth was suitably disgusted by this revelation of our subtle greed: until I placed before her a dish of steaming bean-jar (meat-less, of course) which I had previously prepared. Like the angel she is, she had settled the two children for the night, and we settled down to another quiet evening.

1943

To M.H. La Guelle. January 4th, 1943.

More than two months since my last letter. Thank heaven the news is good! The end cannot come too soon, though we have much to be grateful for. We made merry at Christmas with a vengeance. Nan took Peter John for three weeks, and we made up for last Christmas. There were several dances at College and at Sunnycroft in the Grange. Unfortunately, Jerry was too jumpy to lengthen the curfew so all outings stopped at eight-thirty, to allow enough time for everyone to be home by nine o'clock. Curfew was defeated by many people. To avoid spending much of the holiday in prison, we stayed a night at Harry Broughton's, a week-end at Stan Noel's and a night with Biff and Charles, where in each case, nocturnal bridge flourished with changing fortunes. Gwenyth had a friend or so of her own age to sleep each time and so we felt absolved of all guilt at leaving her. How we would have loved to have given the children one of those rumbustious Christmasses of our youth, such as the one when Doris wrote and produced a play for us to perform before the host of aunts and uncles assembled under our roof.

Marie composed the entr'acte music, I recall one of the tunes on the instant. I must have been very young at the time, for all I remember was that we were living at La Couture in Collings Road. I took the part of a nurse but the gist of the play is long forgotten. I only know that prizes were awarded after the votes of the audience were counted. The girls had expected George to win the first prize and had duly bought him "Tom Brown's Schooldays" for the presentation. But the critics had cast their vote in my favour and George cast a baleful eye at the Cobo Alice Doll intended for second prize, which I was persuaded to accept. No doubt Marie and Doris expected Audrey to win second place for it was well known that I never was partial to dolls, whereas Audrey made them her abiding pleasure. Anyway, I could surely borrow the coveted book after George had read it. Poor Bill! His Oscar was a "Jack-in-a-Box" which he eyed with a pout and tearfully exclaimed: "I didn't want a 'Jack-in-a-box' I wanted a motor car!" You must remember well the tone of juvenile petulance employed by us all throughout the years, when anyone bemoaned an unwelcome object, be it food or whatever: much to Bill's disgust.

We were always made to perform our concert pieces at these family gatherings. Marie on the fiddle, the boys and I to sing and even our kindergarten Audrey managed a nursery rhyme or two (as the Press would say — with great acceptance).

Doris's perennial epic, "The Ride of Jennie McNeil," always enthralled me, whatever its reactions on the rest of the audience. My pounding heart would rise to an almost unbearable crescendo with the storm, hailstones and bullets on that perilous ride as "the grey horse did his duty well" and my spirits plunged to the depths of despair when "all at once he stumbled and fell, himself escaping the nets of harm but flinging the girl with a broken arm" — My raging heart reached bursting point when "she jumped once more to the saddle-bough" saying: "Good horse, one more trial now" — the suspense re-gathered its momentum as, "galloping down the hillside steep, she gained on the Troopers at every leap" until "they were a furlong behind or more when the girl burst through the Colonel's door" just in time to warn him of the imminent approach of the enemy before "fainting to the floor she sank." The said Colonel's escape was only in the nick of time to save me from collapsing with poor Jennie — O the curse of being highly strung! Strange that we have lost the origin of this party-piece. It would be rather fun to run it to earth after all these years and to see what impact it would make on our own children.

The recalling of these Christmas incidents has been a refreshing escape from the present travesties of Christmas celebrations. If you are reading this in the distant future, it will call up memories of those days which you always declared to be your happiest.

I now belong to two bridge-clubs. To-day I was at Nan Gaved's. Tilly Guilbert, 'Bob' Hargreaves and I sailed, rather than cycled, out to Cobo in teeming rain. We were obliged to feel our way home in blinding sleet and howling gale — such is our appetite for diversion!

Some time ago a certain foreigner of alleged Dutch origin became a frequent caller at our Arcade shop. A civilian, he claimed to be an overseer of the Dutch section of Todt workers, forced to build German fortifications. He called himself a "welfare officer" on their behalf. Peter, taking him at his word, invited him up to La Guelle one evening for a chat (on neutral subjects, of course!). This gentleman brought a scrumptious fruit cake for our joint refreshment, which, as you might guess, immediately endeared him to us. A few weeks elapsed and Peter saw him no more. A few days ago, another Dutchman called on Peter who politely enquired about the welfare of his compatriot. On hearing the name and description of our guest, this new customer astounded Peter by revealing the fact that we had been entertaining a member of the dreaded Gestapo! We had obviously entertained an 'angel' unawares. A mercy that our Occupation guard has taught us how to fence with words, whatever the company! 9.30 p.m. And I must conclude — Peter and Gwenyth are now reading and knitting (in that order) by the fire. Peter-John returned to us yesterday from Bordeaux. We could barely contain our excitement. No doubt you must deem us awful parents loaning him for Christmas. Nan's entreaties to have him always overcomes our reluctance: and we feel it is our only chance to get out and about without imposing on Gwenyth. A thousand pities, Nature decreed that Nan should be the deliverer of many babies and yet remain barren herself: adoring them as she does to the point of obsession.

Recently we have received several messages from you, Diana, Father and Doris. Another batch reached Guernsey a day or so ago. I do hope that Father has fully recovered from the ailment you mentioned. You must all return in fine fettle, so that he may play golf again and wallow in his cherished home life and his precious garden, which he must sadly miss. There will be no groping for diversions to rescue us from the snares of boredom, when as Vera Lynn sings: "You may come home once more." This year may see the birth of a new era. So, good-night sweetheart, I must away to 'pot' your new grandson — and so to bed.

To M.H. La Guelle. 24th March, 1943.

More internments have taken place with Emil and Elsie, Margaret and Jack Giraud in the last batch because, it seems, that all ex-officers of the '14-'18 war were an alleged hazard in a possible Allied Invasion on these Islands. We spent the last few hours at Garrivoe, where Emil and Elsie invited us to stay for lunch. They had hoarded a precious tin of meat and, with hot vegetables, we prepared for their final fling. We stood around, drooling while the meat tin was opened, and we soon realized that it must have been *bien mal acquit* for it turned out to be a revolting grey apple purée. We stood aghast as the swindle took effect, a real camera study of a complete family of imbeciles, as we resigned ourselves to grace the modest repast with the Bachmann sense of humour.

Not wishing to waste a moment of our last hour together we persuaded Elsie to leave the clearing up to Blanche and ourselves: as we sat chatting over necessary details for the safety of their home during their internment. Very naturally they were sad and reluctant to be torn from the home they had enjoyed since their marriage. The last hour passed all too quickly before the half-filled bus, sent to collect them, drew up at the gate. What feelings clutched us all as, final embraces over, amid forced badinage, we saw them off on their journey — to what end? The question still hangs ominously in this age of darkness.

I never dreamt I should miss writing your Birthday letter but, as I wrote early on, time and inclination do not always synchronize. For long intervals, during the mechanical details of day-to-day living, it seems that our faculties lie fallow, waiting for peace to come and equip life with a purpose. Then, a great weariness engulfs me as I sit down to write, and I find the elusive spell of spiritual contact has drifted away. This I much regret when, later, things clamour to be written, the urge to set them down is strong within and, alas! I find myself geographically powerless to set pen to paper. The tragedy is that were I to rush back home from some necessary expedition, or to stop bathing our son and forage for pen and paper, the time and energy involved in this crazy procedure would have wiped my mental slate clean and I should be bereft of the very words which had caused the panic. I should be left either with an unaccomplished mission or a goose-pimpled infant giving vent in fine voice.

Perhaps you received our Birthday Greetings sent to you at Christmas. It might even have arrived on the appropriate day, just as mine did from Diana last year.

I am sitting up in bed while Peter reads beside me. Peter-John is with Nurse at Bordeaux for a few days. The real reason for his absence was caused by German manoeuvres. The area of town and the usual places frequented by mothers and children are declared out of bounds, while the Germans indulge in artillery practice. The noise is terrific and, as instructed, all windows remain open against blast damage. All inmates of the Town Hospital, including the sick and dying, have been brought up here to the Victoria Hospital, which has not been occupied nor aired all the winter. All inmates of the Town Asylum have been bundled into the Mental Department of the Emergency Hospital. We saw no reason to alarm our infant who could not understand the situation and Nan jumped at the chance of a spell with him on her own.

We now receive a steady flow of your messages. We devour every item about Diana. A pity she is unable to write from school or billet.

Next day: Well, here we are in '43. The end which seemed so near in November seems as far removed as ever, as we enter the fourth year of war. Meanwhile life drones on, with an endless round of work and sacrifices which only help the wrong side. At times we are possessed by an abnormal longing for the abnormal, whatever its nature, to charm(?) us out of this pall of monotony, now threatening us with spiritual annihilation. Surely these are but the ravings of our frustrated interiors as each succulent mirage recedes into nothingness.

Our plight is not helped by the brutal posters in Candie Road and elsewhere, with their garish display of delectable dishes, flaunted before our very eyes in vivid colours depicting nature's now forbidden fruit, so taken for granted in bygone days. The pyjamad man astride a Bovril bottle on a choppy sea, still ironically extols the ability of its contents to prevent that sinking feeling: in competition with the Bisto kids on the next poster, sniffing exotic kitchen aromas. The rare juicy morsels which come our way seem all-sufficient on arrival, but they are only succulent crumbs in the desert of famine, and all the more missed when their precarious source dries up as your cruse of oil did long ago.

A number of Todt labourers are leaving Guernsey, much to our relief. Not that their departure will augment our food supplies. By all accounts the poor wretches exist on sour German bread and watery soup, which makes us ashamed of our luxurious fare. Unfortunately, Guernsey men are being forced to replace them. May the rest of our men be spared this ignominy, but no predictions are possible in this state of flux.

To M.H. La Guelle. March 28th, 1943.

As soon as the notice for Emil and Elsie's internment arrived, it was decided in family conclave that Jim and Dorothy should fulfil their ambition to marry. They had been trying to find a house, and this seemed a good chance to kill two birds with one stone; for them to marry and also to save Garrivoe by occupying it till the internees return. A few days elapsing between their exodus and the wedding, Peter agreed to sleep at Garrivoe in order to protect it from marauders; Jim remained with Dorothy's people, where he had lived since Winnie and Arthur evacuated. Nan returned at night to sleep at La Guelle, where we kept the old bell handy to summon George from next door in the event of hostile prowlers.

Peter's opinion of Emil and Elsie's bed almost defies description. He vows that he found himself sleeping in an outsize pudding basin; his feet and head pressed on the bed ends with a chasm between, his torso either poised in mid-air supporting the bedclothes, or sunk in the hollow in the crouched position of an unborn child. After a night or so bereft of sleep, and a constant battle with the bed, Peter finally gave up and decided that Garrivoe must take its chance, as every bed in that house seemed to have been designed to defeat the soothing balm of sleep.

The wedding on March 4th was blessed with heavenly weather. Jim had slept at La Guelle on the previous night, so that he might not see the bride before the ceremony. George took a snapshot of Peter and Jim in their tails and toppers standing on your lawn with me in a black suit and small black hat, borrowed from Audrey's extensive wardrobe. We looked rather like the "three black crows upon a tree" in the Paddy McGee song. No cars being available we travelled by horse-drawn landau in the brilliant sunshine to St. Stephen's Church, where the Rev. Collard waited to officiate. The journey back to Dorothy's home was quite something. It was a treat to hear the old-time clatter of horses' hooves with the line of carriages. A convivial reception was highlighted by the Brides' piano solos, but I shall never forget what seemed an incongruous item, as she played Sibelius' Valse Triste there being no sign of sadness in this day of revelry. As on other rare occasions of "Occupation" frolics, we were most reluctant to break up the party. Joy unconfined, being elusive indeed!

Needless to say since those with wanderlust had their wings clipped years ago, the honeymoon will be spent in Guernsey. We drank to the absent ones who were surely with us in spirit.

I well remember the time when you would read to us all, accounts of local weddings reported in the *Evening Press*. Those were the days in our youth, when all wedding guests and gifts were mentioned (a) by name and (b) description: (How ghastly when one recalls this social exposé!). We would all be convulsed by the satirical innuendoes which you employed to add relish to your recital. I also remember the account of one wedding, whose blushing bride was the luckless recipient of eighteen! evening hand-bags, brocaded, beaded, diamantéd or otherwise garishly decorated. You read each item with a different inflexion, until you had us rolling in the aisles.

My joy was often short-lived on those evenings when, because of my tender years, I was escorted upstairs by a senior sister who was detailed to see me settled in bed. There I lay, terrified by the darkness as the adult footsteps receded and I heard the closing of the sitting room door. Then I would creep from my bed and scurry in terror to my niche in the winding granite staircase of our ancient farmhouse. There I would listen wistfully to the merriment below, taking care to keep my eyes glued to the streak of light under the sitting room door, in readiness for the first sound of the turning handle, in order to make a speedy retreat to escape detection. Only once was I literally caught napping, when both my fear and my will-power had fought a losing battle with my leaden eyelids. After that rap on the knuckles which Father administered according to his misguided principles, I took good care to keep a sharper watch, for the punishment had done nothing to assuage my terrors. From then on I managed to guard my guilty secret, though you little knew that only sheer fright kept me shivering on my nightly vigils.

Heaven knows what inhibitions were engendered during these silent watches, or if they accounted for the ghastly dreams which would end with me sitting bolt upright, clutching the bedclothes, surrounded by ghoulies and ghosties and long leggetty beasties, (a childish version of *delirium tremens*) even when, later on, my big sisters were asleep in the same room—Matthew, Mark, Luke & John must have been busy blessing other beds than mine, for they never seemed to heed my supplications. "*Hélas! si vous m'aviez compris, nos cœurs unis seraient heureux*" or, at least, I should have been provided with a night-light.

How you loved to read aloud to us all! There were books at home to suit all tastes. Among them, such old-fashioned stuff as "Sisters Three", "The Ingle Nook", "Harum Scarum" and "Paddy the next best Thing". Then came an enormous mahogany bookcase, bequeathed you by Cousin Ann Winter Head from America. This contained a whole set of Dickens beautifully bound, now in the breakfast room. Ann Winter's timely legacy just before Audrey was born, inspired you to name her Audrey Ann Winter in posthumous gratitude.

I remember also Dean Penfold, who prepared us for our Confirmation with the Trouteauds, and others whose names escape me. I see him now, rotund and smiling, in St. James's Church; his hands clasping the front pew over which he leaned as he spoke, a signet ring with a blood-red stone adorning one chubby hand. After the final class, he took us all back to his house (on foot of course) at Cambridge Park, where we were all presented with a book prize for mastering the complexities of the Catechism. He then summoned his housekeeper, who dispensed cups of tea and buns.

I still have my "Life of Christ" while one of the boys had an enthralling book about gold-diggers in the Sahara, which, in my pagan heart, I much preferred. There was one book in our bookcase, whose spine only I saw from outside the closed glass doors, for I durst not remove it from its shelf. The blood-curdling title was enough to freeze me with horror, it was "The Curse of Carne's Hold". With adolescence I graduated to Florence Barclay and Ethel M. Dell, as Doris, an avid reader, finished them. Maturer years found me under the spell of H. G. Wells (from Audrey's collection) whose "Soul of a Bishop" I have read and re-read. I never can resist his subtle parodies on pomp and circumstance, although you will be relieved to read, I long ago eschewed his pagan views, for you and Father certainly did your parental homework on our Church and Sunday School attendances. Where the Day of Rest came in we never could fathom. It was spent in dressing up in our best finery and walking to and from church, with Father in top hat and tails in the current fashion; and Sunday School at least twice on a Sunday. Inevitably trouble brewed when in our late teens we began to rebel and play truant and tried to argue our case with Father, by asserting that we could worship just as well under the blue dome of Heaven, as we rambled through the lanes when we were supposed to be at church or in Sunday School. One could write a tome on this theme.

I must away to the kitchen, where I cook for my household of six. I emerge from my labours, bearing a cornucopia of camouflaged vegetables, with an occasional fish and barley-flour pudding made with skimmed milk and water, laced with a spoonful of 'ersatz' cocoa from France, or a portion of macaroni. Sweetening of any sort is seldom available but the aching void is filled, when the cries of Little Mary give way to escaping gaseous noises uncontrollable from both fore and aft, which even the doctors seem incapable of stifling. We were tickled pink when one fastidious old lady recounted her conversation with her doctor. Apparently she begged him to restore her self-respect, when she was suffering from dysentery or to give it its local name "The Guernsey Bug". When he expressed himself unable to cure anyone of this, including himself, she exclaimed "O but Doctor, it's so odorous!" You may imagine how often this prize remark recurs in a humorous family, already grasping at straws for a chance of merriment, however ribald.

Embarrassment is a luxury of refinement not to be indulged in when cries of anguish clamour to be heard from within, and will not be denied.

To M.H. Les Dunes. 30th July, 1943.

Almost as I wrote my last words the German order came for us to leave La Guelle. They gave us five days to clear everything. As you may imagine, a gargantuan task. Nearly seventy drawers and cupboards had to be waded through and thinned out, the weeds from the tares. No need to ask you to compare the size of "La Guelle" with "Les Dunes", which could not take one half of your furniture and effects. Mr. Mahy offered us one room in his house; Mr. McCathie loaned a corner of a room in Bucktrout's cigarette factory in Cornet Street; Allie Marquand kindly offered to take the tall-boy from the landing, complete with your linen, furs and hats, which George stored in her garage, covered with a dust-sheet. He had a dress-shop rail made to stand in his Mother-in-law's bedroom, laden with evening gowns, skirts and blouses. We brought the rest in a series of van-loads to Les Dunes. Peter-John sleeps in his cot in Diana's bedroom, now virtually a furniture mart.

Imagine the huge mahogany bookcase and dining suite from your breakfast room, the black carved-oak suite and overmantel of similar dimensions, from the dining room; to say nothing of the sitting room and bedroom furniture, all of which must perforce be emptied of all contents, to deposit into their various lodgings, and you will begin to see the complexities of our exodus.

We were obliged to sift the things worth salvaging and those that must be discarded, much of it old-fashioned, or obsolete, which even you could not have unearthed for years. The list was interminable and no furnishers' assessors had time to take a separate inventory for each destination of the goods. Lovells made large wooden cases, wherein Nan and Peter packed all your china. Thus the normal chaos of house moving was magnified far beyond all general experience. On seeing the mounds accumulate, Peter said: "It's of no use, we can't take all this stuff, you'll have to be more drastic." George made a list of things we were obliged to sell, and left it in your Bank with the proceeds. We refused to take the path of least resistance and allow Lovell's to store it all in their depository, for the Germans are prone to visit these places and to help themselves to whatever takes their fancy. That is why Peter and Emil sold all the old people's belongings from Havelet, which valuable old stuff realized a mere hundred pounds, since no one will buy furniture anyway, while there is the slightest risk of their house being commandeered with all its contents.

You may imagine my feelings as, with the aid of Peter and Gwenyth, who had endured the loss of her family's belongings, we plodded through our reluctant task. The cruel poignancy of it all was accentuated by the shattering news of Father's death, which came to us via Gwenyth's parents in their internment camp in Germany, in the midst of this upheaval.

As I looked back for the last time, the empty house, haunted by you all, seemed like a mausoleum. Vague rustling sounds echoed everywhere. No doubt our obsession with food brought back visions of our last Christmas season party of nearly thirty guests, when the huge doors separating the drawing and dining rooms were opened and the two large dining tables, fully extended, ran the width of the two rooms. The table groaned with its load of good things. A crown of pork graced one end of the table for Father to carve; whilst an enormous joint of beef waited at the other end for George to deal with. Steaming dishes of hot vegetables, sauces and gravies were served by a hired waiter and waitress. The crackers were the size of rolling pins. A few days before the party you met A. H. Brice in town, who jokingly stated that he fully expected oysters and champagne to be served at midnight. He should have known that, faced with such a challenge, you would rise to the occasion. Great was the reception of this *pièce de resistance* at the appointed hour. But, as so often during these reminiscences, which I have recorded to remind you of our good times together, the picture faded whilst I was steeped in the past; until a reluctant nudge from Peter, jerked me into the bleak reality of the present with my new bereavement to remind me that another era had passed which even Peace will not restore.

This ordeal of moving over, I am now glad that it fell to our lot, for it will save you much pain when you return. What will be the fate of Dr. Sutcliffe's furniture which the Germans intend to bring to La Guelle, heaven alone knows.

A few weeks after our return to Les Dunes, George received a call from Mr. McCathie, saying that Bucktrout's factory had been looted, and asking George to check your belongings in the store. Without a detailed inventory, impossible at the time of the eviction, George could only hazard a guess as to the presence of every item there deposited. Mr. Mahy, on the other hand, with his meticulous Court Row mind, and having your things constantly in his possession, will probably have a complete list of every item, while those in our care are here displayed at Les Dunes, awaiting your return.

I wonder if you have received our Red Cross message which runs: in reply to one of your own—" Left La Guelle. *Crampen ordered us, take Basil & Dudley with us. Knew you'd appreciate the effort " which, properly deciphered, should have spoken volumes.

I only managed to rescue the carpet from Doris's bedroom at the risk of deportation. The Germans' foreign maid told me to leave it where it was, as it had been given to her by a German Officer. Greatly daring, and quite exasperated, I exclaimed: " It was not his to give. It is coming with us! " I must confess to some degree of tension for a day or so but we heard no more of the affair, and concluded that she had been bluffing in her threats to report us.

On the arrival of our eviction notice, Peter visited the Billeting Office to seek other accommodation. He learned with great relief and joy that, after eighteen months of Todt Occupation, " Les Dunes " was empty and also " Le Touzel " further up the lane. He returned to tell Gwenyth and me the glad tidings, and to ask Gwenyth if she would care to take " Le Touzel " for herself and Hugh-John. She was as ecstatically happy as ourselves, for this meant the end of community-living and we were at last to be restored to our

* *Crampen*=Father's name for a 'Jerry' pot and Basil & Dudley are the Christian names of our furnishers.

own home. We furnished "Le Touzel" with our own salvaged pieces and thus made room in Les Dunes for the rest of your furniture. The Billeting Officer, on offering to drive Peter down to L'Ancresse with our key, warned him that we might find the house in an appalling condition. Peter replied: "It will have to be damn bad for us to resist it!" I guarantee that you would have shared his sentiments. Damn bad it was (with apologies to Father who, bless him, vigorously resented the mildest form of swearing).

Mr. Chapple, faithful to us, as he had always been to you, dug himself in like a true Briton and cycling down here each day from Victoria Road, often in an easterly gale, set to work with a will. Nan took Peter-John once again to live with her at Bordeaux away from the wet paint and the filth of the undecorated rooms which had been cleared of the Todt straw beds. Our precautions regarding our son were soon justified for one day when Nan brought him on a visit, Mr. Chapple appeared leading Peter-John into the shed with what seemed to be a green glove on one hand. It appears that Mr. C. dangling a paint tin in one hand had been stretching up to paint a window-frame, when he suddenly felt a movement in the tin. He had turned to behold Peter-John with his hand totally immersed. There was nothing for it but another immersion in turpentine!

In a weak quixotic moment, lest he hesitate to accept the job, I offered Mr. C. the bait of lunch every day, while Peter had a dish of vegetables at the temporary café in town, known as "The Special Aid". Then ensued more brain-cudgelling to devise those meals, so hastily promised. I wish you could have seen the two of us at our *tête-à-tête* lunch day after day, amidst the welter of goods and chattels stacked in the centre of our small dining room, so that Mr. C. might have clear access to the four walls.

The linoleums left by our late tenants were heavily pockmarked by hob nailed boots, while gaping holes stared balefully at us like giant eye-sockets from the centre of each chimney breast, now bereft of the hefty pipes which had been attached, as in the German manner, to their stoves in the centre of the rooms.

As you may imagine, this put a full-stop to my hopes of writing, especially as I had to get down to the massive job of scrubbing each floor as Mr. C. finished a room. Water and elbow-grease were my sole scrubbing aids, and when my last ounce of energy petered out, I had still to create a *cordon-bleu* supper for my famished husband, who would cycle into the garden and, jumping off his machine, would lean over the saddle with head bowed while he retrieved breath and energy to walk into the house. But the joy of living in our own home far outweighed all trials and privations, and I know that you would still willingly change places with us.

As we sat up in bed on that first night, Peter asked: "What will you do in the middle of the night if a face appears through that hole in the chimney breast? "

It took the industrious Mr. C. over three months to complete the resurrection of Les Dunes. Hundreds of nails in the window frames had to be removed, and their holes plugged before painting could begin. These had been used to fix the Todt black-out materials and, judging by the numerous holes, the tenants had probably been in residence on a series of short 'lets' over the eighteen months, and taken their own black-out stuff with them in each case. No sentiment was used, none expected, as they had in turn ripped off their handiwork. It would have been a daunting task to anyone who lacked the stout heart of Mr. C. The lounge is distempered dreadnought grey over the remains of the existing paper, while our bedroom revels in a bright orange hue, the only colours available. Mr. C. still had a few pots left over from Audrey's sea-green bedroom paint, which he said would please me. Yes, he was a most likeable and discerning person.

Our table-talk shuttled between past and present, as he recounted the happy times he had had when working for the family. He also said that his wife could not accustom herself to the constant approach of planes. She would say: "Ark! " every time they droned overhead. He would reply: "For Gawd's sake stop arkin! " "But it's no use she can't 'elp it"; I felt that he had become an intimate friend and I did enjoy his vivid brand of speech, although I still have not discovered his Christian name. However, he survived my vegetable brawns and carrageen jellies, swearing that he never tasted the seaweed flavour. Peter says: "I shouldn't wonder if seaweed contains some health-giving properties."

To M.H. Les Dunes. 24th August, 1943.

Italy still totters on the brink of capitulation, but one supposes that Germany continues to bolster the incubus of the Berlin-Rome-Axis, in order to preserve her own prestige in the eyes of the world in general, and the morale of her own people.

This correspondence has become so spasmodic. I seem to store up news and views until I find sufficient time to make a captain's pull, then frantically ply my pen at terrific speed before the next diversion brings me to a full stop.

In two days' time Peter-John will have reached his second birthday and, once again, you are all absent. Perhaps you will be here for the third celebration. Heaven grant it be so.

I find that I spent a lot of time on the eviction from "La Guelle" but I wanted you to have a detailed account of the whereabouts of your furniture and "effects" should Fate decree that—among other possibilities—we shall be absent from Guernsey when you return. Nothing is predictable, as you will have discovered by now. We may as well be realistic.

Twelve noon finds us sitting out by the foghorn beach, in perfect weather looking past Les Fougères Lighthouse towards Alderney, with France visible on the far horizon.

Unfortunately, with Peter just starting a week's holiday the Germans have forbidden us all access to the beaches. I only wish they could tell us how to explain this penance to a child of two years, whom we have to rush and retrieve each time he reaches the bracken near the beach.

One day last week when I was rambling in these parts with junior, we looked up from picking wild flowers to behold a German soldier standing a few paces away. Peter, always ready for a new thrill, eagerly rushed into his outstretched arms as though he were a long lost uncle. Imagine my dilemma with or without the possible raised eyebrows in upper windows along our lane! There was our little renegade fingering the German epaulettes and hat displaying the Eagle of The Third Reich as though, here at last, was a completely new diversion exactly to his taste. The German, his broad smile revealing his gold-filled teeth, looked for all the world as though ready to include me in his fond embrace.

Now I long ago discovered that cheap heroics only let down those who display them, whilst doing nothing to enhance the prestige of one's country, and so with, I thought, an admirable mixture of good nature, firmness and aplomb, I said to Peter John: "Say Good-afternoon": which he did. I then said: "Now say Goodbye" which he also did, somewhat reluctantly. This done, the German took the hint, put him gently down and, clicking his heels, Heiled Hitler and departed, seemingly unoffended and quite unabashed. I was satisfied that honour had been served on both sides for, after all, let us give tribute where it is due, I was also satisfied that in case of possible witnesses, only the most gossip-starved could have made anything of the incident.

The slightest sign of encouragement and the German would have accompanied us back home and probably become a frequent visitor: we should then have certainly been branded as fraternizers, if not actual collaborators, which we decidedly are not. Needless to say, like a dutiful wife, I told my husband of this encounter. His only comment was: "The poor devil—he is probably missing his own youngsters." Our son was far more voluble as he described his great adventure to Peter and Nan. To think that he had seen these men all this time, never have spoken to one at all, suddenly to find himself in the arms of a German—'Oy' was just terrific. The reason why he calls them 'Oys' (pronounced 'Boys' without the 'B') is as obscure to us as it will be to you.

The Germans are now very pessimistic about their chances. They seem to expect an Invasion here and in Europe at any time. Peter hears much of their views in Town and, like everyone else, keeps his ears ever open for their fluctuating moods. How much of their own propaganda they credit or not is somehow reflected, even '*malgré-eux*'. We wonder if your optimism rises by comparison and dispels all fear of their landing on British soil. We are even aware that we may be in the firing line, if and when the Allies land in France.

The Order concerning the beaches is the outcome of an escape from Guernsey by certain fishermen in a Mr. Corbet's boat. Alf Bougourd went as a passenger. Later on, Stan Noel was arrested for aiding and abetting their escape. It was alleged that he had overhauled the boat's engine. One can imagine 'Weazle's feelings on hearing this news. Because of this escapade, daring but thoughtless, in view of the threatened reprisals on the rest of the population, should any further escapes be attempted, all local children are deprived of their greatest enjoyment, and fishermen of their living. It was most dangerous to defy the German edict headlined in the Press long ago. Already the escapees have landed many relatives and friends in prison. Stan, as accessory, spent a month in prison, and was allowed out on 'bail' (ironically!) so that he might settle his affairs, prior to his internment in a German Camp. He spent a night here with us, when more talk than sleep prevailed. We found him weak in both body and morale, after his starvation diet and inquisition, during which he had obviously not satisfied his inquisitors of his innocence. We parted with gravest misgivings, all unspoken, and wished him godspeed. Regardless of any folly or misdemeanour, we can only pray for his safe return and reunion with Weazle.

My menfolk now returning from their romp with Kala, we must leave this peaceful spot and return to Nan, who took over the cooking this morning, at which she leaves me in the shade—insisting that I get out into the fresh air while the gorgeous weather lasts.

1944

To M.H. Les Dunes. January 4th, 1944.

More than four months have passed since my last letter! Every day I inwardly vow to write before nightfall; but somehow time and the urge drift away amid the insistent round of household chores. "*Si mes vers avaient des ailes.*" Mistake me not; the urge and the hour '*voulont*' I am never happier than when I take up the pen and spend an hour with you all. The afternoons are all too short and we retire by 8.30 p.m.

Back in '42 when Mr. Churchill and others predicted our reaching parity with the Germans by '43-'44, we could not imagine our survival thus far, but the date of this letter leaves no room for comment on that point. "Any minute now" has become a sick joke despite the more cheerful news.

All last week the air buzzed with humming planes. On Friday I saw a "dog-fight" nearby between Les Fougères Lighthouse and Fort Le Marchant. From my grandstand view I saw two or three planes plunge into the sea, one of them rolling over and over out of control. I strained my eyes for the markings and held my breath for our precious heroes, but it was impossible in the scuffle to distinguish friend from foe. No doubt Peter would have been able to identify them. At such moments one feels the blind folly of it all. What will be the ghastly aftermath for both sides? And will the supreme sacrifice of all these sons, brothers and husbands have been in vain? The wisdom of Solomon will be needed to face all these imponderables and to come up with the right solutions.

Recently a Flying Fortress came down in the sea between Guernsey and Alderney. Two airmen were captured and marched through the Town under escort prior to imprisonment in Germany. It is said that they spoke to Guernsey people on their journey, saying as they passed, that our local men could be in Khaki by the Spring.

The Germans talk freely to Peter about apathy in Germany, and the general feeling is that the end is in sight.

At this time last week, we were faced with yet another crisis, which obliterated all thoughts of war. Following two heavy colds, Peter-John developed ear-trouble. On December 31st Dr. S. was sufficiently anxious to suggest a visit at any time, be it day or night. On the Sunday morning P.-J.'s temperature, having rocketed to 104.2 and he appearing delirious by his ramblings—even refusing to have Nan near him—which broke her heart—we did call Dr. S. who, on arrival, telephoned the hospital to make ready a bed. In fact he wasted no time with ambulances but, by-passing poor Nurse, who had become incoherent, told me to wrap P.-J. in a blanket, and himself drove us out to the Emergency Hospital for the baby to be examined with the right apparatus. On the way he told me—with reference to Nan—"It's a great mistake for a Nurse to become emotionally involved."

Having settled the baby in his cot, I awaited the return of Dr. S. who was making treatment arrangements with Matron. We knew by P.-J.'s agony that mastoids were suspected.

For two or three nights he had slept in my bed so that I might calm his fears during nightmares. By day I sat continuously with him in my arms on the settee, while Nan hid behind a screen, for he could not recognize her except as some evil and terrifying threat to his safety. Peter and Nan cut up my food, which I ate with fork only, using my one free hand. As I deposited him in that hospital cot, he held up his hands in frantic appeal saying: "No more bye-byes" over and over again. As you may imagine, in terms of sheer emotion this was an equal blow to our loss of Diana. When Dr. S. returned to lead me away I told Peter-John that I was just going to speak to another sick little boy on the verandah. I prayed that he might not permanently associate me with this deception, when his cries failed to bring me back. Had I learned in time, that I could have insisted on staying there all night, wild horses would not have dragged me away, for I felt that the strain of parting with the one person who had given him the deepest sense of security during the past few days, could only aggravate his condition. And so it seemed, when we heard on the following day that his temperature had reached 105°.

Dr. S. mercifully sustained me with desultory conversation all the way home, where Nan and Peter had a kettle boiling for a cup of tea. Nan almost defeated our valiant attempts at self-control, until Peter finally exploded: "Nan! you're a menace!" This broke down the tension and we all collapsed in a fit of hysterics. This proved to be our salvation, though it was that blessed "laughter which is the other side of tears". It was as necessary as the long-awaited bursting of a boil and it steadied us to face the ensuing days of anxiety. An abscess in each ear gradually responded to the magic of M & B tablets so recently discovered, and saved the crisis of a critical operation for which we had been prepared during a few days of great anxiety.

Nan cycled out from Bordeaux each day just to peep at him through a crack in the door. On one occasion Matron Hall met her on her journey between wards. In answer to Nan's anxious enquiries, Matron exploded: "It's of no use coming out here tearing your hair—we're doing all we can. How long have you been nursing?" Nan replied sheepishly (as everyone does when Matron Hall shrivels one with a glare:). "Fourteen years", at which Matron retorted, "Then you should be ashamed of yourself!" Slightly recovering her balance, Nan's typical reply was: "Ah! but this is the first time I've been in love."

Needless to say, all the nurses were captivated, as every parent thinks—with our Supreme Effort, especially since he called them all "Auntie". Astounding how a small child can take one's heart and tear it to pieces. We also cycled out a few times and peeped at his comical attempts to stand in his cot, but were persuaded to remain out of sight as he seemed to have settled down so well, and we were not eager for any more emotional partings.

The cause of the trouble lay in the tonsils, which must be removed when the weather is warmer.

Should the war last much longer it is no exaggeration to say that a number of people will die of mal-nutrition. Last week our grocery list ran thus:

2 oz. grey salt (almost unusuable)
3 oz. of butter
14 oz. of sugar
a small bag of macaroni.

Our 'bread' ration is 4½ lbs. a week and the potato ration 2½ lbs. The rest of our diet consists of vegetables only. Green vegetables being very scarce, most people live on carrots, parsnips, swedes, leeks and beetroots. The milk ration is ¼-pint of skimmed milk (each) daily.

With sufficient money and the right contacts, there are those who can occasionally buy Black Market goods. This, presumably, comes from members of the Todt Organisation and the soldiers who make a tremendous profit from these dangerous transactions.

Butter	from	30/-	a lb.
Sugar	„	16/8	„
Bacon	„	34/–	„
Flour	„	12/6	„
Tea	„	£17	„

Many people sell treasured possessions in order to get a share of the contraband. Needless to say, we dropped out of the fiercer aspects of this competition long ago. Some time back, when Felicia had been very ill in hospital, George heard of someone who still possessed a twelve-pound case of tea! As a great concession this person sold George 4 oz. for which she charged him £4! Only the intense relief after Felicia's crisis—which indeed it was, as you will hear in the distant? future—extracted this ridiculous sum from your thrifty son. We all thought Peter had taken leave of his senses when, for my Christmas '42 present he had paid £5 for a whole pound of tea. None but the power of love and my abiding addiction to a good cup of tea lured him into such extravagance. Certain civilians buying this contraband have been caught and imprisoned by the Germans. The more daring buy it in bulk at a slight reduction from the intrepid smugglers, who are only too anxious to find a fence, and so wash their own hands of it before the dreaded knock on the door. The fence knows full well that he will still dispose of it with a nice margin of profit. It is said that Siberia leaves much to be desired as a health resort. Hence I strongly exhort Peter to resist this perilous traffic for all our sakes.

To M.H. Les Dunes. January 27th, 1944.

Peter-John returned from hospital on Thursday, January 13th, having travelled in an ambulance full of recovered patients, and was the last to be delivered; Mr. Brice's teddy-bear still tucked under his arm. Mr. Falla of the Blue-Bird Bus Company (now an Ambulance driver) and the nurse in attendance, would have liked a snapshot of their arrival but, cameras being forbidden fruit from earliest days, this would not have been easy.*

Junior looked very pale as this was his first day out of bed and was still unable to stand alone. It was not many days before his energy returned by leaps and bounds, as ours correspondingly diminished. He is most resourceful in discovering things to do, which are either destructive or dangerous, following the pattern of our daughter. At that age I would take Diana into the garden with her favourite playthings and, after removing from her sight all possible sources of danger, I would return to the trivial round and common task (which the hymn-book tells us 'will furnish all we need to ask' sieges or wars of attrition notwithstanding (?) If so, there is certainly 'room to deny ourselves'). However, I digress. Diana had been safely left to enjoy the garden and her toys. Two minutes later, as likely as not, I would look out of the window to find her with a mouthful of gravel or see her flinging handfuls of the stuff all over the lawn for the benefit of the lawn mower.

To fulfil the dual purpose of finding her an outlet and of saving the last vestige of my sanity, I was driven to begin our beach picnics in April each year whenever the weather allowed. We would take her on long rambles on Sunday afternoons in the hope of sapping her energy, and thus having a modicum of peace until her bed time. But she would return ahead of us up the lane, turning cartwheels or leaping up the grassy banks on either side the lane and sliding down again on her bottom. Only when Peter-John is ill or sleeping does peace prevail and when he is ill the silence is horrible. As Peter's (senior's) father would say: "When the devil is sick, the devil a saint will be but when the devil is well, a Devil of a Saint is he."

A few nights after his return from hospital we were awakened by terrified screams. Rushing into his room Peter found to his horror that his face, hands, hair and pillow were covered with blood. In his panic he had rubbed the gory syrup all over himself. It was 3 a.m. before we could dispense with cold compresses, wash his hair clean enough for bed and, by the aid of an aspirin, leave him sleeping in his

* Naturally we took a snapshot.

cot. Dr. S. says it might be due to a burst blood-vessel in the septum which he will investigate during his impending tonsilectomy.

We make potato cakes and steamed vegetable puddings as a matter of course, bearing in mind the countless millions who are far more deprived. The gag writers have turned our menus to good account. At the Central Hall the other evening during the Vaudeville Show the comedian said: "I went to a party the other night. We had Bramble tea and carrot-pudding, carrageen* blancmange, potato cake and vegetable brawn. When I went to bed I dreamt I was a crate of vegetables". Many other quips on the subject of our diet go the rounds. Of course, the best ones escape me now.

The potato ration has ceased for the time being, which entails a further Pelmanizing challenge in the kitchen.

Peculiar things are afoot in high places. Once a month the Flour Controller has purloined a sack of flour for his 'fowls'. Inevitably this caused a local furore, especially as the culprit is a man hitherto regarded as above reproach. The Court gave the accused a choice between a £200 fine or three months' imprisonment. We understand that he has lodged an appeal. There are also numerous funny stories about Black Market activities which would give you great amusement, were it not for the fact that the pen is more dangerous than the sword.

A number of deserted husbands have sought 'solace' elsewhere. This staggered us at first as we clung to the tenets of our Victorian up-bringing. Peter was the first to take a more liberal view saying: "We can't judge. Four, or perhaps five years is a long time to be lonely." Local females there are, of low degree, who have taken too literally the Divine exhortation to love their enemies, with the result that there are many 'hapless Eves despoiled of Innocence.'

Two brothers were recently reconstructing a shed in our garden, which Peter had been lucky to buy for £16. One day I overheard Bill and John in argument on marital fidelity. Bill was most scathing about the conduct of some of their acquaintances, whereat John exclaimed: "Go on! If, when Betsy returns from England you find she've been unfaithful, you'll forgive 'er." "Eh" says Bill "Never!

* seaweed.

I'm pure and I expects 'er to be pure! " The Guernsey-French accent is essential to the full enjoyment of this masterpiece, which has given us many an hilarious moment.

To M.H. Les Dunes. March 8th, 1944.

Your fourth birthday in exile. Many happy returns, back in your dear Homeland far across the sea and—with apologies to the lyric writer—you must know how we all miss you where you long to be. I did my best to keep up the old family tradition. I bought your usual bouquet, as in days of yore. Freesias, hyacinths, soleil d'or, adorned our lounge in your honour. It was my turn to have bridge at Les Dunes, which made things more festive. Allie Marquand came for lunch whilst 'Biff' Roussel (convalescing from influenza) was replaced by Pat Hargreaves, who arrived with her mother, our fourth regular member. When Peter returned from business we drank your health in Cointreau and smoked English Gold Flake cigarettes sent from Germany by Emil. A happy chance brought George a Red Cross message from you, which he eagerly telephoned to me. You seem very optimistic about the war.

Our latest affliction is the rationing of gas. We are allocated 350 ft. a week per household, which is quite inadequate. Like countless other people, Peter had a 'bogey' built in our shed. This is made of brick with a flat iron top about two feet square, with three holes over which kettles and saucepans can be placed for cooking. The fuel for the fire beneath this contraption consists of anthracite dust, which we rescued from La Guelle with cow pats to bind it. This is mixed with tar, delivered by horse-drawn van from the gas works. The two Peters have great fun tramping over the Common collecting the cow pats (or '*bouzieaux*' as the patois people call them) with buckets and shovels. With this concoction Peter fills all available flower pots, leaving them to 'set' sufficiently to turn out into cakes of fuel. A metal chimney runs from the bogey through an opening made in the roof of the shed, for the thick black smoke to escape. Much of it gets away beneath the cooking utensils and smothers the cook, the shed and the gardening tools with a murky black paste. In all weathers I may be seen, sometimes by the R.A.F. amid the blast of gunfire, scampering between shed and house with frying pan or saucepan, to deposit the smoky contents before the family. But why worry? We still have our home, we hear from Emil in Laufen quite hilarious versions of their precarious existence. Now Emil, as we all know, has always been painfully thin. One letter from him runs: "Have just finished scrubbing sixty stone steps—good for the figure! " He and Elsie are with the Bob Chilcotts, The Tom Wyatts (Betty Wyatt of happy hospital memory). I look forward to the Occupation Diary which I hope she has written. It should make interesting reading with internment for the second part.

The deported men and women were separated in France. The men being taken on to Germany while the women were encamped in Compiègne. Elsie, of the stout heart, did write letters of anguish on this cruel blow. She tells of the dirty camp conditions and the indignities of the communal showers and toilets. We felt so sad for her and so ashamed of our home comforts. In one letter she writes: "We dread the arrival of warmer weather, when the flies settle in our filthy bird-cage." Alas! poor Elsie and her luckless companions. They spent three months in this grievous state, without a word as to the fate of their menfolk, before being bundled off to Biberach for a further three months. At last their great day of joy arrived when they all packed for their journey to Laufen where they were to join the male internees. Emil wrote that as soon as Elsie caught sight of him behind the wire she broke ranks and flung herself upon him in paroxysms of joy. For their part they must have felt the war was over. Nothing else mattered, and you may imagine how happy we were on reading Emil's news. He reads all Peter's letters aloud and, I must say, Peter is adept at giving them universal news. We live in an age of 'cloaking and dissembling'* as the Book of Common Prayer will have it. I often tell Peter that he should be doing this task, whose pen is abler than mine but he will have none of it and wants me to continue.

Once again, as I close, my Birthday thoughts are with you.

* '*Cloaking and dissembling*' means the subtle and cryptic way that Peter managed to pass on to them any local news.

To M.H. Les Dunes. April 14th, 1944.

A year since our return to Les Dunes. Ironically, George is back at La Guelle after being allocated Dr. Sutcliffe's house. What a reshuffle! Dr. S. moved into New Street after the news of Dr. Montague's death in England, where he too joined the evacuees on the advice of his medical colleagues. Dr. S. told me his death was "a terrible waste." We shall all miss him, in common with his many other patients.

We spent Easter Monday at La Guelle with Felicia, George and Allie. Peter took Junior in the front basket of their errand boy's bicycle. I rode alongside with our day's rations. George's second son, Michael (whose birth, for some mysterious reason I failed to record in December '43) is a model baby. The three children would be good playmates if only we were in the same neighbourhood.

A few days ago Peter called at the Surgery complaining of pains in his stomach and diaphragm. Dr. S. diagnosed starvation pains and warning Peter of possible ulcers, suggested that he should eat little and often. I am to give him something (?) for mid-morning and afternoon nourishment. In typical fashion Peter turned the joke on me, and tried to make me believe he had told Dr. S. that I am "well upholstered at his expense". Now, if this were even true, knowing Peter's strong sense of loyalty, nothing would inveigle him to betray me (on reading this he says I am making doubly sure of his allegiance!) O cruel satire!

For the next few days these extra snacks did sorely try my already overtaxed powers of invention, until one evening when Peter asked: "Did you have a pudding to-day? No don't bother to answer me. Of course you didn't. I had all the milk at lunch-time. Damn silly, I'll not do it again." No one could take more trouble to be enterprising in the kitchen; but our dinners are nearly all meatless beanjars or plain vegetables covered with milkless 'sauce' a disguise which fools no one. The meat ration is reserved for Junior. A little fatless beef, I roast or mince it raw and with a padding of breadcrumbs, onion, herbs and a little water it makes tasty meals for him for most of the week. It would barely provide one meal between five of us, including Enid our new maid, whom Peter wanted me to train against the sad day when Nan must leave us. Occasionally Peter takes his vegetables to Le Noury's to be cooked. It amazes him to see what enormous appetites some of the patrons have. Masses of potatoes, carrots and parsnips are heaped on their plates, all taken to Le Noury's as they arrive for work in the mornings. Peter swears that he could not consume nor digest such large quantities in one sitting. This contention was borne out yesterday when dear old Colonel Milbourne came over from next door, asked if he might come in and told me he had heard of Peter's starvation problem. He had been remonstrating with his wife and daughter against their habit of dumping massive portions of vegetables on his plate twice a day. He welcomed Dr. Sutcliffe's opinion that he should eat little and often and returned to his house armed with this medical support for his argument.

For some days Peter took a few cooked vegetables in a basin to re-heat at lunch-time but after one murky experience, he gave up the idea. His account of this episode was too comical even to appear pathetic, let alone lurid or blasphemous, as it appears his language had been (not altogether in character I might add). But who would condemn in such an extremity?

His custom was to warm the concoction over a gas-jet in the basement, and to carry it up the four flights of stairs into the attic, where, across the roof tops of the Midland Bank, there is a magnificent view of the Harbour and Islands. There he would sit with his bowl and a book in grandfather Head's rocking-chair, stored there as our last ditch of concealment when all other hideouts were bulging with the rest of your possessions. Generations of dust lay unswept on those tattered linoleum stairs, unnoticed, day by day by a series of workmen attending their lathes, plating machines, smelting pots or whatever lay mysteries are to be found in such places.

On this occasion Peter set off with book and bowl, no 'jug of wine' being available in that wilderness, to climb those winding stairs. He had reached the middle of the last dusty flight, when he stumbled and fell, the bowl and his face finding the next step in perfect unison. There he lay, like a very sea-sick passenger in the gale-swept channel, his suit and his stupefied face plastered with the late contents of the bowl.

The first shock over and finding his bruised bones intact, he got to work with his knife, scraping the horrible sludge from his face and clothes into the basin. To this he added what he could retrieve from the stairs and stair-rods together with centuries of dust. Retracing his steps to the basement, he cleaned himself as best he could, reheated the obscene mess which somehow had to be eaten, with or against the grain, for there was no one in all the town to replace his '*cordon bleu*'.

This recital, as you may guess, Mother, was neatly interlarded with gales of laughter at frequent intervals. Knowing Peter's unquenchable sense of the ridiculous, I swear that he would find something to enthuse over, even in a mortuary.

Recently, in common with many other folk, 'Biff' and Charles have experienced a bad spell of health with boils, septic knees and fingers, besides influenza and dysentery. A few days ago Biff left Charles and the children in bed and, feeling groggy herself, set off to collect their medicines from Dr. Gibson's surgery. When, on her return, Charles declined to get up for tea, poor Biff, at the end of her tether, collapsed before his eyes, to the accompaniment of one child yelling for a drink of water. *Malgré lui,* Charles dragged himself from his sick-bed where he had spent some days, and was obliged to rouse himself to take over the reins. After helping Biff into bed, he decided to do the most urgent chores, settle the children and return to bed and his ailing wife. At 7.15 p.m. he was back in bed for the night—or so he thought—when there came a knock at the door. In a weak voice Biff asked Charles to open the window and tell whoever might be down below to go away, as they were ill and wished to be left in peace. Charles opened the window, but the message was never delivered. There on the doorstep was the wife of Bernard Amy (himself in prison for black market activities against the Germans) begging Charles to come across the road at once to help save her house which was on fire. This drove Biff into a fit of hysteria, laughing and crying into her sodden pillow.

The infuriated Charles demanded her to stop being an ass, and to tell him where she had hidden his trousers. Arrived over the way, Charles found that the ingenious female, intending to take a lit fire into her bedroom, had shovelled it from the blazing hearth and flung it lit *en masse* on top of a bucket of mixed coal-dust and tar, thus starting a first-class conflagration. His first action was to open the window and fling the whole contraption into the garden's gold-fish pond, thus effectively cooking the unfortunate gold-fish—alas! lamentably uneatable.

Incidentally, the arrest of Bernard Amy was not entirely without its own touch of irony. He was alleged to have bought some contraband German '*sauçisson*' from a grocer friend in Vauvert. This dangerous mission accomplished, he was on his way home rejoicing when he decided to return and ask his friend to keep them in his refrigerator so that he might collect them as needed. As ill-luck would have it, he walked into the shop with his ill-gotten gains, to find the place being searched by the Feldgendarmerie, who promptly confiscated his precious haul. He received a sentence of nine months' imprisonment, but was allowed home to visit his wife for a given time each day, because she had contracted T.B. and was forbidden even to bath her baby. So the Germans, for whom we hold no brief, have their humane moments.

And now, Adieu. Perhaps the Allies will invade tonight, and tomorrow we shall find ourselves once more in the land of the free.

To M.H. Les Dunes. May 25th, 1944.

An age has passed since my last letter and, even now, I have been detained by two telephone calls. Peter has gone on to bed, instructing me to bring a hot drink. He waits with our supper, which consists of two slices of bread and butter apiece. If there is enough milk (skimmed of course) I shall use the remaining cocoa which Emil and Elsie so generously sent from Germany.

This meal over, I once again take up the pen, reputed to be mightier than the sword. But that must have been in the days before agreements became mere scraps of paper. Like our 'Occupation' ladies-of-easy-virtue, how crudely was our poor Neville despoiled of Innocence at Munich!

We are now recovering from severe colds, our only relief being the occasional guffaw, as we behold one another's distorted countenance. Bleary-eyed, Peter lolls in bed, looking the epitome of debauched and dissolute living, oozing contaminated moisture from every pore and appearing for all the world like an inebriated bull-frog. His description of his once beloved (?) is coarse in the extreme, and too uncouth for repetition! With which retort I now ignore him as: "The big round tears course one another down his innocent nose in piteous chase."

Gone is the dazzling and romantic vision presented the one to the other years ago by a cunning Cupid, revealing the arduous '*amours*' of our salad days for the pale imitations they were. *Néanmoins,* unlike 'Sylvia' I cannot recall many swains—imagined or otherwise—commending me for, as you dear Mother so aptly said, when Peter and I (tennis partners first by accident and then by avid adoption) became engaged: "Well, there's one thing. He may be marrying you for tennis but certainly not for your looks!" "Ah, well!" as Henry would say: "be that as it may"; I shall always be indebted to Father for signing that letter to Gamages which I put on his breakfast plate (at the behest of my conniving brothers and sisters), ordering net, posts and other tennis paraphernalia, a bait for him to lay down our first tennis court, before our friends accumulated and begged him to form a Club; until they numbered nearly a hundred; and our family court was swallowed up by three others to accommodate the vastly increasing numbers, much to our regret. Albeit, no one was ever more addicted to the game than Father himself, he became no mean performer. He and I must have spent innumerable hours playing singles until dusk, and could he punch that ball, as though to say: "Return *that* if you can!"

Once again I leave those glorious days and return to the present. Though no one would be so fatuous as to suggest that this way of life is idyllic, yet to rail against Fate could become a soul-destroying habit, as we see by the chronic victims about us. They flounder in their own private bog of despair, until from sheer impotence, even the Good Samaritan would pass by on the other side. This defeatist attitude is all the more deplorable since we chose to stay here in 1940 and to take our chance. Heaven forbid that we join the drooping martyrs, manfully emerging at the end of the journey, each from his own little crucible. In any case they may as well gird up their loins, for it would be asinine to imagine that the worst is not ahead of us, before Britain and our Allies have saved themselves, and somehow obtained our deliverance. Should they attempt a rescue operation on us first we shall be in the thick of the battle. Then will be the time for us to use our iron rations of courage. We can only pray to be left alone until Hitler decides to capitulate.

Meanwhile our theme must be, as I wrote long ago:

"*Sweet are the uses of Adversity,*
Which, like the toad, ugly and venomous,
Wears yet a precious jewel in his head:
And this our life, exempt from public haunt,
Finds tongues in trees, books in the running brooks,
Sermons in stones and good in everything."

To M.H. Les Dunes. May 31st, 1944.

Junior has been at Bordeaux a whole week, since we were laid low, and now he has an attack of croup. Dr. S. considers it unwise to move him. He was scheduled to be in Hospital on Monday for his tonsilectomy, but this must be delayed.

Diana's fourteenth birthday has come and gone, and the aching void still remains. No doubt she has ceased to miss us, after all this time, surely a natural outcome of youth for which we rejoice, for the sake of her own morale. Thank goodness we brought her up to be adaptable and independent, as a defence against the stigma of being a spoilt only child, with an only child's alleged precocity.

June tomorrow, and still no sign of Invasion, and though Jerry is very jumpy, owing to increased R.A.F. activity over these Islands, one must admit that local suspicions are aroused. Opinions are much divided, but even the most convinced that Britain will not invade Guernsey, for our sakes (as well as the futility of such action), are prepared to admit its possibility. We are still prepared to wait until the Allies are firmly established in France, for this place is bristling with guns, and massive underground fortifications. These would remain intact even though not one building was left standing. Furthermore, it is universally believed that the Germans are determined to resist to the last man.

There have been several minor raids lately. Some Germans were killed at Fort George last Saturday, when our airmen tried to bomb a radar detector. Several houses in that area were riddled by machine-gun bullets and windows smashed. A nursing friend of Nan was with her own sick baby in one semi-detached house when the adjoining house was bombed. She snatched up her child and, in apron and slippers fled from the house in terror. Her panic flight continued until she reached the house of a friend at the Câtel! What a feat with a child-in-arms! Another bomb made a large hole at the top of Colborne Road, having missed the adjacent houses by a matter of feet.

The R.A.F. flew over again this morning, amidst the usual barrage of anti-aircraft fire. I thought they were after a radar-detector, disguised as a tree perched on the rock Colenso a few yards from here, but it remains intact. I fear this lends credence to the current belief that when the Allies invade France we shall be included in the Operation. Peter has improvised a shelter in the garden in case of house-to-house fighting, which would be inevitable. A frightful prospect with a young child.

Arrangements are in hand for setting up Communal kitchens. The R.A.F. have made such a mess of the French Railways (we are told), that gas coal will soon be unobtainable. Electricity rations have been further reduced. The Germans admit to a serious shortage of army food, and this is amply borne out by the amount of crop stealing suffered by the farmers. They are an easy prey after Curfew, when potatoes and other root vegetables are taken from the ground before they have come to fruition.

Jim Stacey and Harry Marley (his lodger since Stan Noel was interned), had a gruelling adventure the other night. Jim's crop of potatoes was being reduced by marauders after Curfew: Together with Harry, he decided to keep watch in the old 'privy' at the end of the field. In the small hours of the night they saw two men of the Todt Organisation arrive with a sack and forks, to begin digging. Very soon our two heroes were upon them; all four men fighting for their lives, potatoes forgotten. The two Germans chased Jim and Harry around the field until Harry shouted: "I'm going to turn round and charge them with a rugby tackle, follow up!" Whilst Harry and his assailant grappled on the ground in mortal combat, Jim set about his companion; after snatching a weapon from his grasp. With this Jim began thrashing his enemy from head to foot until Harry, whose opponent had fled, felt some compassion for the poor hungry fellow, who lay bleeding on the ground. Jim looked up just in time to see Harry collapse in a dead faint, with a wound in his leg. Half-carrying, half-dragging him back to the house in frantic desperation, lest some Todt comrades of the thieves might arrive and really finish our friends off in revenge, Jim and Mrs. Stacey managed to revive Harry and attend to his leg. Harry then became concerned about Jim's victim, and together they stealthily made their way back to the scene of the disaster. To their amazement the wounded man had disappeared. It was inconceivable that he could have vanished alone. Jim and Harry guessed that other Todt men had been enlisted to rescue him, and that they themselves had had a narrow escape of being outnumbered in a second affray, if they had remained on guard. They hoped, in all mercy, that their wounded victim would not fall foul of the Feldgendarmerie over this affair, for their punishment for breaking Curfew would be severe. After all, the poor foreign labourers who by their accent and the odd expletive, H. & J. took to be Germans, were living very near starvation level. Many sins through hunger can and must be forgiven. "A fellow feeling makes us wondrous kind" so one is told, but the poet obviously had reservations for the verse concludes: "but I think the poet would change his mind if, one day, he chanced to find a fellow feeling in his coat behind!"

I believe it was Henry who made a habit of putting this verse in every autograph book proffered him. The fashion for these books has faded, when everyone possessed one and expected a phrase of some sort to accompany the signature. Some people chose to add a sketch, humorous or otherwise.

I have Audrey's autograph book beside me now, in which you wrote:

> *"Do not rashly judge thy Brother,*
> *If he stumble on the way.*
> *Life's beset with sore temptation*
> *He has fallen, and you may.*
> *Oh! I think it ill becomes us*
> *Thus to judge our Brother's case,*
> *Let us wait until we've triumphed*
> *Standing in the self-same place."*

As Peter left this morning, I said: "I've a fortnight's washing to do, without soap, and a dinner to cook for four people with just vegetables." My conscience smote me at once, and I felt ashamed for Peter also had a trying day ahead and we seldom allow ourselves to moan. Things are bound to worsen and we simply must not weaken at this late stage of our self-imposed journey. To keep one's train of thought on the right track requires frequent shunting but there are other helpers if one does not live alone, as many poor souls do. Having sufficiently castigated myself for this pathetic lapse, I hoped that Peter soon forgot it.

Talking of tracks, trains are now running through the deep cuttings in our undulating L'Ancresse Common, hitherto jealously hallowed by successive Committees and fossil Councils. One can scarce forbear to smile at the delicious abandon with which Jerry has cut the red tape, and bye-passed all the furrowed brows and pseudo-punditry, if I may irreverently coin a phrase.

Peter-John is due to enter Hospital at a moment's notice. Owing to a shortage of anaesthetics and other surgical necessities, Peter asked Dr. S. did he not think that this operation was urgent. He replied: "Of course I do, but I have to convince the Medical Board." The poor child has had an uphill fight from birth. No doubt that is why he is so terrified of gunfire and low-flying aircraft. They waken him at night and send him screaming indoors during the day. Yesterday, as the guns roared, twice he fell on the gravel in his flight, arriving at the door with both bleeding knees. We dread to think what effect an Invasion here would have upon him, much as we shall welcome the first British uniform.

I make up for lost time by these rather lengthy epistles when Junior is at Bordeaux for the day, or when Nan is out on one of their excursions, as they are this afternoon.

I now look up to behold a vase of flowers wilting in sympathy with my flagging pen, so I shall adjourn to give them fresh water before death becomes absolute.

To M.H. Les Dunes. June 11th, 1944.

At long last the Invasion of Deliverance is under way! It is still difficult to believe that our brave men have landed in France, whose coast is so often in view from here with the naked eye. How we envy the people of Bayeux. Of course the rumour-mongers are having a series of Field Days. I shall not weary you with their ramblings, which are not very original, and we all know that any or all of them may be right or wrong. One thing is certain. Our Fate is in the balance. Most of us feel, however, that our Allies will leave us a little longer; to test the morale of the Germans here, and to see if they will try to withdraw to Brest or Carteret before it is too late. All is conjecture and we are far too excited to entertain any single idea for long. The gamblers are placing up to Five-Pound-bets upon the conviction that the Allies will land here or not land here within a month. Who knows? These dissertations may be brought to an abrupt end. I only pray that you will be the one to find them in the hiding place I discovered one day by accident. A thousand pities that I am unable to disclose it to you but it defies the most fool-proof code. Yet a simple Safe, requiring neither combination nor key.

The night before D-Day, we had no sleep. The air was alive with roaring planes. We could see through binoculars the Ack-ack display over the French coast; though an Easterly gale was blowing, the sky was clear and the silvery shapes of the planes glinted in the bright moonlight. The Germans rushed about all night erecting barricades everywhere, and we felt that something of great moment was being enacted in the electric atmosphere.

It was no surprise to Peter when, the next morning, he was stopped by a soldier on guard at the end of our lane, who told him that he could proceed no further and that Town was out of bounds.

On June 5th, the day before the Invasion, while the telephones were still in operation, Dr. S. telephoned me to say that I must take Peter-John to Hospital on June 7th. The embargo on the roads I had to take was not in force, so I set out, with him on the back of Nan's bicycle for the long-awaited tonsilectomy.

How does one explain to a two-year old child for the second time in six months that you will soon be seeing him again? and hope that you are not stamping yourself on his mind as a person definitely not to be trusted. I undressed and put him into the hospital cot, where it soon dawned upon him that, once more, I was about to desert him. Resisting his startled appeals and smothering my urge to succumb, I embraced him quickly with a Judas countenance and walked away, looking neither to right nor left until those precincts were far behind me. It was one of those dreaded emotional tasks which only a mother must do, and I felt that if, in cowardly fashion, I had left it to Nan, she would have been cycling blind in both directions. I had reason to thank the stoical resistance engendered in our youth by the callous derision of a big family, for it stood me in good stead in the midst of strangers. Our anxiety was naturally heightened by the uncertainty of Invasion, by the fact that Dr. S. wanted him in Hospital at least a week, and also because we were unable to contact Dr. or Hospital by telephone.

I set off the next day on my five-mile journey to find out if all was well. Junior was still asleep 'under the influence', so I was able to approach his cot and see for myself. Wearing a blood-spattered garment and with a spittoon beside him, he lay without a vestige of colour in his cheeks, oblivious to all around him. However, the deed was done. The nurses assured me that his weeping had ceased the day before soon after I left; but this was belied by Nan's husband (Master of the Mental Department of the Hospital), who went to peep at him at the end of the day. 'Chem' (as we call him) had found Junior still upset (surely by my betrayal), and had been unable to pacify him before he also turned away. Nan tells us that 'Chem' broke down when telling her about it and, blowing his nose furiously, set off up their garden saying: "The little blighter upset me!"

After my visit I saw Dr. Sutcliffe's car outside the hospital and waited for his verdict. He expressed himself satisfied with the operation but, having removed two large septic tonsils, and communications now being so difficult, he emphasised the necessity of keeping him longer than usual, where he could have prompt attention.

This scrupulous care recalled the dismal treatment prevalent in our youth, when the custom was for the family doctor to call at the patient's house and, with neither ceremony nor chloroform (only a mild analgesic) would use upon a child a lethal instrument. This thing of torture was about the size of a safety razor, having at the end a flat surface with a hole about the size of the organ to be removed. Telling the wriggling victim to 'open wide' he would slip the ghastly gadget into the mouth and guillotine the tonsil, amid the blood-curdling screams of his innocent victim. A deed worthy of the Spanish Inquisition!

Doris was the 'candidate' called before me and, when at the tender age of seven years, from underneath the dining-room table I heard her terrified screams, I took to my heels and fled into the farthest corner of the garden, from whence I was carried, yelling in protest, into your bedroom; our everlasting Chamber of Horrors. Having endured the inhuman onslaught on the first tonsil, I launched a counter-attack on Dr. Robinson's shins, while parental arms held me down for the second tonsil to be beheaded. But Dr. Robinson decided to stay his hand, and thus to save my threatened sanity, or perhaps to protect his smarting shins, by saying: "That will do for today". Released, in a dismal condition, I joined my brothers and sisters (all older than myself), in another room, where I found them nursing their wounded throats over a series of receptacles.

All unknowing, sitting before our executioner ere the foul deed began, we must have looked imploringly at you and the doctor much as little Prince Arthur did in Shakespeare's *King John,* when the King's henchmen approached to remove Arthur's eyes with hot irons. I have this picture in the illustrated copy of Shakespeare that you gave me in 1921. Young Arthur raises his piteous streaming eyes to the King's Chamberlain, as he kneels clutching Hubert's legs: "O save me Hubert save me—my eyes are out even with the fierce look of these bloody men!" How you and father must have suffered with us all. *Néanmoins,* I still possess the twin of my lost tonsil, which I hope will remain intact until I hear the Clarion Call.

Peter's ordeal was far more original. His mother had made an appointment with their Dr. for the very day he was invited to a birthday picnic. This he was to forego. On the appointed day Peter's mother entered his room, only to find that the bird had flown. After a thorough search of house and garden, she resigned herself to the fact that Peter had obviously eschewed the operation in favour of the picnic. Why she failed to inform the doctor remains a mystery to this day. At lunchtime there was a disturbance in the hall, where she found Peter accompanied by his hostess. Apparently when the lunch hampers were opened at the picnic Peter declined to eat, much to everyone's surprise. "I'm not hungry" he muttered. When asked if he felt unwell he replied: "I've had my tonsils out!" "When?" exclaimed everyone in unison. "This morning" came the startling reply. Whereupon the nearest cab was hailed and the poor child driven home to his stupefied parents. What courage—to say nothing of a rare sense of duty! I refuse to believe that the rigours of parental discipline could have led him to have honoured the unwelcome assignation with Dr. X before savouring the delights of the day's outing. Incidentally Dr. X's guillotine had jammed, leaving the throat in a sorry state so that he still suffers a yearly bout of septic tonsillitis.

Such are the changing scenes of life. Who could have imagined at the beginning of the road, where and how we should all end? And is the final drama about to be played out? We are just flotsam in the path of the current, as we await the outcome of the gathering storm. This stupendous turn of events has wiped out the stagnation and boredom which had settled on the Island like a pall. High drama has replaced them, whilst numerous reactions scuttle hither and thither in our brains like a nest of disturbed ants. The old grapevine, long ago afflicted with dry rot, and unable to call up or refurbish the old corny rumours, has now taken on a new lease of life. Credible and incredible stories flourish from impenetrable sources. But, inured as we are to a series of reversals, we are deeply suspicious of over-optimistic reports, the probable result of some over-zealous gardener stimulating the grapevine with a double dose of manure.

What a dreadful June! We pray each night for calmer weather to assist the Normandy landings. We are ever mindful of our own brave Guernseymen, who are sacrificing their lives, along with the Allies, for the deliverance of our country and of Europe. Meanwhile, on the whole, the Germans are as eager to fraternize as we feel eager to remain quietly aloof. Recently an Officer has made a habit of calling here, ostensibly on business. As Peter is usually out at these times, I keep the door locked and answer his enquiries at the open window. This could not continue as I did not wish to be branded a collaborator. At Peter's suggestion I intended to remind him that our business premises are in Town, when suddenly the visits ceased. This same Officer called one evening when Junior was afflicted with that ear trouble in January. It was dark when he knocked at the door. As I opened it he brushed past me into the house, to find Peter sitting by the fire with our son in his arms, obviously very ill. "Wolfi" (the name he wanted engraved on a locket), was most concerned and advised us to apply potato poultices on the infant's ears, as his parents had done when he was similarly afflicted in his childhood. This was one of the few times during that ordeal when P.J. showed a spark of real interest in life. He fairly boggled at the sight of the resplendent uniform, actually in our home, as though it were an apparition and, for a moment, he forgot his agony.

Our visitor must have sensed that he was as unwelcome in the evening as he was by day, for no seat was offered him. Finding that we were far too harassed almost to notice his presence at all, he tactfully left us to our own problems. The next day, with tongue in cheek, I admonished Dr. Sutcliffe for not prescribing potato poultices as advised by "Wolfi". As expected he fumed: "These people know everything—they make me sick!"

To M.H. Les Dunes. June 19th, 1944.

Day and night we hear the din of hostilities from the French coast. It is said that Carteret is now in Allied hands. If this be true, we are almost certainly landed for the duration with the Germans, their Todt Organization and their cosmopolitan hordes of slave workers, for their escape will be impossible.

While this makes our position even more precarious, yet we are proud to be holding down a couple of German divisions, which would otherwise be reinforcing the Germans in France. A sharp raid took place over Town at approximately 8.30 this morning. Bombs fell in various places, including the Old Harbour. Almost every shop in Town suffered from the blast, including our own. Peter arrived there to find Bank Clerks and other business people sweeping up the glass in the streets—all irreplaceable of course. Peter estimates the damage at nearly £100,000. Mercifully, there were no casualties since, by German decree, business does not begin until ten o'clock.

We know from War Bulletins that bombing can precede a full-scale invasion, and wonder if this is one of those with relation to Guernsey. Apparently boats are being sunk in these waters; and last evening we sighted two destroyers on the horizon opposite Les Dunes. Long range German guns went into action; and we saw several splashes far out in the bay. The destroyers quickly put down a smoke screen and were seen no more.

Judging by the amount of attention shewn us, we are uncomfortably in the news, whilst a cursory glance at the map, makes us feel very 'front line'. In a few days, poor little Guernsey could be reduced to a heap of rubble. We tremble for our son. What a world we have brought him into! We are ever thankful that Diana is away from it all. Where are those people who scoffed at the evacuees in 1940? They are remarkably silent. We always said: "Time will tell," and that time may be very near. If the High Command deem it imperative to their plans that we should endure the full blast of Invasion, with all its grimmest horrors, then we must indeed gird up our loins, and face up to it as courageously as possible. Other countries have experienced it and endured. Our prevailing regret would be that, after so eagerly awaiting your return for the past four years, and lived through many trials and tribulations, we might not be here to welcome you all. In which case, I again pray that you may discover this book in its secret place, so that love's labour will not have been lost. Enough! No more on this joyful theme.

To M.H. Les Dunes. June 23rd, 1944.

Nothing momentous took place last night. There was great excitement this morning over cases of food dropped by German planes to the troops in Guernsey. For once, the usual rumours were not without foundation. Search parties were out early to find them, even through our garden. One of our neighbours regretted not being up with the lark to gather his manna from Heaven but, alas, the early birds in his garden were in uniform.

We are sitting up in bed at ten o'clock, listening to the booming of distant planes through our open window: A series of Easterly gales having at last subsided. Hundreds of planes must have roared over us all day, while guns rumbled in the Cherbourg area. Like pinpoints of twinkling stars, the sun catches them and throws off their brilliant reflections. Our house literally shook this evening with the Cherbourg bombardment. As usual we bid Goodbye to Nan, and wondered if we shall meet in the morning, or whether some heavy drama will have befallen us during this quiet night. Peter teases me for wanting to sleep half-dressed and with a suitcase of immediate necessities ready to dash to our dug-out. So once more I am attired in conventional nightwear and hope for the best. As in the first days we must continue to 'put our blind eye to the doings', as we say: "Goodnight dear Mother." May we be granted a speedy deliverance if our heroes arrive before dawn.

To M.H. Les Dunes. June 29th, 1944.

Exactly four years since our initial air raid on the Harbour, with its tragic loss of life. Unless our position alters soon, I fear that this correspondence will gravitate, without variations, into the predominant theme of suspended animation. Each day seems an eternity, with the enemy and ourselves living at concert pitch. Surely the War Office will not risk our annihilation, in an effort to secure our salvation, much as we shudder at the thought of another winter with dwindling rations and bleak stagnation. Imagine Churchill with his agile mind and great dynamism, rusting away in utter impotence. The futility of such a life deadens the faculties by slow tortuous degrees. As Dr. S. told us recently, he is certain that he is not '*compos mentis*' and that, when our folks return, they will take one look at us, shrug their shoulders and sigh: "I suppose it must be the Occupation."

Peter-John returned from hospital on June 15th after almost two hours in the ambulance and a week in hospital. He was very wobbly on his feet for a few days, but now seems to have more stamina, and we see a distinct improvement generally. Nan says that it would have been easy for him to slip through our fingers, during one of his many attacks of illness, to say nothing of his hazardous birth.

To M.H. Les Dunes. July 2nd, 1944.

Young George is three years old today, but we see no chance of visiting them at the moment. I wonder how and where Marie celebrated her birthday yesterday. All accounts of the family war-time adventures we are eager to hear. May nothing arise to cause a further depletion in our numbers and finally wreck the joy of our reunion.

We now live in a land of pseudo peace. The guns at Cherbourg are silent, and we seldom see or hear a plane. No doubt they are grounded by this appalling weather. It rains and blows incessantly. When the rain stops awhile, the wind puts down the loud pedal and rises to a maddening crescendo. Last night, for the second time, we saw a number of destroyers far out at sea. Jerry opened up with the usual barrage of guns. Inevitably there appeared in the next edition of the Press the announcement of a crushing victory over the British Navy!

We set off with Junior this afternoon. He was proudly clad in mackintosh and wellington boots, given to him by Nan for Christmas (origin unknown and unprobed but almost certainly the products of a clever barter). P.J. loves to visit one of the quarries in the lanes hereabouts where a couple of wild ducks swim in formation with their family of ducklings around a large clump of water lilies. He could watch them for hours.

Since the last air raid, business is virtually at a standstill. The Jewellers & Silversmiths, having no more goods to display, had long ago ordered nursery plants in tubs to be sent down for window decoration. But, as most of our windows had been boarded up to replace the plate glass shattered by the raid, these were no longer needed. The Midland Bank across the way suffered so much damage that they transferred their business to one of our Arcade shops.

To M.H. Les Dunes. August 8th, 1944.

More than a month has passed, and it seems, with the receding sounds of war, that the Allies have decided to leave us, and to concentrate on penetrating deeper into Europe.

Meanwhile, daily visits from the R.A.F. keep the Germans on the 'qui vive' and even as I write, planes are roaring in strength not far away. This afternoon we were obliged to leave our tea in the garden and scamper indoors, while German guns blasted away, probably trying to repulse an attack on their boats in the Harbour.

I try to avoid the gnawing subject of food as far as possible, for it has become an obsession in these Islands. Having hoped to hold your interest so far, I hate to think that at this late stage you might not read on. Suffice it to say that, given the 'book of verse' we are naturally without 'the jug of wine', and 'sans almost anything else you might think edible'. But, as things are we are more than thankful that you are not "beside us in the wilderness," where Paradise has become merely a figment of the imagination.

To M.H. Les Dunes. August 20th, 1944.

It now seems certain that Doris will spend her next birthday in Guernsey. Diana should be with you for today's celebration.

We hear that the German Commandant has told his troops they are cut off from Europe and completely isolated. Be that as it may, unless their censorship is foolproof! this admission seems somewhat superfluous. The position around Brest for some time now must have made it impossible for them to escape.

This has truly become a war of attrition for an already conquered foe, still armed to the teeth with useless weapons and indestructible fortifications. The invasion of Guernsey seems less and less likely with the approach of Autumn and Winter, during which we shall be much too busy keeping body and soul together, to contemplate what the Spring has in store.

One amusing story runs, that the German Chief sent for Victor Creasey and told him there must be drastic cuts in electricity and gas rations; also that reserves of coal are low. But, as soon as the Germans have recaptured St. Malo and Grouville! supplies will be resumed. The general question now is, if and how V.C. managed to keep a poker face! We needed no confirmation of the dearth of coal for we have to manage on 250ft. of gas per household per week and 1½ units of electricity.

We welcome the news that the Allies are supplying food to the Florentines on a generous scale. They have our blessing and this I say without sarcasm or sour grapes.

Meanwhile our son continues to grow in devilry and initiative. One day last week Peter went to fetch him from his afternoon nap, only to find him brandishing a thermometer and, with cherubic glee, announcing triumphantly "No temp!" Who, we asked one another, had left the thing within his reach. Have our brains really become so atrophied? If so, this should serve to revive them.

Today our thoughts are in France with Meta and her widespread family. We pray that the Liberation of Paris will be swift and merciful. Peter is most anxious about his many French relatives. Now that all Meta's danger of detection is past, I am able to tell you of an incident which took place at the end of 1940 when I was at the business in the Arcade.

One day a Frenchman came in and stealthily asked if I was related to Monsieur Bachmann. Assuring him of my close relationship, I saw him glance furtively about him before producing a letter from his pocket. He said: "Monsr. Bachmann's sister in Cherbourg gave me this letter to give him, and to wait for an answer, if possible. My boat leaves again before one hour. I will call soon for a letter from her brothers." By what low cunning Meta had coerced this man (forced to bring over supplies for the Germans), to risk his freedom, if not his life; by defying German restrictions in this way, we may never know. I flew upstairs and gave the 'hot' missive to Emil who said: "My God! that chap took a chance." Peter, being up in Mill Street, Emil eagerly read all the French family news and set about writing an answer, as fast as his pen would travel. Apparently the French civilians' treatment is the same as ours, provided also, that no German edicts are ignored, and that they conform generally to German demands. Nothing of military value was mentioned, partly because those 'Occupied' are kept in ignorance of German activities and intentions. Albeit, because of the vastness of their country, and their chances of escaping detection, I have no doubt that among their millions some underground resistance will flourish. The chance of such ventures being successful in these Islands do not exist.

As promised, our anonymous hero returned and, thrusting Emil's letter into the same inner pocket, accompanied no doubt by a generous gratuity from a grateful family, he departed. We could imagine the agitated and resourceful Meta awaiting his return in Cherbourg, and devouring our news as eagerly as we had received hers.

To M.H. Les Dunes. August 31st, 1944.

As expected, the Germans and their unfortunate cosmopolitan hordes are now isolated with us: for Brest, their last Port of refuge, has been sorely dealt with by the British. As the days pass, we feel that the Allies will ignore us until a German collapse brings about our automatic liberation. Now that the end is so near, we have to curb our impatience, which only makes each day seem a lifetime. Then, in the stillness of the night, with a familiar sea fog for cover, we sometimes wonder if the Allies will attempt to recover these Islands. Our hopes and fears keep the old adrenalin ever on the move. Our hopes we freely exchange but we merely breathe our unuttered fears. They need no words, where all minds are as one.

Today we were obliged to rush indoors while German guns blasted at the R.A.F. planes which, even as I write, are roaring in strength not far away. For a moment I thought they were heading for the Harbour but the noise is diminishing and the guns are silenced.

On hearing that Paris was free, Peter was delighted for Meta's sake and for her large family. But what of Eva? On the verge of producing her seventh child. The Allies, it seems, are streaming on in that direction, judging by the position of Douai on the map. The people in the South of England must be delighted to hear that the V.1 sites are being approached. All of which activities take the Allies further away from us, though the tension here remains unchanged and September seems to be a popular month for invasions.

With the prospect of a fifth winter of Occupation one wonders how many of the lonely and ill will survive. The hardiest among us are hard put to it already. Those committed on religious grounds to mortify the flesh now have a Hitler-sent opportunity to concede to such a dogma, for rations are almost non-existent.

This afternoon Peter and I were present at Mrs. Turner's funeral. The shocking news must be on the way to 'Weazle'. Her agony will be the greater, because of the tragic separation during the last years of her Mother's life, cut short, according to Harry Marley, by mal-nutrition. Mr. Sauvary was the undertaker. After the funeral he came towards us, whispering as though he had some secret of great moment for our ears alone. As we replied in the same muted fashion, he laughed and said: "You can speak up — I've lost my voice." We spent a most interesting period in a cemetery building exchanging Occupation experiences.* He made nothing of his throat trouble, which he thinks must be laryngitis. Of course he misses his family during these lonely years. Mr. Turner is also now a tragic figure.

Diana will soon be returning to Wales for the Autumn term. We long for a sight of her, and it is such a pity for her to be missing this most interesting stage of her brother's development. Our chances of seeing her for Christmas recede as each week passes. We pray for the long-awaited reunion to become a reality.

* Mr. S. had found an R.A.F. pamphlet in his garden which he hoped Peter would be able to translate. Peter's German lessons with Mrs. Tate enabled him to give us all the gist.

To M.H. Les Dunes. September 8th, 1944.

As I write each letter, I wonder if it is to be the last one under German Occupation.

Now that the forces of America, Britain and Canada are closing in on Germany in the West and those of Russia and Yugoslavia in the South, our war prospects seem very much brighter. Russia has long been held up outside Warsaw but perhaps she is waiting for us to launch the final assault so that we may all march into Germany together. As we hear of the Liberation of each town and village we become very envious, as we face the prospect of yet another winter under these worsening conditions.

The R.A.F. are again paying us some attention, despite awful gales. Propaganda leaflets in German arrive in some profusion but, so far, Peter and I have not been lucky enough to collect one. We lie in bed at night and, when the zooming planes arrive amid the shattering din of blasting guns, we say: "Here comes the '*Evening Standard*'."

We hear that fraternizers in Europe are having their heads shaved by indignant patriots. It is said that one local girl has already been 'scalped' for betraying someone who kept a wireless set, and of other people receiving cards with the words: "You are the next on our list, signed 'The G.U.B.'" (Guernsey Underground Barbers).

Junior has just arrived in my room saying: "Kit, I want my milk!" He always calls me Kit, a familiarity which we allow to run its course. Walking on the Common a few days ago with Peter and me, he watched Kala dive headlong through the glass of a greenhouse after a rabbit, neither suffering any ill effects. Later, however, much to Dad's delight, Kala did catch one, which we removed from his mouth. On the way home Junior wanted to carry the poor little furry beast but we refused his request on the grounds that it might be full of fleas. We forgot his interest in it until, after much apparent brooding on the subject of parasites he asked: "Do angels have fleas in their wings?" Some of his choice remarks, I enter into his log-book. Another one runs: "Do you get cheese straight from the cow?" "Or does it come from his milk?" No doubt there are thousands of fond parents who could cap such delicious phrases, coined by their offspring. It is a source of delight shared by us all — and why not? Every mind is unique, and every infant mind an unblazed trail. Recently he has made friends with two little boys of neighbouring families. They appeared outside our gate, much to Junior's delight. He rushed into the house exclaiming excitedly: "I've just seen two little boys, the same size as my size is!" Then began a daily visit so that Peter-John had at last found companions to amuse him. We thought this was great: until a few days ago, when Peter, Nan and I were loitering in conversation over the lunch-table. Suddenly we were aware of a deadly hush outside. When a search of the house and garden produced no result Nan and I saw Dad disappearing over the hill across the lane and out of sight. We flew upstairs to see him as he fled over the common, where once more we lost sight of him. After what seemed an age, he returned with Junior only. He had found the three young demons swinging on the wire separating the public from the minefields, in blissful ignorance of the board dangling beside them, bearing the skull and crossbones and the words: "Achtung!! Minen!!"

The absence of the other two children was due to Peter's manner of dealing with them, before seeing them take to their heels and make for home. In his terror, Peter had put them each in turn across his knee and had lambasted them.

Needless to say Junior was companionless for some days. His friends thought his Father was an ogre, lying in ambush for their next appearance. All was forgiven, however, when Father visited the parents and explained the situation. Fortunately they were very sensible, commended Peter for taking the law into his own hands and said they would probably have done the same as he did, for it was vital to be dealt with on the spot, and thus indelibly engraved on the minds of the children.

Kala had already been blown up at that spot by an anti-personnel mine, and suffered a broken leg. That had been a shock to Peter sitting behind a rock while Kala hunted rabbits. A loud explosion on that occasion brought the Germans out of their bunkers to sweep the landscape with their field glasses, while Peter grabbed Kala and, hiding him under his coat, made for home in a panic lest they shoot our dog, as they had already shot someone's valued goat for the same offence.

Did I say that we are bored? Well, we can do without this type of diversion, where the life of our son is involved.

To M.H. Les Dunes. Friday, Sept. 22nd, 1944.

Bob Hargreaves* has just 'phoned their latest piece of hearsay. The German General has spent two hours in conference on board an American vessel in the Russel. Also that the German Authorities here are in telephonic communication with our Allies in France. This is alleged to be the outcome of distressing conditions in Jersey, due to the absence of anaesthetics, dressings, disinfectants et cetera. Typhoid and gangrene are also to be found among the German wounded. A neighbour has called to verify this news. They actually saw an American (?) destroyer about two miles away. German officers, with field-glasses were on the jetty; while a small boat went out to the destroyer. Someone saw the American markings on the flag. The bounds of ridicule have so often been surpassed by the inventiveness of frustrated gossips that, even now, we feel these starving eye-witnesses may have been fooled by a mirage. Albeit, one cannot ignore the infectious excitement engendered by these latest reports, coming as they do from such differing sources. Maybe the Red Cross will at least send medical supplies, but we naturally hope for bigger things. One feels quite dizzy at the very thought of Liberation, when we shall at last be able to communicate with you freely.

This evening when I decided to write, there were hosts of things I meant to tell you, but I fear this latest news has swept my mind of everything else, and my feeble brain refuses to budge on any other theme.

* 'Bob' abv. for Barbara.

To M.H. Les Dunes. Sunday, October 8th, 1944.

Our fifth winter begins in earnest with a week of easterly gales. We hear that you are granted permission to use electric heaters and, while we rejoice with you, we wish we could share them together. Our own electric ration is now reduced to one-and-a-half units a week per household. Current is cut off at 2 p.m. until 7 p.m. when the gas also goes to earth for the rest of the day. It is almost dark at seven o'clock, hence we sup by candlelight. The current returns at 6 a.m.

When I last wrote, we were full of hope but whatever the gist of the Allied-German pow-wow, the outcome remains a mystery for there has been no tangible result. Yesterday an Officer told Peter that negotiations are definitely afoot. We were actually mentioned in Parliament last week. Apparently the British Government is satisfied that we are being well treated. If they mean that we are not being physically tortured, they are correct. I doubt if the Germans who are as near starvation level as we are, could summon the energy for sadism, even if that was ever their intention. As I have probably said before, and it deserves repetition, we derive no satisfaction from their pathetic state. If the common soldier thinks of us at all, it is now probably as co-exiles and 'brothers' in adversity. We incline to the same view.

Once more Liberation seems far off, and the manner of our release uncertain. However, anxiety always intervenes in time to save us being bored to extinction. Or is that happy state achieved, only when mental atrophy banishes both boredom and anxiety? Possibly those so insulated are what Hitler calls sheep who, according to Tennyson's '*Arthur*' "nourish a blind life within the brain." Here the escapist comes into the picture. Surely escapism is to sit above the clouds on the mountain top and leave others to do battle in the foothills. But how much of solace and serenity can be enjoyed by such a course? In our chastening experience during these past years, nothing but total participation brings any lasting peace of mind.

Meanwhile Peter-John has energy enough to equip an army. One recent afternoon, Peter sent him upstairs for me to comb his hair in readiness for an outing. Junior arrived at my closed door and bellowed: "Kit, comb the baby's hair, Mr. B. said." The poor child is quite muddled. Dad calls me 'Kit' while Nan addresses Dad as 'Mr. B.' Confusion is inevitable.

They are just returning from another expedition, collecting firewood in the pram, from a derelict building, where they revel as demolition experts. This has become the highlight of their existence as they set off like a couple of conspirators with Kala at their heels.

So concludes this letter as they clamour for supper. One would think that I have only to wave a magic wand or raise my eyes to Heaven for the ravens to bring us bread and flesh. But methinks even the ravens found their way into the German stew-pots long ago!

To M.H. Les Dunes. October 20th, 1944.

And so it goes on. Since my last letter, we hear that the celebrated meeting between the Germans and our Allies in the Russel, was in the nature of a request or demand for the Germans here to surrender. Naturally, it was rejected, if this story be true. Only the total collapse of the Third Reich will suffice for such a document to be signed.

The wireless (yes, we have one!) tells us yet again that we are being properly treated, so we have nothing to worry about. This news threw us into paroxysms of joy, and we all took on a new lease of life. Now you must admit, dear Mother, that seldom, if ever, through these dissertations, have I resorted to sarcasm. Now, I confess, I have fallen by the wayside. But really! How can one, from the cover of security and a comfortable interior, pour such cold comfort into the ear of those who have neither?

Having said this I now humbly relent, for one supposes the announcer to have meant this news to reassure you all in England, who naturally assume that we are without our wireless sets. We have kept one most of the time, though until now, it has been unsafe to commit ourselves on paper. Indeed no one would entrust such a vital secret to a bosom friend. The following story will show you the reason.

One day Stan told me that Winston Churchill would be on the air that night. Now everyone with or without a wireless set knows by bush telegraph when Churchill is due to broadcast. So I took no notice of Stan's remark except to acknowledge it, until he cursed: "It will be on the Overseas Service and we can't get that station on our set!!" Innocently and with raised eyebrows, a vestige of a smile lurking, I replied: "Can't you, Stan?" Whereupon he exploded: "Hell! you could have been — just anyone!" But obviously I still did not reveal that we also had a set with which we hoped to be among Churchill's ardent listeners.

Whenever the news promises to be interesting, we telephone Gwenyth. Lest our 'phones are tapped we ring and say: "We have a nice bowl of 'fruit' if you'd care to collect it." We have to choose the tempting morsel, to fit the season so as to avoid detection. In winter it is 'cake' but Gwenyth is quick to get the message and she arrives post haste, for we hang on to every shred of news, as though our life depends upon it. And Gwenyth longs for news of Gordon fighting with the British in 'furrin parts', according to her news from her folk in the internment camp at Laufen.

On one occasion, before we left La Guelle, George managed to procure a contraband pig which he kept in the stables behind the garages. Tension reigned whenever the Germans arrived to collect yet another lorry, until George felt sure that the grunting swine must sooner or later announce his presence, and have George deported.

He made discreet approaches to one or two of his intimates for its disposal. One day I answered the 'phone to one of the medical fraternity, unaware that he was a prospective buyer. I had forgotten for the moment all about this transaction. Dr. X caught me off guard with his opening words: "Tell George I've found a good home for his 'Alsatian'."* Inured as we have become by instinct to detect the still small voice of caution which says: "Gird thy heavenly armour on, wear it ever night and day; ambush'd lies the evil one . . ." I replied in an imploring tone: "Are you sure he will have a good home?" Dr. X replied: "You may rest assured that he will be well looked after." Thus did we bid adieu to Lily's stable companion. Those breakfast rashers and succulent roasts were nurtured to grace other tables than ours. A syndicate had taken over. Alas! poor little Mary had suffered yet another bereavement.

Thank goodness for sugar-beet syrup. We spread it on our bread at breakfast. Boiled vegetables form our daily dinner-menu: swedes, parsnips and potatoes, unadorned. Our puddings consist of 'ersatz' flour mixed with separated milk and water, with the addition of beet syrup, which costs 3½ marks (7/5) a pound. Acorn coffee rounds off the meal.

One evening recently we read of a barter offer of sugar-beet syrup for clothes. I raked out an old cardigan belonging to Doris and, after replacing the buttons which I thought she might like to keep for their originality, I plied my skill at invisible mending. A pair of those ghastly European stockings previously mentioned and a pair of gloves, completed the parcel. Even should this bring us one pound of syrup we felt it would be a fair bargain. Peter sallied forth the next day, full of high hopes, after speaking to the 'dealer' on the telephone. A quaint little Guernsey woman, of the poke bonnet variety, duly arrived in Peter's office for the momentous negotiations to begin, towards, Peter hoped, an amicable conclusion. Whilst Mrs. X examined the garments, Peter tasted the syrup. Presently Mrs. X began to hum and ha, whereupon Peter turned to her and with a wry face said: "You needn't bother any further. My wife (!) would not accept this syrup. It tastes like parsnips." "Thank you," exclaimed the outraged woman, in her rich Guernsey-French accent: "Parsnips indeed! My syrup is the very best. Everyone tells me." With these words and in high dudgeon, she left Peter to rinse from his mouth the bitter flavour of over-cooked parsnip.

* George did not own an Alsatian.

I verily believe that we had more fun out of Peter's version of this story than ever the syrup could have given us. The clothes await another windfall from a happier issue. That was our second failure to pull off a barter for syrup. The first time we had advertised for a pot or so. One morning I had answered a 'phone call to hear this famous accent from the other end. The caller said: "It's that I understand you are asking for syrup." On this occasion, I thought it was George trying on me one of his practical jokes, in this accent which he was wont to mimic, in a disguised falsetto voice. I was not falling for it this time and very cleverly retorted: "Don't think you can fool me, George." "I beg your pardon?" said the voice. Again I said: "Come off it, don't be an ass. You can't fool me!" "Well!" exploded the caller. "I've never been so insulted in all my life! Thank you!" Down crashed the receiver in my ear. Too late I realized just how 'clever' I had been. When I told Peter he said: "You idiot! Perhaps this will be a lesson to you. Now we've lost the precious syrup." I tried to comfort him by saying it was probably horrible stuff anyway, for we have tasted some obscene imitations.

Yesterday morning we heard Freddie Grisewood speaking on "The Kitchen Front." We fairly gasped when he said that he had actually heard of people refusing their bacon ration because it was too fat!! If we could lay hands on one single rasher of bacon we should be in clover, and the fatter the better! It would flavour our dinners for days. But there will always be grousers in every community. Verily the wireless can be both our best friend and our worst enemy. All part of the "Battle of Life" as Peter's Father was wont to say.

The Jersey Bailiff has written a forthright letter to the Germans, and our Doctors constantly harass them with complaints. Skin troubles abound to add to the discomforts of dysentery; poisoned hands and feet and other ills produced by mal-nutrition.

To M.H. Les Dunes, L'Ancresse, November 19th, 1944.

A whole month since my last letter. Conditions here have rapidly deteriorated in the past two or three weeks.

Lively exchanges have taken place between the German Staff, our Bailiff and John Leale. This resulted in a communiqué being radioed to Germany, asking them to appeal to the Red Cross for help. But did the message reach Geneva? is the question in the mind of everyone. The situation is rapidly becoming grave, and many people will assuredly die this winter unless help is soon forthcoming. In a letter to the Bailiff, Dr. Symons, M.O.H., wrote: "Those will be the lucky ones who die quickly." The Germans are calling with lorries at all our potato depôts and confiscating the contents. The same is being done with other comestibles. The bread supply is expected to cease in a few weeks' time, to be followed by electricity. Gas may last until Christmas. All root vegetables are now rationed, our quota for this week being three carrots and one swede between three of us. Depôts have been set up for the distribution of salt water for cooking at 2½d. for a ½-gallon. The General is reported to be leaving Guernsey, to be replaced by the Commander of the famous Brest Garrison, who is said to have escaped from there by submarine. Apparently he is a person to be dreaded as a fighter to the last man.

Our great hope lies with the two men who escaped from here about ten days ago — this time with our blessing — after they had attended a very urgent and dramatic States Meeting.

We are delighted to hear Winston's after-dinner speeches in the Mansion House and in Paris. He deserves the succulent fruits of his labours. It was in no spirit of jealousy, that Peter and I sang at supper tonight. "They shall hunger no more, neither thirst any more. Neither shall the sun light on them, nor any heat." In fact, Winston, bless him, was not in mind when we burst into song, continuing with the 23rd psalm "Beside the still waters . . ." Just as the men of Arnhem speak of religion coming to them in their extremity, so it bears us on our way.

We still laugh at times at the prospect of becoming slimmer and weaker, so that we shall be doing our bidding at bridge in stage whispers. The last time that Bob Hargreaves and Tilly Guilbert cycled down here for bridge, I was waiting for them in the garden. Presently I heard sounds of hysterical laughter coming from up the lane. I went out to behold two middle-aged females collapsed with their cycles into the grass bank. Totally mystified, I approached them, just as they were sorting themselves out. There in the lane stood the skinny 'Bob' (Barbara) with an enormous bust. I had joined in bantering her about her flat chest the previous week. This time she had stuffed two pairs of 'Younguns'* golf stockings inside her jumper, and apparently they would persist in leaving the usual places where the female bosom is meant to be. All this palaver had been invented to entertain me and Allie Marquand, who had come down in the morning and was waiting in the house. Our comedians flopped into your two armchairs, looking unequal to playing bridge at all, never mind bidding in whispers.

Recently after the very dangerous acquisition of a surprise haul of bread and tobacco — of which I hope more anon — Peter and I cycled to Le Friquet to see if we could arrange a barter with Cecil Arnold for eggs. Our faces fell when he announced that his remaining hens were broody but our spirits revived, when he tendered his only offering — a goose egg!! Naturally (to use Peter's pet phrase) we 'didn't loiter' over the transaction. We gave our fragile prize, cotton wool and kid glove treatment all the way home, as though it might have been the Koh-i-Noor itself. Anyway in her present state of health Little Mary would find no use at all for diamonds of any price.

* Her husband's nickname.

To M.H. Les Dunes. November 24th, 1944.

A few lines in waiting for my two Peters to arrive for tea. Since my last letter, a change, too wonderful to be believed, has come to these Islands. The Red Cross has heard our appeal and have promised to help us. Dare we credit this announcement in our German-censored Press? Needless to say the gossips are off at a tangent. A berth has been barricaded at the White Rock* for the arrival of the mercy-boat on Monday(!) A house is being made ready for the Red Cross Representative to live in Mount Row (!) and thus the fickle rumours fly. Long ago we decided to take

* The local name for our Harbour.

these stories with a pinch of salt and to abide by Mr. Asquith's famous 'wait-and-see' policy which, whatever its merits or defects at that time, is the only reasonable course to be adopted now.

In my last letter I referred to a dangerous haul which Peter had discovered by accident. A certain preamble is unavoidable to put you in the picture.

One day in town, Peter chanced to meet an old country friend and, fuel being such a major problem, Peter inquired if, perchance, he had an old tree for sale. "No," there were no trees available, he said, but he did have two or three old houses situated towards the top of Constitution Steps, which he was prepared to sell. Two of them had been partially destroyed by fire, though a lot of wood remained; while the third house, though unburnt, was also derelict. Contracts were duly signed for the site and salvage. Without delay Peter arranged with Eugène, Martin, Bill and John Guilliard — the 'Four Just Men' as he calls them, to help him cut out the remaining timber from the burnt houses. The weather being bitterly cold, and the Constitution Steps covered with snow, they slid the big stuff down those numerous stone steps of considerable gradient, from whence sundry locals eagerly collected the smaller pieces in baskets, barrows, prams or other conveyances, rejoicing at their sudden windfall.

Peter disposed of the wood among friends and relatives and, after keeping enough for our own needs, he set out to try his luck at bartering the rest with likely farmers for a little corn and potatoes. Sometimes Junior accompanied Peter and Eugène on their bartering expeditions, when he was allowed turns of driving "Cocotte," Eugène's faithful white horse. You should have seen P.J. muffled up and with radiant face, as they set out on these journeys. Very little food, I fear, came out of it from this land of famine, but the wood was invaluable and it had both given the 'men' a much-needed diversion and joy to all the recipients. On one occasion they returned with four pounds of grain, which I 'minced' with my inadequate kitchen mincer (you should try it sometime!) but I was able to make a little porridge and a few cakes for Junior, husks notwithstanding.

The dangerous outcome of this affair came later. Peter returned one morning to look over the remaining house, left untouched because it was too sound to demolish. On this particular morning Peter found that a large hole had been ripped in a bedroom ceiling since his last visit. On investigation he saw, and dragged out of the aperture a sack containing, of all things, loaves of German bread and a quantity of cigarettes and tobacco!

Literally trembling with excitement and apprehension, he retraced his steps to the Arcade to fetch his bicycle with its large errand boy's basket in the front, and filled it with his tremendous 'find'. (It would have been sheer lunacy to have walked through town carrying a sack). Covering the loaded basket with paper and odd fragments of wood, as a makeshift camouflage, he lost no time hanging around for the possible return of the plunderer, but struggled down those precipitous steps with his loaded bicycle, with heaven-sent energy and on to a safe journey home.

I fairly shook with fright when he arrived, and I was most reluctant to have this dangerous contraband in the house. I begged Peter not to return to that site until the war ended, for I felt that some desperate character might find him there and take drastic measures to silence him. This may sound dramatic but, I assure you, that the spectre of starvation can transform a man of peace into a veritable demon. My pleading proved to have been providential for, some weeks later, Peter unwisely revisited his property to find that the aforesaid desperate character had returned. He must have gone berserk at the loss of his booty, for practically the whole ceiling had been torn down in his frenzied search. Peter hurried away, and has promised to give that place a wide berth until after the war. The bread was rather sour and mouldy, but after I had trimmed off the worst of it and destroyed any possible interior fungus by a thorough heating, we managed a few meals from it.

Before I leave the subject of bread, I must mention another lively incident. One day Peter arrived home and plunging his hands deep into his now baggy trousers, he brought forth a large German loaf! Hungry though I was I said this was going a bit far, and that I would have to sterilize it in the oven. "I should if I were you," said Peter nonchalantly, "for the Pole who brought it in to me carried it in the same way." My fastidious streak now sorely affronted, I smartly removed the whole crust, baked that for

Kala and thoroughly cooked the rest of the loaf. Peter had borne it home tied with twine to his braces. On walking up the hill leading from the North Cinema he was aware that two Germans had dismounted their bicycles and were walking behind him. At that moment the loaf parted company with the string and Peter was obliged to climb the rest of the hill as though crippled by some ghastly deformity. Thus he plodded on as the load shuffled from one groin to the other, until the Germans passed him, and he was at last able to manoeuvre himself and his benign swelling, on to the saddle of his bicycle.

To M.H. Les Dunes. December 4th, 1944.

I mentioned before certain correspondence which had passed between our Bailiff and the Germans. The outcome is the following message sent by German Wireless to the Red Cross on November the 5th:

Secretary-General,
International Red Cross,
Geneva.

Conditions rapidly deteriorating here. Will soon become impossible. We appreciate difficulties but civilian population need urgent supplies of essentials. We urge immediate visit of Red Cross Representative. All rations drastically reduced.

Bread finishes Dec. 15th.
Sugar " Jan. 6th.

Fat production much below subsistence level. Ration of milk reduced to one-third of a pint per head by end of year.

Soap and other cleansers—stocks completely exhausted.

Vegetables generally inadequate to supply civilian population through winter. German consumption heavy. Salt exhausted.

Clothing and footwear stock almost exhausted.

Fuel, gas and electricity finish end of year. Coal stock exhausted.

Wood fuel inadequate.

Many essential medical supplies finish.

(Signed) VICTOR G. CAREY,

Bailiff of Guernsey.

From personal knowledge this letter contained under-
:tements in many homes.

Despite the appearance of a German notice in the Press
ne days ago, stating that the Red Cross had replied and
omised to send parcels of foodstuffs, soap and medica-
ents, nothing more has been heard. The general feeling of
bilation has once more subsided.

Peter now takes our dinner to be cooked in a neighbour's
rze-oven. We place the parsnips and swedes (and carrots,
any) in a stone jar, which we stand in the middle of an
amel tin, around which we arrange the potatoes, with a
tle water. As you may know, the dried furze (or gorse)
put into these brick ovens and set alight. When it is all
ırnt, the door is opened and the ashes are shovelled out of

the red-hot oven. It is then filled with the customers' tins of vegetables.

The complete absence of meat or fish could well have been added to the Bailiff's Red Cross message, for they have long since been absent from our menus.

The German Officer, who acted as interpreter between Guernsey and the Red Cross, when our S.O.S. was broadcast, went into the shop a day or so ago. He had once before discussed our position here with Peter. He now asserts that the message has been answered, and that he interpreted it. He also says that the wording of the Red Cross promise of help was even stronger than that now published in the Press, but that it was moderated in the interpreting. Perhaps he was averse to raising false hopes, for, if help is not forthcoming, Doctors predict a rapidly rising death-rate over the next few months. Alas and alack!

Nan arrives each morning and, in an agonized tone, inquires: "Mrs. B. where are the Russians?" I am never able to give her the answer which she so longs to hear, though she no longer expects a miracle to have taken place overnight. Her question is just a daily formality.

Diana will soon be with you again for Christmas. This both gladdens and saddens us, because you cannot all be with us — until next year!

To M.H. Les Dunes. December 14th, 1944.

God save the King! May he enjoy many happier returns.

Since my last letter, the Island has been seething with tales of our 'Ship' coming home. According to the Germans she should have left Portugal about two weeks ago. The rotting grapevine whispered that —

(a) she had left;

(b) she was due in three days;

(c) she had put into various ports for shelter. (Incidentally we prayed for her through a week of gales);

(d) she would be here in three days;

(e) she had been seen coming down the Russel! (Biff 'phoned this gem to me and, like a credulous idiot I tore upstairs only to disillusion myself);

(f) she was off the Casquets;

(g) off St. Martin's Point;

(h) off the Hanois Lighthouse!

And now, ironically, the B.B.C. announces that she is due to leave some time next week!! It would seem that a fleet of ghost ships has been haunting these waters. Alas! those taunting mirages have besotted their starving and gullible victims. That 'Necessity is the Mother of Invention' is all too apparent. I wonder if some particular circumstance inspired the author of this motto? Never before could it have been more apt.

I now hurry to catch the remaining daylight. In a few minutes it will be dark, and I shall have to finish this by candlelight. The very last day for gas also is December the 20th. Our 'turkey' must perforce be cooked over a wood fire.

People with wooden gates on their property are obliged to lift them off their hinges and house them for the night, so many have been stolen for fuel, including the gates of your field opposite "La Guelle". Our meagre bread ration is composed mainly of husks, like the sweepings of some barn. Felicia struck the right witty note when she said: "One needs a chaff-cutter to cut it, and a spittoon beside one for the husks."

I hope that I have written what I had in mind, for I certainly cannot now distinctly see what my pen has recorded. The light is failing, so I shall bid you, *Adieu Chérie. Reviens Bientôt.*

To M.H. Les Dunes. December 27th, 1944.

Our last 'Occupied' Christmas has surely come and gone, for which we are truly thankful. The end cannot be far away.

The gas was finally cut off three days before Christmas. This produced further chaos and improvisation, especially as the 'Bogey' in the shed no longer had cow-pat and tar sustenance to maintain its usefulness for Christmas Day. Each household, through German munificence, was allocated one pork chop for the entire family. Most of us hereabouts put this ration in the tin for the furze oven, which, given peacetime fare, excels all other methods of cooking.

That Christmas dinner was quite something, and its memory will linger on. On Boxing Day we resumed our meatless fare, which Peter collected as usual, this time with a disastrous outcome. The kitchen which houses the furze-oven contained several benches around the walls, where the public sat and chatted during the cooking, while the uncooked dinners waited on trestles for the oven to be emptied and reheated. A few people, for reasons of their own, had saved their chops for Boxing Day. Peter chatted as usual with our neighbours whose dinners were almost cooked. The *esprit de corps*—as always throughout the Island—is excellent, and such a boost to morale.

It was a bitterly cold day and the north-east wind rushed into the room whenever a new arrival opened the door. Presently a customer entered, and was battling to close the door against the howling gale, when Kala, who had tracked Peter's footsteps like a Bisto kid—pushed his way between this person's legs. Peter made a frantic dash to help push Kala back into the icy blast—but, before he could say 'Jack Robinson' the starving animal had snatched a pork chop from a waiting dinner and made his escape. Horrified, Peter set off after Kala down the road in the opposite direction from Les Dunes, which Kala wanted to avoid until he had polished off this rare tit-bit. Finally, Peter caught him, dragged the tattered remains from his mouth, and, finding it a tangle of skin and grizzle, shrugged his shoulders and (quote) "gave it back to the poor little devil!" Neither could he find it in his heart to chastise him.

Imagine poor Peter's feelings as, with unwilling feet, he made his way back to that roomful of people, to ask who had owned the missing chop. He set off, with bowed head, to find the owner, a Mr. Bichard. Fearing a storm of justified invective from his victim, he knocked on the door of the house, and asked the housekeeper(?) who opened it, if he might speak to Mr. Bichard. Peter tells me that he felt like a naughty schoolboy, entering the Head's study, for six of the best. "Ah well," said his host, on hearing of his grievous loss, "there it is. Have you anything to offer in exchange?" Peter replied that we had left, a one-pound pot of calves' foot jelly, to which he was welcome. (This was indeed, the only item of our original store which we were keeping as Junior's iron ration). But this fact Peter did not reveal to his host. "Well," said he, "I'll have to be satisfied with that, and if you can get my watch repaired we'll say no more about it." Needless to say, such was Peter's sense of relief, that the watch was, luckily in these days of few spare parts, restored to its owner in perfect working order.

This incident recalled the day, years ago, you remember, when P.C. Browning arrived in our yard, driving before him one of our pigs. This creature he had 'apprehended' in St. John's Cemetery, of all places, doing sacrilegious damage to the glass wreaths on the graves. Surely this must have been the first and last time a farmer was to be charged with harbouring an infidel pig. I forget what the verbose jungle of the law made of this affair but, should a roving pig of whatever denomination enter our property at this moment, we would fall on its neck before reluctantly slitting its throat.

To M.H   Les Dunes. December 30th, 1944.

One more tale I really must make the effort to recount, as well as memory permits from George's lively version, for it seems likely that life may become truly hectic in the New

Year, and my letters much curtailed. A brief preamble is unavoidable to put you in the picture.

Soon after we were evicted from La Guelle, George's bungalow was also commandeered. He was allocated the house of Dr. S. who had returned to New Street where he intends to remain.

George was allowed to retain the farm and outbuildings at La Guelle for which the Germans had no use. Lily had been spared to George for some time after I had written her epitaph. Methinks the local authorities turned a 'blind eye' until the Spring, when Lily ran dry. After all, the bulk of her now small yield was destined for German gullets.

George returned each day to milk the cow and to check whether the remaining two lorries — out of the original two dozen — had also been purloined.

One day George arrived to find the heads of his few remaining hens strewn about the yard, a mortal blow indeed! No doubt the Germans had been busy after Curfew. Earlier on I mentioned their foreign maid, whom they called Ellie. (They pronounced it to rhyme with 'daily'). She managed their household at La Guelle, and generally sported with them in scanty attire, like Amaryllis, in the shade of your mulberry tree. Now, Ellie decided to replace George's hens with a batch of her own, plus one fine rooster, a garrulous fellow with gay plumage. These she encouraged to run wild, and to create general havoc in the garden, which had hitherto been Father's pride and joy.

We were spending the day with Felicia and George in their new billet, when George told us his story.

Looking up from his plate of gravyless boiled vegetables he said with mock sorrow: "By the way, Ellie is in great distress, you'll be sorry to hear that she has lost the new cockbird."

"I'm jolly glad!" cried Felicia.

" Good luck to whoever finds the thing! " I added, " I only wish we had him."

Without looking up from his plate, George muttered, with a fair attempt at ventriloquism: " We'll have him for dinner on Sunday." Before coming in for lunch he had slunk upstairs and hung the bird in the attic.

That morning he had arrived at La G. as usual, just as Ellie's resplendent cockbird came strutting round the stables. " Here's a bit of luck! " thought George, the memory of his own slaughtered hens still very green. Stealthily he stalked his prey. Then pounced! One deft twist of his expert fingers and the bold chanticleer departed this life, with no more sound that a tired gurgle.

Whipping his jack-knife from his pocket George darted into the stable, and proceeded to bleed the poor creature into the stable drain. No sooner had he completed the bloody deed when, to his horror, George heard nearby Ellie's shrill voice calling: " Cockee! Cockee! Vere are you? "

Quick as a flash George was up the loft ladder and had pushed the dead bird under some straw, and was down again to cover with sand the bloodstains on the floor. Thankfully he heard Ellie's footsteps pass the closed door on the way into the field and on to the quarry which lay beyond.

There was not a moment to lose. She would soon be returning. The body must be disposed of before her suspicions were aroused by the presence of George's bicycle, left propped against a shed. Nothing would have pleased Ellie more than to have set the Germans on his track.

Leaping once more up the ladder, George seized a rusty five-pot milk-can long ago discarded, and proceeded to cram the dead rooster, with all his finery, through the narrow neck of the can (no small feat, as anyone acquainted with the Guernsey milk-can will appreciate).

George says that he felt much as a murderer must feel, when packing a dismembered victim into a suitcase, prior to abandoning it on some lonely moor.

Down the ladder again, a quick glance from the stable doorway and, in an instant, George was across the yard and had flung his hard-won booty over the wall of Harry Marquand's garden, fervently praying that he would be the one to retrieve it.

With a thankful sigh that his luck had so far held, he turned to face the returning Ellie with as much composure as he could muster. She was still calling the ill-fated 'Cockee', and was almost in sight, when George glanced down to flick away any bits of straw or dust which might be adhering to his clothes. To his renewed horror he saw that his suit was bespattered with the rooster's blood. Without a moment's hesitation he leapt into a disused pigstye, or rather on to the piles of timber which he had neatly stacked in case of acute fuel shortage; just as Ellie came in sight. Had she been less distressed over the loss of her bird, she must surely have marvelled at the maniacal frenzy with which George was flinging planks of wood indiscriminately into the yard, in a desperate effort to conceal the tell-tale bloodstains from her malevolent eye.

Ellie stopped by the growing pile of timber to ask: "Have you zeen Cockee?"

Not daring to look up, George replied: "I'm afraid not. Have you lost him?"

"Yes," she said. "It is veree annoying and ve have only had heem a few days."

Still concentrating on his task, George agreed that it was certainly vexing. He hoped she would soon realize that nothing was to be gained by standing there, but the stubborn woman was not to be put off.

"Vere do you zink he could be?" she persisted, dodging the flying bits of wood.

Confound the woman! Would she never move on? George could not keep up this masquerade indefinitely. "Perhaps," he ventured, "he has returned to his old home. They sometimes do you know."

That Ellie was satisfied with this naïve suggestion, George very much doubted but, mercifully, she walked off at last, still calling the ill-fated 'Cockee'.

Puffing and panting, George leaned against the pigstye wall and surveyed its emptiness with disgust. All that timber would have to be re-stacked another day. He had neither time nor energy after his ordeal, and was naturally anxious to be gone. George milked the cow, and left the place as quickly as possible, with the smaller can prominently displayed on the handlebars of his bicycle. If Ellie was watching she would see that 'Cockee' was not going with him. Roguishly he reflected that, whereas many a decoration was being acquired at that very moment on many a foreign strand, for lesser deeds of daring, his reward promised to be purely gastronomic.

George set off to keep his next assignment with the deceased. In the unlikely event that Fate might even now be devising some scurvy trick to rob him of his prey, at least he felt safe from the dire consequences of Ellie's wrath, for the Germans, having no sense of humour, and a total disregard for poetic justice, would have treated this little episode as a major piece of sabotage, and would have dealt with it on that level.

George wisely ignored the camouflaged hole in the hedge, through which we and the Marquand family had often visited one another after Curfew, and cycled round the block to their front entrance. He hoped they would not be at home, on the basis that the fewer his confederates, the better. His star was still in the ascendency, for he found the place deserted, and there, reposing on the lawn, at the far end of the garden lay 'Cockee's' round and rusty coffin.

Nonchalantly, for the benefit of any interested neighbours at upper windows, George sauntered down the garden, ostensibly admiring our friends' herbaceous border, and casually strolled back again with his prize; his heart, at every step, resuming the even tenor of its ways.

The rest you know: and that about finishes me for the day, written for the record, at odd intervals, with George's blessing, now that all danger of reprisals is over.

1945

To M.H. Les Dunes. January 18th, 1945.

Mother! those parcels have arrived! They were welcome and good. God bless the Red Cross.

We began with a delicious spread of cheese, dried milk and a knob of butter, melted over the fire. Two slices each for supper, followed by a slice of bread, butter and marmalade. A bar of chocolate melted in a glass of hot milk, and the war was over! When the *Vega* brings flour, it will round off this meal to perfection.

We are told that the Red Cross representative was horrified, when he tasted a sample of our Occupation bread, which is usually sour, husky, damp inside and of a muddy grey colour.

When the good ship *'Vega'* berthed, cheers went up from the ecstatic crowd, barricaded some distance away. The crew came up on deck, including the cook, who waved his frying pan. This eloquent action promoted a tremendous roar from the crowd. When the grand news of her arrival became known, few persons throughout this benighted Isle remained unmoved. All day long streams of people cycled or walked towards the east coast, to catch a glimpse of her.

We told Peter-John that Diana had sent his parcel. He was so excited, that he wanted to open all the tins at once. In going to bed, we drank cups of tea, which kept us awake all night; but why worry, excitement would have had the same effect anyway. Certainly tea is a stimulant. In our wakeful hours we planned our reunion, and our day was crowned by the splendid War news.

To M.H. Les Dunes. February 1st, 1945.

Grand news from the Russian Front continues to thrill us. Peter really thinks that Diana may be home by the fifth Anniversary of her departure on June 20th.

Last night Major Lewis Hastings could ill-conceal his excitement, which we found infectious.

Yesterday, a German soldier told Peter "*Ve are Kapput*". Their capitulation is all we need. One German called on Jim Stacey at the farm and tried to do a barter for potatoes, with a bottle, purporting to contain whisky.

Jim gave it another name, and advised the fellow to "hoist the White Flag, then the British will bring all the food you need." When Jim was reported and given a prison sentence, he said: "I can't go to prison now, I have a cow due to calve, and you want the milk." He was ordered to return in three months' time to serve his sentence. He reminds us that the haymaking will then be his excuse, and banks on the war being over by June. Anyway, I doubt if there are any vacancies in our over-crowded prison.

Only a few officers still display any signs of arrogance. One blond, pompous specimen in this district, passes us by with too-studied an indifference to be convincing. Under the tilted peak of his braided hat, and with head in air, and half closed eyelids, he proudly looks down his nose, as though he might still be the victor and we the vanquished. With tongue-in-cheek, we only just forbear to smile as he prances by. The men in the ranks make no attempt to conceal their abject condition. One of them, in conversation with Peter at business this week, openly conceded defeat, whereupon Peter assured him that we have nothing against the German people in general, except that they always seem to pick a bad Government.

One of our staff found the head and skin of a cat in the Arcade this week, and recently Farmer Sarchet arrived home to find a similar ghastly sight. Marauding for food by our starving 'visitors' is prevalent on a large scale after Curfew, as well as in broad daylight; even to the extent of entering occupied houses during the daytime. A housewife near Cambridge Park found a German rummaging in her house: her husband almost literally kicked him out. Her neighbour discovered a German entering her kitchen; stuffing parsnips into his jackboots, he seized her only carrot, which she managed to snatch from him as he fled. It is common knowledge that many soldiers have died of starvation.

We have now received a second food parcel. For some reason the '*Vega*' brought eighteen hundred fewer than last time. The Distribution Committee decided to leave out all children of four years and under — not, as Dr. S. most emphatically assures me — because children of that age do not need the food — but because they have two parents in the Island. Thus, two parcels at least will go to the parents and one each to the older children, if any. This sensible method of selection ensures that all who live alone receive a parcel. We are officially notified that these parcels will be replaced at the next consignment. Inevitably, there has been some bitterness and heart-searching over this. It is a thorny subject, but we are prepared to share the sacrifice this month, which, we must admit, is being placed upon us with good reason. Naturally (as all parents do for their children), Peter-John is given a large share of our parcels, even when we each receive one. We rejoice in his tea ration which stimulates our ever-rising spirits. We barter a tin of meat for a neighbour's pot of jam. He is a diabetic and is in a dreadful state, owing to the absence of insulin in the Island. The extra sugar in the jam is a boon to us for, naturally, our sugar augments Junior's still inadequate allowance. We have devised a system of self-rationing from the parcels, and find that they give us approximately five ounces of food each day spread over the month. One young man nearby was so thrilled by his first parcel that he ate the whole lot at once. Needless to say, the ambulance collected him in the night. Rolling in agony and, by the aid of a stirrup-pump, he and his precious cargo departed company without ceremony.

A few nights ago we were settled in bed, when Kala started barking furiously. We then heard the sound of heavy boots running up the path. Leaping from bed, we were just in time to see a German soldier bound over the

gate, great-coat, jackboots and all, as though the hounds of hell were at his heels, instead of one small shaggy brown mongrel who, his mission accomplished, sat down on one haunch and scratched behind his ear with his free paw, bearing a "That's that!" look about him. Peter discovered the next morning that the lock of the shed had been tampered with.

To M.H. Les Dunes. February 25th, 1945.

Two hours of electricity left! It is almost 8 o'clock and the light goes out at 10 p.m. — permanently! Peter has put in a 100-watt bulb so that we might have two hours of blissful seeing. The final bread-ration (one pound apiece), Peter collected from the depôt on the 13th of this month. Until the *'Vega'* arrives with flour, we shall be at grips with our worst mass blow for many moons. That the parcels are a Godsend nobody denies, we could not even exist without them — but they are lamentably inadequate without bread and potatoes. A spoonful of jam or butter, or salmon, or a forkful of meat cannot suffice and people with growing children must be in dire distress. Infants of under two years of age have their milk ration reduced to one and a half pints a day and children up to 14 years have one pint.

We hear that certain outraged parents have contrived to pin a notice on the door of the German Headquarters at Grange Lodge Hotel as follows: "You have taken our children's milk and butter. The war is nearly over. We will not forget." There appears to be a shred of truth in this, for on that day, German guards were posted at both ends of the Grange.

Recently the Germans have been searching houses for hidden stores of food. They found a large hoard in the house of two prominent people. Of course, this was no concern of the Germans, whatever we may think. Nevertheless, these hoarders must feel rather squalid when they collect their New Zealand and Canadian Red Cross parcels, which they must do if they are not to arouse suspicion. Whether all this food is still part of their original store — or has been syphoned into their homes via the Black Market over these past years, Heaven alone knows.

The *'Vega'* is expected on the 5th of March so, with luck, we may have real bread on your birthday.

To M.H. Les Dunes. March 8th, 1945.

Many Happy Returns! This day will always stand out in Guernsey's history! For bread came to us over the waters, and our souls rejoiced!! This blessing was indeed bestowed to us all on this, your Birthday. For three barren weeks, Guernsey's children had walked to school, many with feet wrapped up in cloth for shoes, and with empty bellies, or stayed at home for lack of energy. The official bread ration begins next week but this was an especial sample of things to come.

It is now 9.15 p.m. as we sit up in bed with a candle between us. Our minute wireless set always at the ready for news. It is the size and shape of an electric light switch. Peter has rigged up an invisible complicated earth and aerial, which have to be dismantled when not in use. The single head-phone he improvised from one of the business telephone receivers. When he called on the 'dealer' who made it, the latter brave fellow said: "I think this will have to be the last one. I have made eight hundred of these, so I think it's time to call a halt, before I get caught."

After assuring himself of their British loyalty, Peter had been providing a number of people with marcasite to use in place of a crystal.

One day a local policeman entered the shop and quietly said: "I understand you have been providing certain people with marcasite." Peter was about to offer his wrists for the handcuffs to be clamped on, when our P.C. X whispered hoarsely: "Can you let me have a piece?"

All the War Correspondents have been a tower of strength to us, and, of course, so has dear old Winston, with his buoyant speeches, on which theme I have written before. Colonel Britain with Beethoven's 5th Symphony has set our hearts throbbing with its dramatic beat, which will have a new meaning for us each time we hear it when Peace comes. It must have had the opposite effect on the Germans—more like a death-knell, which is easy to imagine if one is on the losing side.

And now I must stop, being in my own light, which somewhat cramps one's style.

To M.H. Les Dunes. March 26th, 1945.

A whole month we have been without electricity. It seems like a year; however, the lighter evenings are a great help. The Germans advanced the Standard Time by one hour, which gives them and ourselves daylight until 9 o'clock.

A wonderful evening, and the news is magnificent. We may see you this year after all. This thought helps us to forget our morbid obsession with food.

At one time we were in possession of three wireless sets, in different places of concealment, until a friendly cryptic 'phone call warned us that the Germans were about to search our area. I took one set out into the shed and, half-emptying a sack of wood, I thrust the 'object' into the sack and refilled it. Peter dashed off to Jim Stacey's farm and between them they added our largest set to his own, in the middle of a hay-rick. When not in use the third one which we have kept, rests with this book in its secret hiding place. As long as we can survive they will be safe. Failing which

"It matters not how strait the gate, —
How charged with punishment the scroll"—!

we shall be beyond their power to chastise.

Needless to say the Germans did not pick on Les Dunes, but others were not so lucky. Numerous amusing stories are constantly circulating — all quite credible. To wit — a certain native was listening in one evening when the Germans knocked on his door. Dashing his set into its hideout, the poor man opened the door to be met with the familiar staccato: "You have a Vireless set!" "No," pleaded our trembling ally: "I have no set." Again came the dread accusation, and again came the denial. "Then," roared the German, "Vy are you vearing a headphone?" The quivering victim was arrested, and prison claimed another inmate. A mother and daughter were called on one evening, when the same routine was repeated. Whilst the daughter answered the knock, the Mother, in desperation threw the set into a saucepan of pseudo soup on the fire, just as the Germans entered the room. During the search the daughter lifted the saucepan lid and began stirring the soup. Looking up at her Mother, she exclaimed: "What have you put in the soup?" The mother mumbled "Bones!" "Bones?" queried her daughter. "I said 'Bones' you idiot!" The mother's withering look silenced her offspring and, fortunately, the Germans being either too engrossed or too 'dumb' to grasp the situation, the women were spared, but we assume, the next bulletin and many others were lost to them. There are few families in Guernsey who have not their own fund of similar stories all equally amusing.

I end to-day with the latest amusing, and quite credible Barter story going the round. A local wit was attracted by a notice-board on a certain property at St. Martin's which read: "This House for Sale." In an inspired moment he wrote beneath it: "Or would exchange for Rabbit." This, I thought, caps the priceless notice in the barter column of the Press, which reads: "Two nightgowns for a breeding-doe"!

To M.H. Les Dunes. March 27th, 1945.

Our spirits are still in the ascendancy despite my present head-cold. We rejoice that, having suffered most of the forms depression takes, we have survived and are now feeling more optimistic about our non-invasion.

We must remember those who have not been so blessed. The countless victims of this terrible war; those, over whose country the battle has raged, and the many horrors and crimes, which have been perpetrated upon innocent people. The history books and even the Bible are ridden with accounts of these senseless wars and their ghastly consequences. The world seems destined to suffer and endure them till the Crack of Doom —

"Why is all around us here
As if some lesser god had made the world?
Where blind and naked Ignorance
Delivers brawling judgments unashamed
On all things, all day long."

Before this eloquence of Tennyson one cannot too humbly bow. How can we read these words of his and remain unmoved? Especially in the position wherein we find ourselves to-day.

To M.H. Les Dunes. Tuesday, April 10th, 1945.

The problem of P.J.'s footwear is almost insoluble. We bandage his blistered heels daily. At last Peter has found a cobbler who consented to make a pair of shoes. This was achieved by a semi-barter, one of the most difficult to date. The cobbler required 10 lbs. of root vegetables, a bottle of oil, four boxes of matches, two packets of cigarette papers and 17/-. To this Peter was obliged to add the leather elbow-pieces from his golf-jacket. The vegetables, oil and papers were not obtainable for love nor money. The end product of Peter's bartering and gentle persuasion, was an apology for shoes which one would normally decline to accept as a gift. I spent last Saturday afternoon reinforcing the straps as best I could, but Junior was delighted with the result.

Owing to a great increase in burglaries and breaking-and-entering, we now take our precious food upstairs at night. Peter takes this on a tray whilst I follow with a garden fork! Peter is determined to attack any prowlers with this implement. I tell him that he will cut an elegant figure standing at the top of the stairs in his nightshirt, fork poised for pitching at the intruders, but he is quite resolved to use it for, if these parcels and the odd vegetables are stolen from us, they are irreplaceable until the '*Vega*' returns. It is literally a matter of life and death.

When first I heard of the spate of lootings and assaults I refused to leave the house for our daily rambles with Junior, in order to stay and guard our food, come what may. Peter finally came up with an idea: "If I can find a hiding place to your satisfaction," he said: "Will you come out with us? You can't stay indoors indefinitely: and if you do I might very well return any day and find you bound and gagged or simply laid out!" Before this charming prospect my heroism evaporated, so I agreed to his plan.

When P.J. was in bed we moved the settee, rolled back the carpet and Peter set to work, sawing a section of wood from the floor. Among the foundations of Les Dunes we pushed our tins of food. Peter replaced the floorboards and we now sit over our sacred fund of sustenance like expectant fowls. "Anyway," said Peter, "before anyone finds the stuff they will have to tear the place to pieces."

To M.H. Les Dunes. April 26th, 1945.

The horrible feeling returns, that these blighters will not give in until they are forced to it. Yesterday an Officer told Peter that as long as Hitler is at large, there is very little hope of surrender here.

One night last week, George's next door neighbour had a gruelling experience. A German entered his bedroom during his search for food. The two men grappled and finally rolled down the stairs together. I think George was more immersed in the story of this fracas than in the fate of the neighbour's food parcel, or perhaps he failed to inquire, for I am still unaware of the outcome. Indeed, amid the welter of these current adventures, which are certainly prevalent, it is not surprising if we are confused.

At least two people have been battered to death. This re-opened the question in the public mind, were Mr. & Mrs. Sigwart murdered a few weeks ago, or was the verdict of homicide and suicide correct. Guernsey people are far from satisfied on this point. Mr. Sigwart was of a most mild and gentle nature, the epitome of 'one of Nature's gentlemen'. He just may have been driven to desperation and despair, by malnutrition and the grim battle for survival, with dwindling strength. We were very sad at the Business in which he had given us invaluable help as an interpreter.

The Germans would like to lay the blame for our new troubles at the door of the Russian element here. Georgians who were taken prisoner by the Germans and who turned traitor and joined forces with them when they were convinced that Hitler would win the war. It is not difficult to imagine what their sorry fate will be. But they are lucky to escape those barbaric and ghastly Concentration Camps, whose existence have now come to light. Surely many generations must pass, before the soul of Germany can feel purged of the guilt and degradation of this real-life version of Dante's Inferno.

No fate can be too bad for the hideous, inhuman specimens who ran these places and fed the gas chambers. The dreadful martyrdom of those pitiful, innocent victims must now, with sorrow and unashamed emotion, be in the minds of the whole civilized world; they make our little Calvaries look very mean indeed.

No one can doubt that, "as they passed over, all the trumpets sounded for them on the other side."

To M.H. May 5th, 1945.

Norway, the Channel Ports, and the Channel Islands await with bated breath the word that means Liberation. Each time we pick up the earphones, we wonder if that word has been given. We are keyed up to concert pitch. Almost 3 o'clock, so I pause for a moment to listen to the latest news.

Well, there is nothing new on the wireless, but our brightest hope lies in the fact that Admiral Doenitz has said: "Further resistance to the Allied Powers in the West is senseless." Will the tough German Commandant here, surrender in the face of this announcement? Surely he will not decide to make a last stand after all, as he has threatened to do, regardless of orders to the contrary.

When, lying in bed last night, we heard that the Germans in Denmark, Holland and the Frisian Islands had surrendered, Peter gasped: "Well, I'm damned! they've forgotten us". A few minutes later there came a loud rapping on our door. Kala bounding around the house, gripped the pants of the caller. It was, Peter discovered, on leaning out of the window, our next door neighbour, telling us that, "it's all over!" Other neighbours had run to tell them the great news. They must have mistaken Frisian Islands for Channel Islands. Peter visited these people this morning to correct the mistake. They told him that the old lady delivering the news had fallen in the wet grass in her nightclothes. Anyway, for once they had all enjoyed a sleepless night.

Looking up from my writing, I have just seen in the lane, a German soldier foraging in a hole where someone has dumped refuse. He put his 'find' in a handcart which his friend was guarding, and twice returned for more!

Those once full-blooded "Assyrians" who swooped on us in 1940, "their cohorts gleaming," and flaunting their laurels of victory over the weaker countries of Europe, now haunt our streets like the ghosts of those same Biblical hordes who were struck by the plague. The Pride of The Third Reich, fallen low, now stoop to rummage in the dustbins of little Guernsey, and scrape the ground from our discarded cauliflower stumps. These they munch as they slouch along in their shabby field-grey uniforms, while the Nazi Flag with its Swastika, under whose ægis they once so proudly walked our streets and byways, still limply flutters in the breeze. These are the poor shrunken relics of those powerful hosts, who crucified so many millions on their way to rule the World, spurred on by the bizarre ravings of their devilish rulers.

These poor wretches were merely the pawns in the game and—unbelievably you may think—we are no longer capable of any feeling save utter and profound pity for their abject state. We feel no unctuous pride in this, partly because we are just too plain weary to feel otherwise.

As in Biblical times there has, for some time, been a famine in the land. Gaunt walking skeletons about us (both British and German) have become a familiar sight. With empty bellies the soldiers wait for their superiors to hoist the White Flag. Then, verily shall we see this "legion of the lost ones join the cohorts of the damned—"

To M.H. Les Dunes, Sunday, May 6th, 1945.

On this, the third Anniversary of Audrey's death, the coming surrender in the Channel Islands was mentioned on the wireless. Amidst all the jubilation I cannot but wish that Father and Audrey had been spared a few more years to enjoy the Liberation with us. But, as I wrote long ago, this is no time for yearning. We have much to be thankful for, and we look forward to reunion with you, Diana and the rest of the family, with great joy and thanksgiving.

Looking back on the turmoil of the Evacuation, one has often wondered over the years, what became of Guernsey's scattered thousands. We know, through cryptic messages, that many joined the Services; others drove ambulances through the blitz, or joined in other operations as their fathers did before them in the First World War, fighting for King and Country, and the relief of their beloved 'Sarnia'.

Peter's two brothers fought with the R.G.L.I. (Royal Guernsey Light Infantry) in that first global débacle. Emil was gassed and taken prisoner, while 'Kit' was killed at Cambrai. Peter was at Boarding school in Jersey, when the Principal sent for him to break the news. Mercifully their mother was spared all the anxiety and grief, for she died that August of 1914 just before the war was declared. But the double blow left his Father a broken reed.

Ironically Emil now finds himself interned in Laufen, a prisoner for the second time. But this time he is sustained by Elsie, and some of their very good friends.

To M.H. Les Dunes, Thursday, May 10th, 1945.

Yesterday at 8 a.m. a Token Force of British Troops landed in Guernsey.

We all cycled into Town to join in the excitement. The Island had gone mad with joy! We spoke to many soldiers, robust and sunburnt from various foreign campaigns. Peter-John was highly delighted with the whole affair.

On Tuesday The Germans surrendered to our Bailiff. This was made official at midnight. We were at Bordeaux with Nan, when, during one of the day's bulletins, Winston Churchill alluded to us as: "Our dear Channel Islands." We were all shaken by his touching words and, for some moments, were quite speechless.

During that evening, Jim Stacey and Harry Marley came to say that British ships were at anchor in the roads, and that their lights could be seen from the hill behind Les Dunes. Together with Nan, we all traipsed through Col. Milbourne's deserted and derelict property and scrambled over the hedge to see the welcome lights in the distance. Jim Stacey was helping me over the hedge in the darkness, to join the others who had merrily gone before, when the sound of stamping and snorting close at hand stopped us in our tracks. It was Yve Toudic's bull, obviously objecting to our presence. Farmer Stacey, being the right man for the occasion, said: "I'll deal with the bull and occupy his attention, while you make a run for it."

As we joined the others, and regaled them with our latest adventure, I reflected upon the irony of the situation. After almost five years of divers impending fates which could have befallen us, the final straw would have been to meet my end on the eve of Liberation, literally on the horns of a new dilemma in the shape of an enraged bull.

However, this seemed to add extra spice to the excitement, as we all stood together to feast our eyes on the twinkling lights of the flotilla. A wondrous sight for sore eyes!

So ends one era of our lives, as we await the dawn of another. We are told: "It is better to travel hopefully than to arrive." This saying has always baffled me. For our part we have had enough of 'travelling' for the moment. We have arrived, and our hopes are realised. Thank Heaven!

One thing remains: To greet you all with Diana, and to witness her first meeting with her long-awaited Brother.

Castle Cornet—Liberation Day 1945.

* * * * * * * * *

EPILOGUE

On reading these letters, our returning relatives, and a few intimates, failed to understand why this diary had ended so calmly. They had expected vivid ravings of ecstasy and unbridled joy.

This was better understood when I reminded them of the mass of daily correspondence which passed between us all from the moment of Liberation until July 10th when, at long last, my Mother—my abiding Inspiration for these letters—set foot on her native soil. Our post war letters were not even begun until past midnight each day: after the last of the British soldiers, who practically haunted our ever-open house, had returned to Camp near Fort Le Marchant.

Each day, at the crack of dawn, Peter-John fled from home to return with a party of soldiers. Equipped with towels and shaving-kit, they luxuriated in the bathroom, whilst I prepared breakfast. Then followed endless stories, generously larded with banter between us all, over numerous cups of tea. Each batch of men was replaced by another of their Company who were guarding petrol supplies and rounding-up German prisoners.

One soldier weighed over 20 stone and was indeed so corpulent, that he was exempted from route marching. He loped about in dancing-pumps, his massive bare chest brown as a bun, his braces down and flapping around his hips. A typical story ran as follows. One night this soldier returned home on leave, just before a 'doodle-bug' exploded perilously near his house. His wife's screams almost drowned the noise of the explosion. Going in search of the terrified woman, he yelled "Are you 'urt?" "No" came the reply. "Then wot the 'ell are you 'ollering for?" he blared. No doubt in the same rich Cockney accent, interspersed with the ripe expletives used in this recital to us.

Another 'Tommy' spoke of the old man whom he had found, groping about on the edge of a vast bomb crater, where his house had stood a few minutes before. On snatching him to safety, the soldier asked: "Wot yer lookin' fer Grandad?" The old man replied: "I seem to have put my specs down some place and can't see to find 'em".

The soldiers were as eager to hear our Occupation stories as we were to hear of their war adventures. And so the hours rolled on. Time seemed unimportant. The whole rosy future of freedom was ours.

We were loaded with tins of meat, jam, and fruit and much else: which, besides our three months' double rations from Britain, we were quite unable to eat or digest, after years of enforced abstinence. When we asked other liberated friends, how they were coping with all this fare, the answer was always: "We just can't eat it!" All our eagerly awaited feasts suddenly lost their exotic appeal. Nobody was more surprised than we were at our own indifference in our new-found Canaan. Mouths had stopped watering for milk and honey: stomachs had shrunk to pigmy proportions: and although our energy was nil, we soon realized that our batteries must be re-charged in small doses.

On the 26th of May the British Forces gave a magnificent Victory Ball for us at the Royal Hotel. Peter and I went along, in almost the only available taxi. It was afterwards used by King George VI and Queen Elizabeth, during their Liberation Tour of Guernsey on June 7th.

After dancing with a Col. Wilkinson (?) I was led by him to the tables which groaned under the weight of numerous dishes, laden with exotic food. When I asked him what he would like to eat (as though I were the hostess!) he replied: "Nothing at all, thank you. This is all for you." O dear! he must have marvelled at my seeming lack of appreciation, when my appetite failed to come up to his expectations. I hoped he did not think that we would hurl ourselves bodily on to those tables and wallow in a gastronomic frenzy.

This gallant told me that if I showed him a map of Guernsey, he could pick out our house as he knew from reconnaissance photographs, every stick and stone of L'Ancresse, and the number of planes which had been at the ready, for a massive pinpoint bombing if our Brest Commandant had refused to surrender. I thanked God again that this determined character, had been led to see Reason.

To have invented a date for a pseudo letter, after the hectic life which prevailed throughout the Island during those first weeks of freedom, in order to give five years of correspondence a sensational climax, would have made a nonsense of all that had gone before.

Predictably, mental and physical lethargy became the gradual reaction common to us all. The concert pitch of ecstasy could not be maintained—nor re-kindled with any hope of credibility.

LIST OF CHARACTERS PORTRAYED IN "THE PREY OF AN EAGLE"

M. H.	—	Author's Mother, Minnie Head
Audrey	—	Author's Sister
Doris	—	Author's Sister
Marie	—	Author's Sister
Henry	—	Author's Brother
George	—	Author's Brother
Bill	—	Author's Brother
Peter	—	Author's Husband
Diana	—	Author's Daughter
Peter John	—	Author's Son
Felicia	—	George Head's Wife
Lily	—	Bill Head's Wife
Emil Bachmann	—	Peter's Brother
Elsie Bachmann	—	Peter's Sister-in-law
Winnie Bell	—	Peter's Sister
Bubbles & Ted	—	Emil's Children
Jim & Dorothy	—	Winnie's Son & Wife
Meta Noyon	—	Peter's Sister
Flo & Ted Griffiths		
Unice Le Maitre	—	L'Ancresse Tea Rooms
Winnie Spearpoint	—	L'Ancresse Tea Rooms
"Weazle" & Stan Noel		
Edna Veal and her mother.		
Charles & "Biff" Roussel		
"Pam" de la Mare.		

——— — ———

"La Guelle"	—	Author's parents' house.
"Les Dunes"	—	Author's house.